# The Socialist Ideas of the
# Alternative Economic Strategy

Baris Tufekci

# The Socialist Ideas of the British Left's Alternative Economic Strategy

## 1973–1983

palgrave
macmillan

Baris Tufekci
Queen Mary University of London
London, UK

ISBN 978-3-030-35000-0      ISBN 978-3-030-34998-1   (eBook)
https://doi.org/10.1007/978-3-030-34998-1

This Palgrave Macmillan imprint is published by the registered company Springer Nature
Switzerland AG
The registered company address is: Gewerbestrasse 11, 6330 Cham, Switzerland

*To my parents*

# Acknowledgements

I am extremely grateful to Judith Bara, Madeleine Davis, Patrick Diamond, Andrew Gamble, Michael Kenny, Ray Kiely, Tom Quinn and Raj Veerasekaran for their advice and feedback on all or parts of this project. All its errors, however, are the author's alone.

It was a pleasure to speak about my research with Ben Fine, Geoffrey Hodgson, Stuart Holland and Bob Rowthorn, each of whom once supported the economic strategy that is the subject of this book. I am grateful for their time and recollections.

It was also a pleasure to work with Anne Birchley-Brun and Ambra Finotello at Palgrave Macmillan. Their editorial guidance and suggestions were invaluable.

Much of my work on this project was carried out at the People's History Museum in Manchester, the Working Class Movement Library in Salford, the Trades Union Congress Library and the Senate House Library, both in London. I am thankful for the abundant help and advice that I received on each visit.

Finally, my deepest gratitude is due to my parents, without whose support and encouragement this book could not have been written.

---

The original version of book author's affiliation was revised: The affiliation has been updated with the changes. The correction to the affiliation is available at https://doi.org/10.1007/978-3-030-34998-1_8

# CONTENTS

1 Introduction: A New 'Marketplace for Ideas'                    1

2 Class and Party: The Historical Context of the Rise
  of the AES                                                     11

3 Reform or Revolution: The AES as Socialist Strategy            39

4 Planning the Market: The AES and Capitalism                    65

5 A Britain Oppressed: The AES and the Nation                   101

6 Class Conflict and Class Collaboration: The AES
  and the Working Class                                         131

7 Conclusion: The AES, New Times and the Death
  of British Socialism                                          175

Correction to: The Socialist Ideas of the British Left's
Alternative Economic Strategy                                    C1

Afterword: Corbyn—A Socialist Rebirth?                    207

Bibliography                                             219

Index                                                   245

# LIST OF FIGURES

Fig. 7.1    Total number of working days lost to strikes in the UK,
1945–2015 (*Source* Office for National Statistics)     196
Fig. 7.2    Number of trade-union members in Great Britain,
1945–2015/2016 (*Source* Department for Business,
Energy and Industrial Strategy)     197

# CHAPTER 1

# Introduction: A New 'Marketplace for Ideas'

Few periods in the Labour Party's history intrigue the British political imagination more than the years leading up to the 1983 general election. Routinely characterised as a time when ownership of Labour fell into the hands of its hard left, the lasting impression has been one of a party signing its suicide note before an electorate increasingly bewildered by its 'loony left' excesses. As subsequent Labour leaders have come to appreciate, almost nothing is seen as more politically damaging than their association with the dismal memory of June 1983, when electoral disaster apparently succeeded a progressive, decade-long over-indulgence in left-wing nostrums. For many on the Conservative right, meanwhile, Labour policies which deviate from the 'pro-market' New Labour approach established since the 1990s—particularly with regard to public ownership—are to be condemned as threats to take Britain 'back to the 1970s', to a time of crisis and uncertainty seen as a direct consequence of a socialist mismanagement in government.[1]

Among some sections of the left, however, an alternative narrative has also emerged, defending aspects of the Labour left's agenda in those years as viable responses to economic crisis. One account endorses the Labour left's economic strategy, points to Tony Benn's 'crucial and at times heroic role' in challenging the 'British establishment', upholds Labour's 'social contract' and the union leaders' role in maintaining it, while commending the self-restraint shown by British workers in the face of capitalist crisis.[2]

© The Author(s) 2020
B. Tufekci, *The Socialist Ideas of the British
Left's Alternative Economic Strategy,*
https://doi.org/10.1007/978-3-030-34998-1_1

Other commentators have also sought to 'revisit' Labour's 1970s strategy in favourable terms[3]; and, with the rise of Labour's Jeremy Corbyn in 2015, 'Old Labour, not New Labour' appears to have become a slogan among those on the British left seeking to recapture some of the radicalism in Labour's politics in the 1970s and early 1980s.[4] Indeed, with 'Corbynism', the politics of that period have been presented as something of a benchmark, a standard of Labour-left radicalism against which to measure the radicalism of Corbyn's agenda.

While the Labour left's politics of the 1970s and early 1980s expressed support for a variety of causes—feminism, anti-racism, anti-militarism, unilateral nuclear disarmament—at the heart of its agenda was the Alternative Economic Strategy (AES), its programme of economic reforms that informed the Labour Party's official economic platform between 1973 and 1983. With support and input from the Communist Party of Great Britain, left-wing trade-union leaders, left-wing economists and sections of the New Left, the AES was the rallying point for the bulk of British socialism. Demanding economic reflation, import controls, price controls, public ownership in profitable firms and sectors, compulsory planning agreements, industrial democracy and a withdrawal from the European Economic Community (EEC), the AES presented itself as a radical and, at times, even a revolutionary response to the deep crisis of British capitalism. This self-justification by the AES, at the level of its policy and rhetoric, has played an important role in the Labour left's subsequent representation as a radical force in this period of Britain's post-war history—by political lore, the contemporary left and, as discussed below, the academic literature.

The aim of this book, therefore, is to determine the extent to which the AES has been mischaracterised. Focusing on the political and theoretical ideas of the strategy, it questions the predominant view in the academic literature that the AES represented a radical left-wing break with the moderate, revisionist politics that dominated Labour's approach in the two decades after the Second World War. Locating the rise of the AES in its historical context, it examines the political ideas with which the prominent proponents of the AES responded to Britain's economic crisis and the concurrent breakdown of the post-war 'Keynesian consensus'. It aims to show that the AES was characterised by a high degree of involvement with radical left-wing ideas, and that several of its key advocates sought to justify their strategy through the language and theoretical frameworks of Marxist theory. However, through an examination of AES approaches to socialist strategy, the capitalist economy, Britain's economic decline and the rise of class conflict, the book also argues that existing academic accounts have significantly overstated the radicalism of the strategy. What was perhaps more notable about the AES, especially in the light of its stated 'revolutionary' aims, was the extent of its moderation—its continuities with post-war Labour revisionism, its marked reluctance to look beyond the market economy, the degree of its preoccupation with Britain's global-economic status, and its inability to break with Labourist politics of class co-operation in the national interest. While the book will argue that the AES was the last mainstream political strategy in Britain identifiable as a 'class politics' socialist initiative, it will also point to some of the ways in which its ideas perhaps prepared the way for New Labour in the 1990s.

## PROMINENT ACADEMIC VIEWS ON THE AES

The academic literature has tended to emphasise the left-wing radicalism of the AES. According to Tomlinson, the AES 'represented a violent break with the whole of post-war British approaches to economic policy'.[5] Seyd argues along similar lines: the 1970s saw a 'radical rethinking of the Party's previous commitments'.[6] Thompson argues that the AES 'represented, *au fond*, a fundamental challenge to the ethos, principles and practice of capitalism',[7] and that 'the overarching macroeconomic rationale of Keynesian social democracy came in for a severe pounding from the [AES] Left'.[8] According to Shaw, Labour's 1983, AES-derived general-election manifesto was 'highly ambitious' and 'stuffed with left-wing ideas'.[9] For Panitch and Leys, the AES marked an attempt to break with Labourist tradition: it wanted to 'pull the party out of the failed patterns of its past behaviour', and its development belonged to 'a broader attempt on the part of a remarkably creative British Marxist left...to transcend the limits of both Labourist parliamentarism and Trotskyist and Leninist vanguardism'.[10] According to Cronin, Labour's 1973 party programme 'made clear the new, or recently clarified, polarisation of British politics and called for a dramatic shift of power and wealth to working people and a major expansion of public ownership'.[11] Although the arguments regarding the radicalism of the AES are often qualified, an underlying message has been that it represented a highly significant shift leftward in the Labour Party during the 1970s and early 1980s. As Jones argues, it 'amounted to a clear repudiation of a revisionist social-democratic approach to economic strategy'.[12]

An important work on the AES, its book-length study by Wickham-Jones, calls it an 'extremely radical' strategy.[13] While the AES policy of reflation was 'conventional', Wickham-Jones argues, its policies of public ownership, economic planning, price controls, industrial democracy and import controls were original, radical and innovative.[14] For Wickham-Jones, the radical nature of the AES is evidenced by what he sees as its Marxist foundations:

> The main theoretical influence for the argument about monopolisation was not Keynesian economics but Marxist in orientation. Elements of the theory such as the focus on the concentrated structure of the economy, the pressure on firms to maximise profits, and the role of classes and class conflict drew on Marxist economic analysis. It was not an orthodox Marxism but one which stressed the monopolistic nature of capitalism.[15]

The party's understanding of 'economic developments owed more to Marx than Keynes'.[16] Labour 'jettisoned the Keynesian social democracy' which had previously characterised its economic strategy, for an economic theory based on a 'modified Marxism'.[17] Together with his association of the AES with Marxism, Wickham-Jones places it outside the reformist tradition. The AES was 'far removed' in its content and objectives from Labour's previous policy pronouncements, going beyond the 'moderation of reformism' and the limits to social-democratic radicalism described by Przeworski.[18] With the AES, Labour 'abandoned one kind of social democracy for a qualitatively different and more radical version'.[19] In its latter version, social democracy entailed 'a transformation of society based on the development of new relationships involving accountability and industrial democracy'.[20] Wickham-Jones strongly disputes the argument that Labour remained 'a moderate party constrained by capitalism'.[21] The Labour left 'did not recognise the unyielding domination of the economy by capitalists'.[22] The AES represented a politics outside the kind of ideological framework within which previous Labour politics was bound: it was not a 'mild strategy' nor was it 'developed within the framework of Labour's existing commitments'.[23]

Wickham-Jones's book is a well-researched account of the rise and development of the AES within the Labour Party. Its claims about the political and ideological nature of the AES, however, receive limited substantiation. This is partly because its focus is policy formation rather than policy content, a history of party-political processes and events rather than an analysis of ideas and theories. While Wickham-Jones does address counter-arguments regarding the ideological orientation of the AES, he does so mainly in his concluding chapter and without an in-depth focus. His argument that the AES was an 'extremely radical' strategy of 'modified Marxism' therefore appears unconvincing and at odds with the focus chosen for his study. For example, his position that AES emphases on economic monopolisation and class conflict were examples of the strategy's Marxist foundations (however partial) is left unsupported in his study; it is merely assumed that a strategy with such emphases must necessarily have had a theoretical affinity with Marxism.

In Thompson's case, the political content of the AES is considered in greater detail, but his characterisation of the strategy is also unconvincing. His book *Political Economy and the Labour Party* shows that the AES favoured selective nationalisations, aspects of industrial democracy, increased state planning, the stimulation of demand and controls on imports, but it does not explain why these policies should be considered a challenge to capitalist 'ethos, principles and practice' or 'a radical socialist alternative'.[24] Indeed, Thompson goes on to assess AES positions as a 'Keynesianism with attitude' because they entailed reflating the economy and implementing policies such as 'extended public ownership, industrial democracy and purposive economic planning'.[25] It is not adequately explained precisely why this variant of Keynesianism represented a challenge to capitalist principles any more so than the Keynesianism that had been the economic orthodoxy of the advanced capitalist economies and very much an accepted constituent of their 'ethos, principles and practice'.

Likewise, Thompson credits the left-wing AES economist Geoffrey Hodgson with seeking a radical break with Keynesian social democracy,[26] yet his own analysis of Hodgson's politics arguably shows that they were not against market exchange, competition and international commerce. Thompson cites Hodgson's calls for 'parallel and competing public firms', a 'solution [which] implies competition and...a market'.[27] Again, why such proposals ought to be considered a 'fundamental challenge' to capitalism remains largely unanswered in Thompson's account. While Thompson makes interesting comparisons between Labour revisionism and the Labour left, his intention seems to be to establish the radicalism of the AES simply by contrasting it to the political moderation of the right. Indeed, at times, academic accounts have considered the AES as an ambitious left-wing strategy based on the fact that it received hostile opposition from British industry or that it 'thoroughly alarmed' the right-wing of the Labour Party.[28] Wickham-Jones, for instance, seeks to support the radical credentials of the AES by pointing to the capitalists' 'overt and extreme hostility towards it'.[29] But whether that factor alone necessarily sheds much light on the ideological orientations of the AES—any more so than what its supporters thought about the strategy—can be doubted. Many proponents and opponents of the AES saw the strategy as far-reaching and radical, but unless their perceptions of the AES are to be taken at face-value, they need to be subjected to a greater degree of objective scrutiny in order to establish the nature of the strategy's ideological foundations.

## A New 'Marketplace for Ideas' in the 1970s

A study of this kind is also apt in the context of a recent growth of interest in 1970s Britain, an area which, as Black and Pemberton argue, has been 'comparatively ill-served by historians'.[30] As Cawood points out, the first focused study of the 1970s, Alwyn Turner's *Crisis? What Crisis?*, appeared only in 2008, and concentrated heavily on the decade's cultural developments rather than offering a 'detailed analysis of the politics of the crisis'.[31] Turner's history was followed by a number of other books on the decade: Beckett's engaging journalistic account *When the Lights Went Out*, published in 2009; Sandbrook's 2012 general history of the latter part of the decade, *Seasons in the Sun* (which became the basis for his BBC Two documentary series, *The Seventies*); Black, Pemberton and Thane's edited volume of essays, *Reassessing 1970s Britain*; and Medhurst's more polemical account *That Option No Longer Exists*.

The latter two books feature the AES as a major focus. Medhurst's contributes to the idea that this period represents something of a golden age for the British left, and upholds the AES as 'the only viable option [in the given circumstances] for those working for achievable social and economic change'.[32] He rejects the presentation of the 1970s as a 'grey decade of decline and defeat', and depicts it as a period fertile for the rise of radical and alternative economic and political ideas. This idea also appears in Black et al., who build on Peter Hall's characterisation of the decade as expanding the 'marketplace of economic ideas'. Hall argued that the second half of the 1970s saw the British Treasury's loss of influence due to a growing political disenchantment with Keynesianism, which broadened the arena of debate around macroeconomic management to increasingly include the media, financial institutions, economic research institutes and also the wider public.[33] For Hall, this battle of ideas was principally between a Labour government identified with Keynesianism, and increasing numbers of individuals on the right advancing monetarist solutions.[34]

According to Black and Pemberton, however, the 'marketplace for ideas' concept can also apply to 'the quest on the left of British politics for an "alternative economic strategy"'.[35] In addition, they argue, the 'marketplace' concept could be widened beyond economic policy:

> it seems to us that one of the significant features of the 1970s is the breadth of the 'battle of ideas', a battle fought in the media..., in publishing..., in the much expanded higher-education sector and, of course, in the political arena.[36]

An interesting question arises, therefore, as to what extent the AES reflected this broadening of the 'battle of ideas' in British politics in the 1970s. To what extent did it take advantage of the apparently growing crisis of Keynesianism in order to advance a radical politics of the left? In addition, to what extent did the AES draw on radical-left ideas outside the repertoire of dominant Labour thinking in the 1950s and 1960s?

Black et al.'s volume—although containing chapters by Stuart Holland, the dominant theorist of the AES, and Mark Wickham-Jones, its academic scholar—does not analyse the broad ideological ambit of the strategy and the extent of its involvement with radical-left ideas and debates. Holland's chapter is mainly a review of his role in the development of the AES within the Labour Party, and a summary of his main economic proposals,[37] while Wickham-Jones's chapter—'The challenge of Stuart Holland'—also focuses on Holland's role and policy ideas. Indeed, Wickham-Jones argues that, 'From the left's perspective, in the marketplace for ideas, [Holland] exercised, for a time at any rate, a near monopolistic domination'.[38] Yet, although Holland's economic theories were, of course, central to the AES, the 'marketplace for ideas' that the strategy represented perhaps extended considerably beyond the views of a single individual. Indeed, Holland's positions—as a figure previously associated with the right of the Labour Party—and particularly the ways in which he framed them, were arguably influenced considerably by his awareness of counter-positions from individuals and groups to his left, both within and outside the AES. Without the left-wing resurgence in and around Labour in the 1970s, it is perhaps less likely that Holland would have packaged his economic policies (also previously associated with the Labour right) in the markedly radical terms in which he came to present them, i.e. as 'revolutionary reforms', as policies for the revolutionary transformation of the capitalist system. In this sense, it is necessary to consider the influence of the expansion of the left's 'marketplace for ideas' in the 1970s on the ways in which the policies of the AES were posed and justified by its prominent advocates—i.e. in increasingly left-wing terms.

## Outline and Arguments

This book will focus, therefore, on the political ideas of the AES to evaluate the kind of socialist strategy that it represented. Although it will situate the AES in its specific historical context, by concentrating on ideas rather than events it aims to assess the ideological content of AES analyses and policies. In short, how radical was the AES's socialism? To what degree did it diverge from the more moderate conceptions of socialism previously dominant in the Labour Party, and from perhaps more radical conceptions both within and outside Labour?

Since the book focuses on the ideas of the AES, its main sources are the published texts in which they were propounded and discussed. The AES belongs to a socialist tradition of abundant written discourse, polemic, pamphleteering and published theoretical discussion, incorporating a variety of left-wing individuals and groups both for and against the strategy. As suggested above, this feature of the AES has arguably been inadequately explored and documented in the academic literature. To reiterate, however, this focus is necessary to assess the ideological content of AES approaches and their relation to other left-wing approaches. As such, this book, as an intellectual history, is primarily a critical analysis and discussion of the numerous books, pamphlets, manifestos, programmes, essays and articles authored by key proponents of the strategy.

Structurally, the book is divided into six further chapters. Chapter 2 will discuss the historical context in which the AES emerged, focusing on the breakdown by the early 1970s of the relative stability of class relations that had characterised Britain in the 1950s and early 1960s. It was in these new conditions that the AES advanced solutions that would aim both to regenerate working-class enthusiasm for the party and to secure trade-union co-operation through a strategy of reforms in the interests of the working class as well as the British economy. The following four chapters will be organised thematically. Chapter 3 will discuss the AES as a socialist strategy, focusing particularly on AES discussions around the old strategic question of 'reform or revolution'. An aim will be to illustrate that the

AES, despite its 'reformism' and the apparent incompatibility of its political and economic aims, involved a prominent attempt to justify itself in revolutionary terms, to renounce Labour's 'gradualism', and to assert its socialist radicalism through a dialogue with Marxist theory.

Chapter 4 will examine the economic approaches of the AES, focusing on Stuart Holland, the strategy's dominant economic theorist. It will consider whether the AES represented a radical break with Keynesian economic strategy and Labour revisionism, and the extent to which it was, as Donald Sassoon has suggested, 'a policy of *co-existence and partnership* with the private sector, aimed at improving the latter's performance'.[39] Chapter 5 will discuss AES approaches to the nation, and in particular to the role that Britain should play in the world economy. It will argue that Britain's economic decline was a central concern of the AES, which advanced protectionism not only as necessary for the implementation of progressive policies at home but also to re-establish Britain's standing abroad as a major economic power. Chapter 6, through a discussion of the ideas for industrial democracy and workers' control, will consider the role of the working class in the AES. It will discuss whether AES approaches saw the empowerment of workers in the workplace as a means to embolden working-class militancy or to engender improved industrial relations via closer class collaboration. Chapter 7, in summarising the arguments of the book, will contrast AES approaches to those which succeeded them in the 1980s and 1990s, addressing the question of whether the AES can be considered the final project of a mainstream British left identifiable as belonging to a socialist tradition.

## Notes

1. For example: *Telegraph*, 'Revealed: Corbyn's Manifesto'; *Mail Online*, 'The NEW Longest Suicide Note'; *Express*, 'Labour's Leaked Manifesto'.
2. Medhurst, *That Option No Longer Exists*, pp. 137, 154. His italics. See also Medhurst, 'The Myth of the 1970s'.
3. For example: Jones, 'Those Crazy Days of "Socialism"'; Bailey, 'Not all "The Bad Old Days"'; Reynolds, 'Labour's Alternative Economic Strategy'.
4. *Telegraph*, 'Death of New Labour'.
5. Tomlinson, 'Economic Policy', p. 12.
6. Seyd, *The Rise and Fall of the Labour Left*, p. 22.
7. Thompson, *Political Economy and the Labour Party*, p. 5.
8. Thompson, *Left in the Wilderness*, p. 35.
9. Shaw, *The Labour Party Since 1945*, p. 167.

10. Panitch and Leys, *The End of Parliamentary Socialism*, pp. 73, 154.
11. Cronin, *New Labour's Pasts*, p. 136.
12. Jones, *Remaking the Labour Party*, p. 91.
13. Wickham-Jones, *Economic Strategy and the Labour Party*, p. 77.
14. Ibid., pp. 5, 53.
15. Ibid., p. 58.
16. Ibid., p. 80.
17. Ibid., pp. 81, 193. Wickham-Jones has more recently qualified this point somewhat, arguing that Holland's 'approach owed as much to Marx as to Keynes', even if it was not a 'dogmatic or even a particularly coherent' Marxism. Nevertheless, Holland 'drew heavily on important strands from Marxist economic debates', notably in his 'emphasis on monopolisation and on the role of multinationals', as well as in his analysis of the power of capital, which 'was underpinned by notions of class and of class conflict'. (Wickham-Jones, 'The Challenge of Stuart Holland', pp. 129, 135.)
18. Wickham-Jones, *Economic Strategy and the Labour Party*, p. 84.
19. Ibid., p. 83.
20. Ibid.
21. Ibid., p. 194.
22. Ibid., p. 84.
23. Ibid., p. 195.
24. Thompson, *Political Economy and the Labour Party*, pp. 5, 234.
25. Ibid., p. 195.
26. Ibid., p. 234.
27. Ibid., p. 233.
28. Shaw, *The Labour Party Since 1945*, p. 113.
29. Wickham-Jones, *Economic Strategy and the Labour Party*, p. 196.
30. Black and Pemberton, 'Introduction', p. 15.
31. Cawood, 'Crisis? What Crisis?'.
32. Medhurst, *That Option No Longer Exists*, p. 152.
33. Hall, 'Policy Paradigms', p. 286.
34. Ibid., pp. 283–7.
35. Black and Pemberton, 'Introduction', p. 15.
36. Ibid., p. 15.
37. Holland, 'Alternative European and Economic Strategies'.
38. Wickham-Jones, 'The challenge of Stuart Holland', p. 133.
39. Sassoon, *One Hundred Years of Socialism*, p. 525. His italics.

# CHAPTER 2

# Class and Party: The Historical Context of the Rise of the AES

The party is clearly ready for change, and those people who are prepared to take the time (and make the effort) to put forward new ideas may be surprised to discover how responsive the party is likely to be to them...By 1973 at the latest, this machine has got to be preparing itself for the next general election and that means that the decisions will have to be taken quite soon.
—Tony Benn, 1971[1]

The next few years are decisive. Those who are 'lulled to sleep' by any temporary calm in the storm of class struggle in Britain will be violently awoken by conflicts and clashes which will put in the shade even the General Strike of 1926.
—Labour Party Young Socialists, 1973[2]

## INTRODUCTION

This chapter discusses the political context in which the AES emerged. While Chapters 4 and 5 will consider the national and international economic situation to which the AES's ideas sought to respond, this chapter will focus on what was arguably the central development of 1970s British politics—the breakdown of the relative stability of post-war British industrial relations. It will relate the rise of the AES to the Labour Party's need to

© The Author(s) 2020
B. Tufekci, *The Socialist Ideas of the British Left's Alternative Economic Strategy*,
https://doi.org/10.1007/978-3-030-34998-1_2

adjust itself politically and organisationally to maintain its relevance to this new social and political environment, one which saw not only an explosion in industrial militancy but also the early erosion of Labour's support base in the working class. This is crucial to understanding the AES in its historical context, since, as discussed below, the AES informed the approach of a Labour government that based its core legitimacy on its self-professed capacity to foster industrial harmony due to its unique relationship with British workers.

The first part of this chapter will outline the post-war class conditions in which the AES's predecessor, Labour revisionism, dominated the party's politics. With economic growth and the relative stability of class relations, Labour witnessed an increased party interest in loosening its association with the working class. Labour's leading revisionist theoretician, Anthony Crosland, believed that post-war Britain had entered a new phase of social and economic development distinct from 'traditional capitalism'. This idea coincided with a broad intellectual trend, in the 1950s and early 1960s, declaring the end of class conflict and the left-right ideological struggles which class conflict had engendered and sustained. Although these theories of an emerging conflict-free society turned out to have been mistaken, they were also intellectual reflections of the large degree of relative class harmony characterising post-war Western society.

In Britain, this era of relative stability ended in the late 1960s, as the decline of the relative economic growth underpinning the post-war political consensus gave way to the emergence of economic crisis and a large-scale intensification of industrial conflict. Although significant instances of labour unrest had occurred in the 1950s—including national strikes in shipbuilding and engineering[3]—it was typically smaller in scale, and industrial relations lacked the degree of direct political significance that it came to acquire by the late 1960s. With this politicisation of industrial conflict, greater political space was created—both in the Labour Party and in national politics more broadly—for the view that government intervention in workers' economic interests was a legitimate option to manage the intractable war taking place in British industry. That this notion had been placed on the national political agenda gave added encouragement to the rise of a Labour left to devise a strategy for the alleviation of industrial conflict via government action in favour of the working class.

However, the late 1960s and early 1970s also witnessed a weakening of Labour's working-class support, at a time when Labour's need of its working-class ties had increased. As explained below, there were three facets to this problem: the decline of Labour as a mass organisation, a result of growing disillusion with the party during the 1960s Wilson governments, which led to a significant exodus of members from the party; a growing electoral crisis, as the 1970 general election called into question post-war electoral stability and the reliability of Labour's working-class electoral support base; and the rise of tensions between Labour and the trade unions, as the rise of workplace militancy challenged Labour's ability to maintain a working relationship with British trade-unionism to obtain its co-operation with Labour's pay policies. If Labour was to present itself as the party uniquely able to secure industrial peace due to its close relationship with British workers, by the early 1970s it had become clear that Labour required an alternative to the old politics that had helped produce the increased tensions between the party and its working-class base.

The final part of this chapter will briefly outline the Labour government's approach to class conflict in the 1970s, focusing particularly on its implementation of the 'social contract', Labour's strategy for industrial peace devised via the AES, which continued to inform official Labour policy until 1983, a number of years after the strategy's stark failure in the late 1970s to meet the expectations of the AES left. This will provide a background to the discussions of subsequent chapters, which will explore the ideological and theoretical tensions within AES approaches, considering whether, in the light of its limitations, the AES contained the scope to produce practical outcomes fundamentally different from those of the 1974–1979 Labour government.

## Labour Revisionism

Labour revisionism emerged in the specific social and economic climate of the 1950s. Associated with the Labour right, it was the dominant ideological orientation of the Labour Party in the first two decades after the Second World War. As its name suggested, revisionism sought to re-think what it saw as Labour's outdated traditions and ideological nostrums. Although Anthony Crosland, the chief intellectual architect of Labour revisionism, expressed his inspiration by Eduard Bernstein and claimed to be refuting the sacred cows of Marxist theory, revisionism's main target was Labour's long association with nationalisation, state intervention and the working class. Unlike German social democracy (Bernstein's target), Labour had not had a Marxist past. What it did contain, however, was a longstanding left-wing association of socialism with an economic transformation via the state's agency. Thus in Crosland's revamping of the socialist project the need for this transformation was demoted in importance or relevance to Britain as it stood in 1950s. As Warde points out, this was 'a new kind of socialism', requiring 'less a change of social structure than a change of attitude: the socialist project was so re-defined that Crosland could explicitly exclude, as policies of social advance, free social services, nationalization, more economic control, and heavier direct taxation'.[4] Indeed, for Crosland, 'traditional capitalism' had been 'reformed and modified almost out of existence' with the changes effected by the post-war Labour government (full employment, welfarism, selective public ownership), and socialists now faced a very different type of society.[5]

Accompanying its claim of qualitative systemic change was the revisionist assertion of the increased redundancy of social conflict, in particular the antagonism between social classes. As Thompson puts it:

> A certain cross-class, aspirational consensus was seen by some as having emerged, something that militated against class conflict and thence the kind of policies that such conflict had previously implied. Consistent with this was Crosland's view that increasing affluence, regardless of relative impoverishment, would progressively eliminate the material basis of social antagonism.[6]

This is not to say that Crosland had quite come to embrace a form of the 'post-class' type of political analysis that, as discussed in Chapter 7, found favour on the British left in the 1990s. He did not disagree that there would 'always be potential conflicts between management and labour', and that these 'harsh facts' could not be 'spirited away by moral rearmament touring troupes, or luncheons of progressive businessmen, or syndicalist castles in the air'.[7] He saw labour as one of the two sides of industry, and argued that the 'workers' side must have an untrammelled Trade Union movement to defend its claims'.[8] Yet, with improved management, as well as greater working-class affluence, industrial relations would see the weakening of class tensions: 'greater or lesser harmony is largely a function of the quality of management'.[9]

In a sense, the argument that increased working-class affluence would alleviate class tensions did not neatly correspond with the reality of post-war industrial relations. As Allen argued, strikes in fact increased during the post-war period of relative prosperity, and statistics on manual workers showed that 'the most prosperous ones, the dockers, the miners and motor car workers, are also the most strike prone'.[10] There was little reason to assume that the benefits of greater affluence, such as a better educated workforce, would automatically reduce industrial unrest: 'the newly emerging strike prone groups are the draughtsmen, school-teachers and clerks. In the past apprentice-skilled craftsmen were always better educated than other manual workers and at the same time were more effective in their industrial action'.[11] If trade-unionism remained regarded by workers as the most effective means to defend or improve their economic situation, there was perhaps no necessary causal relationship between greater prosperity and reduced class conflict in capitalist society.

However, the revisionist account did, to an extent, reflect the material realities of its historical period. As David Coates argues, from the perspective of subsequent decades the climate of industrial relations in the 1950s seemed 'particularly serene'.[12] Unemployment was low and job security was high. Many of the industries that had dominated the interwar economy were still booming until the late 1950s and there was a rapid expansion of new industries like light engineering and motorcar production. For the first time, annual wage rises became the 'accepted norm', and demand for newly mass-produced consumer goods (televisions, vacuum cleaners, refrigerators) began to encompass 'wider and wider sections of the employed population as living standards, though still low, steadily began to rise'.[13] As another account puts it:

> If class conflict was never abolished in all this, it was nonetheless substantially reshaped…At the centre of this enactment was a complex new workplace compromise between big capital and much of organised labour, in which certain more vicious exploitative practices gave way to rising wages and greater work security, in exchange for labour cooperation to enhance productivity.[14]

With the rise in living standards, the establishment of the welfare system after the war and the easing of class tensions, the political salience of class came into question. With rising prosperity, many felt that Labour's apparently cloth-cap, proletarian image had become outmoded, and Labour's identification with the trade unions and the working class was seen to have become an electoral liability.[15]

Recognising that the competing ideological visions of left and right had been closely associated with competing class interests, several intellectuals also wrote about growing affluence causing the end of ideology. The prominent American sociologist Daniel Bell argued that left and right ideological rivalry meant little in a post-war world where workers were 'tamed' by 'consumption society' and 'escapist fantasies' of owning a small shop or petrol station.[16] It was argued that class conflict had waned or even disappeared as a result of 'embourgeoisment', the 'affluent society' or the redistribution of wealth through state intervention. Another American sociologist, Seymour Martin Lipset, represented this mood in 1960 as follows:

> the fundamental political problems of the industrial revolution have been solved: the workers have achieved industrial and political citizenship, the conservatives have accepted the welfare state, and the democratic left has recognised that an increase in overall state power carries with it more dangers to freedom than solutions for economic problems. This very triumph of the democratic social revolution in the West ends domestic politics for those intellectuals who must have ideologies or utopias to motivate them to political action.[17]

The idea was that a new historical epoch had emerged, one fundamentally different from that of the previous one hundred or so years since the industrial revolution had spawned the modern class conflicts and their representative ideologies. Though such accounts turned out to have been deeply flawed—with their tendency to interpret the historically specific social and political developments accompanying post-war economic growth as permanent and stable[18]—as intellectual reflections on post-war realities, they were based on an element of truth: post-war growth had produced relative social and industrial stability in the 1950s, and post-war politics, including Labour revisionism, was to a large extent a product of that stability.

## EARLY CHALLENGES TO REVISIONISM

This is not to argue that opposition to revisionist dominance did not occur until the 1970s, or that there was no Labour left in the intervening period. Left-wing Labour politicians like Aneurin Bevan, Richard Crossman, Barbara Castle and John Strachey made attempts to challenge the dominance of the revisionist right. However, these attempts were primarily at the level of polemic and made little impact as an organisational offensive against the revisionist leadership, or even as a systematic critique of revisionist economic ideas. As Wickham-Jones points out, the Labour left's economic ideas 'lacked the coherence of Revisionism and seemed to be rooted in the past', i.e. in the 'fundamentalist' politics of state nationalisation and planning.[19] In addition, the Bevanites' primary focus was on British foreign policy, particularly nuclear disarmament, rather than the economic foundations of revisionist thinking.[20] Furthermore, as Panitch argues, the Bevanite left was almost wholly a parliamentary phenomenon, and one whose socialism was characterised by a 'parliamentary paternalism' which laid little emphasis on working-class agency or participation.[21]

This has been linked to the constitutional restrictions that Labour had placed on internal factions prior to the 1970s, which encouraged Bevanite activities to be 'almost solely concentrated within the PLP'.[22] Whatever the case, Bevan proved an inconsistent ally of the grassroots left, both in the anti-nuclear-weapons movement and the trade unions. In 1957, having accepted the role of Shadow Foreign Secretary the previous year, he reversed his longstanding support for unilateral nuclear disarmament, and in his final speech in Parliament, in November 1959, he lamented Labour's inability to 'persuade the ordinary men and women that it is worth while making sacrifices in their immediate standards or forgoing substantial rising standards to extend fixed capital equipment throughout the country'.[23] Although subsequent generations of Labour-leftists continued to herald Bevan as the archetype of the Labour radical, by the time of his death in 1960 he had made a large degree of peace with the revisionist party leadership.

Despite the limitations of its intra-party opposition, however, the revisionist movement did not proceed without setbacks. Its thwarted campaign against Clause 4 under the revisionist leadership of Hugh Gaitskell, upon Labour's third successive general election defeat in 1959, was a prominent example of the limits to revisionist 'modernisation' of the Labour Party. Indeed, according to Minkin, it was in 1959 that the 'golden age' of Labour revisionism ended, giving way to a new 'crisis of reinforcing tensions' between the Labour leadership, its internal factions and its trade-union allies.[24] Along with their retreat on Clause 4, the 1960 Labour conference saw the Labour leaders defeated on the policy of nuclear weapons, as the Transport and General Workers' Union (TGWU), with the support of other unions, voted in favour of unilateral nuclear disarmament (a Conference decision which Gaitskell rejected and reversed in 1961). According to Minkin, this event marked a break with the unions' post-war practice of restricting themselves to industrial matters and abstaining from public interference in the political decisions of the Labour leadership.[25]

However, Labour's essentially revisionist strategy, central to which was the ongoing attempt to weaken Labour's association with the working class, continued into the 1970 general election, in which Labour stood with a manifesto dominated by the revisionist ideas of the Labour right.[26] Some saw Labour's 1961 policy document *Signposts for the Sixties*, with its rhetorical attack on a 'small ruling caste', as a potential starting point for a socialist renewal in the party[27]; but, as Minkin points out, by the time of Labour's 1964 general election win, 'most commentators agreed that the Party had lost its "cloth cap" image. It now appeared as a classless and meritocratic party with a special appeal to the new white-collar salariat'.[28]

It was only after the experience of Labour's 1964–1970 governments that a Labour left found itself in a favourable position to challenge the old revisionist right and assert viably the need for a class-oriented Labour politics. First announced in Labour's 1973 party programme, each Labour general-election manifesto between 1974 and 1983 pledged a fundamental change 'in the balance of power and wealth in favour of working people and their families', representing a significant shift of tone in Labour's political pronouncements. The following section will consider some of the factors that made this shift possible.

## The Erosion of Labour's Working-Class Base

The backdrop to Labour's reorientation to the working class in the early 1970s was the erosion of its working-class support from the late 1960s. As mentioned, there were three features of this decline of working-class support: Labour's organisational decline, its electoral decline, and the deterioration of its relationship with the unions. As discussed below, this decline was a significant threat to the party because, by the early 1970s, the union-Labour alliance had come to represent a renewed and heightened importance for Labour. With the rise of class tensions in that period, along with the detrimental impact that this rise was widely perceived to be having on the British economy, Labour recognised that a strengthened relationship with the working class had acquired a new significance for its political purpose and electoral success.

### Labour's Loss of Members

Labour's individual membership had peaked at around one million in the early 1950s. By 1964 that figure had fallen to around 830,000, and by 1970 it was less than 700,000.[29] Although these figures were themselves large overestimates due to the manner in which the party calculated individual membership, they nevertheless demonstrated a steep downward trend.[30] According to Forester's estimate of the party's actual membership, it had more than halved between 1951 and 1970,[31] while for Pimlott it had dropped by one third during the 1964–1970 government alone.[32]

Workers formed a significant portion of the party's deserters: in *The Labour Party in Crisis*, Whiteley argued that a large part of the Labour membership's decline could be attributed to the departure of working-class members following the Labour government's failures in the late 1960s.[33] In Hindess's well-known account in 1971, the fall in working-class political participation reduced Labour's orientation to working-class concerns, which in turn led to a further fall in working-class participation, since workers were less likely to see Labour as a party for their interests.[34] Whatever the case, the late 1960s saw a significant weakening in Labour's standing as the mass party of British workers. For Pimlott, Labour was 'withering away at the grass roots'.[35] According to Minkin, Constituency Labour Party (CLP) organisations had 'shrivelled to a skeleton during the period from 1966 to 1970'.[36] As Seyd put it: 'A combination of social change, neglect and political disillusionment almost destroyed the Labour Party as a mass party'.[37]

Along with the erosion of its mass membership, by the end of the 1960s there were signs that Labour was losing its attraction to left-wing activism in the country. With widespread left-wing anger at the 1960s Labour government, left-wing activists were increasingly looking to rival groups to the left of the Labour Party, in particular the Trotskyist organisations, whose memberships saw some growth in this period.[38] Although the numbers lost to these organisations were modest in absolute terms, as an electoral machine Labour had always had a dependence on highly motivated individuals who, despite constituting a minority within the party as a whole, were crucial to the maintenance of its mass base. As Richard Crossman put it in a frequently cited passage, Labour 'required militants' to organise party support—'politically conscious Socialists' who, though excluded from power in the party, were necessary 'to do the work of organising the constituencies'.[39] Ralph Miliband also highlighted the importance for Labour of its activists: in contrast to the Conservatives, Labour had a particular dependence on its activist base due to the financial pressures under which it had to operate, and thus 'could not but welcome and encourage' the commitment of activists who, on a voluntary basis, performed the 'activities, tasks and chores' central to building support for the party.[40] By the late 1960s, however, after two decades of Labour's domination by revisionist centrism, it appeared that Labour's appeal to the wider left had diminished.

The rise of Labour leftism in the early 1970s occurred within the context of this decline of Labour as a mass party. As Panitch has argued, this new left recognised 'that the traditional loyalties underlying Labour support were fraying severely and that the only way to remedy this was not to attempt to reassert old "parliamentary paternalism" of a social democratic welfare state in crisis, but to turn the party into an agency of social and political mobilization'.[41] In line with this agenda, the 1970s saw the formation of Labour-left organisations seeking to reverse the decline of Labour's support base within the working-class, as well as to attract new activists to the party. Benn emerged as a key figure in the Labour left's attempt to appeal to working-class militants as well as radical leftists outside of the Labour Party.[42] As one left-wing critic noted, the Bennites' aim was to 'initiate a campaign to recruit activists who would otherwise be drawn into revolutionary politics'.[43] The Campaign for Labour Party Democracy (CLPD) was formed in 1973 with the aim to democratise the party to make its leadership more responsive to the demands of its party base, and the Labour Co-ordinating Committee (LCC) was formed in 1978 to develop Labour into a party of mass campaigns and mass organisation, particularly within the trade union movement.[44]

The organisational scope of these new groups differed from that of postwar left-wing factions like the Tribune Group of Labour MPs, which, as Seyd points out, had confined its activities mainly to parliamentary business.[45] Seyd argues that the new Labour activists involved in the newer groups were less interested in sustaining in office a Labour government which failed to implement the policies adopted by the party while in opposition.[46] Arguably, however, sections of the Labour leadership understood the advantages of this re-energised activism, which could serve to breathe new life into the party at a time when Labour's ties with its electoral and activist base had weakened. The Labour leadership tolerated Labour-left factions in the 1970s, where it had not done so in the 1950s.[47] This was partly because of the increased strength of the Labour left in the 1970s, but perhaps also due to an appreciation within the PLP leadership that the alternative was the party's increased irrelevance and deterioration in the face of the highly dynamic and uncertain political climate that had emerged by the 1970s.

## The Decline of 'Class Voting'

Labour's electoral crisis was highlighted by the 1970 general election, after which the long-term decline in Labour's electoral base in the working class became a growing political focus for the party. A key feature of the relative economic and political stability of the first two decades after the Second World War was the stability of the electoral realm, the pattern and structure of post-war voting. In those two decades, about 90% of the British voters voted either Labour or Conservative, and electoral behaviour seemed driven by the predictable basis of voters' sociological locations in class society. As Franklin put it in *The Decline of Class Voting in Britain*, in this period

> the extent to which parties gained or lost seats from election to election was quite small, and continuity of political patterns was evident even when government changed hands. During most of this period governments enjoyed relatively stable levels of popularity between elections and, above all, there were only two major parties contending for power.[48]

Whereas in the interwar years class-party alignment had been relatively weak, the 1950s were the peak years in the electoral association between classes and parties.[49] Pulzer's famous assertion that class was the basis of British politics and that all else was 'embellishment and detail' was widely accepted.[50] According to Alford, an association between class and voting was 'natural and expected' and it would be 'remarkable if such a relation were not found', given 'the existence of class interests, the representation of those interests by political parties, and the regular association of certain parties with certain interests'.[51] Class was 'pre-eminent among the factors used to explain party allegiance in Britain'.[52] Individuals from certain classes would vote for certain parties: so strong was this belief, that individuals who voted otherwise, i.e. for parties other than their 'natural' party, were labelled political 'deviants', and a range of theories were devised to explain such deviations from the class-voting norm.[53] Moreover, the assumed reality that parties were the class representatives of a socially stratified electorate was promoted by some as a source of democratic wellbeing. As Lipset wrote, 'a healthy democracy requires consensus on the nature of the political struggle, and this includes the assumption that different groups are best served by different parties'.[54]

The 1970 general election drew attention to a long-term electoral process that political scientists came to call a 'class dealignment' in British politics, an election in which 'Labour first lost a large proportion of voters from among social groups which had previously supported the party'.[55] The breakdown of the post-war Keynesian consensus (see Chapter 4) coincided with significant changes in voting. The stability that had characterised voting behaviour in the two decades after 1945 was replaced by the increased volatility at the ballot box of the 1970s. The two elections held in 1974 saw Labour and the Conservatives' combined share of the vote fall to around 75%.[56] By the 1980s, academics and commentators from across the ideological spectrum began to describe what they viewed as a clear process of transformation in the class nature of politics and society generally.[57]

In their 1974 book *Political Change in Britain*, Butler and Stokes referred to an 'aging' of the class and party alignment, which they saw as a product of growing working-class affluence.[58] Yet, as Crewe et al. argued in 1977, the common academic explanations given in the 1960s for the decline of class politics—such as 'affluence' and the 'end of ideology'—rang less true in the changed economic and political circumstances of the 1970s. After all, class-party electoral alignment was weakest in the interwar Depression years and strongest in the 'relatively prosperous and ideologically bland 1950s'.[59] The rise of class tensions and economic instability in the years leading up to the 1974 elections had not given rise to greater class-party alignment. On the contrary, these developments showed that 'the class basis of party support...could continue to wither away regardless of the downturn in the economy and the resurgence of ideological and class conflict'.[60]

What had developed by the 1970s, therefore, was the decline of Labour's working-class base at a time when class had arguably acquired an *increased* political significance. To a political-science mindset so strongly influenced by a sociological understanding of the relationship between class and politics, a decline of party-class alignment at the ballot box tended to indicate a decline in the political salience of class in general. But the 1970s were also a decade in which class conflict played a crucial if not decisive role in the fall of three governments—Wilson's in 1970, Heath's in 1974 and Callaghan's in 1979.[61] Trade-union membership in Britain, while stagnant for much of the post-war period, had never been higher by the end of the 1970s. In 1975, the Conservative Party chose a leader who saw the elimination of the social and political power of organised labour as among her principal tasks in domestic politics; and her defeat of the year-long miners' strike of

1984–1985 proved to be a watershed in British political history, with far-reaching consequences for both main parties, as discussed in Chapter 7. It was clear that class had an importance for party politics beyond its salience for voting behaviour. The late 1960s to the early 1980s saw not the reduction in the political importance of class but the struggle of the Labour Party to maintain its relevance to workers at a time when the relative stability of British post-war class relations (including its electoral expressions) was being unravelled. It was this challenge that the AES rose to meet, attempting to address the political imperative to strengthen Labour's working-class alliance by re-establishing Labour's identification with the working class, repairing the damage seen to have been caused by the revisionist leadership of the 1960s.

### Workplace Militancy and Labour's Union Alliance

This 'damage' was arguably most apparent in the sphere of industrial relations, as was the breakdown of post-war class stability. In addition to its electoral and membership decline, by 1970 Labour confronted increased tensions in its relations with the trade-union movement due in part to a politicisation of industrial relations that had developed in the 1960s. According to Coates, this occurred in two broad stages. The first stage, between 1961 and 1973, saw British politics becoming 'increasingly dominated by the emerging weakness of British industrial capital, and by the threat that emerging weakness posed to the full employment basis of the post-war settlement'.[62] These problems were compounded in the second stage, beginning after 1973, which was characterised by a declining American dominance of world capitalism and a consequent 'generalised crisis of Keynesian demand management'.[63] The first stage gave rise to a corporatist, tripartist response from British governments, whereas the second stage saw the rise of monetarist policies from the late 1970s. The corporatist response entailed a 'social contract' which sought to maintain the class equilibrium of the 1950s, the close negotiations between the government and 'peak organisations of capital and labour' that had characterised that decade. The monetarist response, on the other hand, sought a sharp break with the post-war settlement, rejecting Keynesian policies for full employment and 'eschewing the cosy "beer and sandwiches" relationship of Labour Ministers and trade unionists'.[64] Both stages, however, were characterised by the politicisation of industrial relations, as British governments searched for solutions to the increased strain placed on the terms of the post-war settlement (full employment, welfare provision, rising living standards) by the growing structural weakness of Britain's economy.[65]

In the face of a declining British capitalism, with rising inflation, slow growth and lack of competitiveness in the international market, the Wilson government introduced a wage freeze in July 1966 and a devaluation of the pound in November 1967 accompanied by cuts in public spending.[66] Wilson's National Plan, pledging increased investment and technological innovation, was thereby derailed, and by January 1968 unemployment had doubled under Labour.[67] With the growth of an increasingly self-confident workplace militancy in the late 1960s, as workers rose to defend their jobs, wages and conditions against economic decline, the Labour government responded initially with *voluntary* incomes policy, and in 1968 the majority proposals of the Donovan Commission (see Chapter 6) recommended measures to strengthen the official union leadership's control of the union rank and file rather than legal sanctions against unions. In 1969, however, against the backdrop of increasingly disruptive strikes (prominently those of the seamen in 1966 and the Liverpool dockers in 1967) and growing concern among international finance with Labour's ability to govern, the Labour government effectively rejected the Donovan proposals in its notorious White Paper *In Place of Strife* (drafted by Wilson and the Employment Minister Barbara Castle), which called for a legislative restriction of union power.[68]

Although, as discussed below, its intensity should not be exaggerated, the trade-union opposition to *In Place of Strife*—along with that of Cabinet members, including leading figures in Labour revisionism (such as Crosland and Roy Jenkins), which had acquired an association with the principles of union autonomy during Labour's close alliance with the right-dominated TUC in the post-war period[69]—was enough to convince the Labour government against further pursuit of a strategy based on direct statutory attacks on the unions. The strikes against *In Place of Strife*, though involving a small minority of workers, were the first against state policy since the general strike of 1926.[70] For their part, trade-union leaders were concerned to protect their most basic powers and prerogatives against statutory challenges from *any* government—and the fact that this was a Labour government underlined the extent to which union-Labour relations had been dented under Wilson.

This was not, of course, the first time that Labour ministers had threatened legal action against workplace militancy; strikes were regularly broken up by the Labour government in the 1940s, for example, including through the use of British troops.[71] As Seyd argues, however, *In Place of Strife* was arguably the first major challenge by any British government to the post-war political consensus, to the 'Butskellist' emphasis on co-operation and bargaining that had characterised the 1950s and early 1960s.[72] Trade unions were a cornerstone of Britain's relative stability in the post-war period. Labour had played a major role in Churchill's war ministry during the Second World War, and the loyalty of trade-union leaders like Ernest Bevin, Minister of Labour during the war, was critical to the maintenance of labour discipline and working-class co-operation. After the war, close government-union collaboration remained vital to the maintenance of industrial order. With Labour elected to government in 1945, trade-union representation on government committees grew from 12 in 1939 to 60 in 1948 and to 81 in 1951.[73] Despite the austere economic environment, including Attlee's maintenance of rationing, only seven million days were lost to strikes in the first three years after the war, over twenty times fewer than those lost in the first three years after the First World War.[74] The unions had become an 'estate of the realm', a part of the state apparatus: though negative press portrayals of unions were common, as an institution the TUC 'retained a rather different image—a stodgy carthorse, respectable, moderate and accommodating'.[75] The post-war union leadership was committed to maintaining its standing as a moderating force. As the union leader George Woodcock put it, the official union machinery was the best defence against 'recalcitrants': 'Without giving any guarantee that we can smooth every difficulty, we offer the best prospect there is in this democracy of dealing with people who do not conform'.[76]

Yet a basis for the co-operative approach of post-war trade-unionism was the relatively stable equilibrium of British class relations. In the 1950s, the TUC leadership was dominated by the union right, and the tenets of Labour revisionism found general favour among the right-wing union leaders. As long as there was 'no direct challenge to any [union] rule-book tablets of stone', revisionism appealed to a trade-union leadership satisfied with the structural changes of the post-war settlement.[77] By the late 1960s, however, the situation had changed. The end of the relative economic stability underlying revisionism and right-wing trade-unionism had given way to a level of rank-and-file union militancy unseen in Britain since the 1920s. As Minkin points out:

> a Leftwing union political strategy, which many in the unions thought had been buried in the 1920s, began its resurrection. In the late 1960s, the

growth of membership, the increase in union militancy, the spread of union action, the emergence of the 'flying picket' and the election of militant shop stewards and officers strengthened a new Leftwing and neo-syndicalist current.[78]

The rise of this militancy had a significance for union leadership, making it 'much more difficult for union leaders to count on their members' acquiescence to deals struck at higher levels'.[79] To maintain its ability to regulate rank-and-file activity under the new conditions of growing militancy, trade-union leadership underwent a shift in personnel, policy and rhetoric, one which at the minimum could enable it to relate to the growth of rank-and-file union organisation and unofficial union action, resulting in part in 'increasing numbers of militantly-inclined conference delegates and executive members; in part [in] the desperate efforts of normally cautious leaders, afraid of losing control to unofficial activists, to *sponsor* and hence contain membership militancy'.[80] The effect of this leftward drift in union leadership was to facilitate the containment of rank-and-file union militancy within the bounds of basic trade-union responsibilities and modes of practice, particularly those in relation to the Labour Party. This process became, as discussed below, increasingly prominent after Labour's election in 1974, as the Labour government and the union leaders adopted a mode of co-operation legitimated by a new left-wing strategy based around the AES.

## The AES in Power

As mentioned, the management of industrial conflict was central to the Labour Party's political purpose in the 1970s, and the AES rose to official Labour policy within this political context. The early 1970s saw key victories for British trade unions, culminating in the collapse of Edward Heath's Conservative government in February 1974 after a national miners' strike crippled the country's fuel supplies and forced the government to implement a three-day per week limit on the commercial consumption of electricity. If Heath's election slogan, 'Who governs Britain?', sought to take advantage of a popular feeling that the country had become ungovernable due to excessive trade-union power, the Conservatives' substantial loss of votes in February 1974 indicated a lack of popular confidence in a Conservative solution. With manifestos derived to a large extent from the AES and calling for 'a fundamental and irreversible shift in the balance of power and wealth in favour of working people and their families', Labour won two general elections in 1974. Its victories were not prodigious: the February election produced only a minority Labour government, and in October Labour won by a majority of three seats in parliament. However, they indicated a lack of popular enthusiasm for the head-on collision with organised labour that had characterised the 'Heath course' in the period between 1971 and 1974.[81] In place of the unsuccessful coercive approach of the Heath government, as well as the failure of Labour's own statutory approach in the late 1960s, Labour in the 1974 pledged union co-operation through the 'consensual' approach of the social contract.[82] As Wilson put it in his foreword to the February 1974 manifesto, it was stubborn 're-fusal by an arrogant Conservative administration' which stood in the way of '[getting] the country back to work'.[83] In the October manifesto, this time as Prime Minister, he again pointed to the Conservatives' inability to deal appropriately with the industrial relations problem, with their 'policies of confrontation and conflict and "fight to a finish" philosophies'.[84]

This was not a new position for Wilson, or indeed for Labour: it had long presented itself as the party to reduce class confrontation, as it did in its manifesto for the 1922 general election, in which it declared itself the 'best bulwark' against revolution, 'violent upheaval and class wars'.[85] This was the political tradition within which Wilson explicitly placed himself in 1970, when, as leader of the Opposition, he warned parliament that Heath's Industrial Relations Act would serve as a 'militants' charter' that would only further incite 'the revolutionary situation' in the workplace, reproaching the Conservatives for '[showing] as much understanding in the revolutionary situation as the court of Louis XVI or Nicholas II, or even King Farouk'.[86] In this vein, Labour's main pitch to the electorate in 1974 was that it was uniquely placed to halt the class warfare of the period. As Cronin has pointed out, Wilson

made Labour's supposed ability to secure union co-operation in tripartite bargaining central to the government's programme for growth and industrial modernisation...The very legitimacy of the Wilson/Callaghan governments of 1974-79 was based on the claim that Labour would govern in a partnership with the unions and thus avoid conflict, and the impasse over economic policy that marked the failed regime of Edward Heath.[87]

Labour's answer to industrial conflict was the 'social contract', a policy for national unity around a set of initiatives that would engender economic revitalisation by fostering a spirit of industrial co-operation. Devised in the Liaison Committee, in which the party and the unions co-formulated Labour policy, the social contract was the basis of Labour's approach to the working class in the 1970s. It was, as Cronin writes,

> a deal in which the party agreed to refrain from statutory incomes policy while in office, to restore and augment union rights and, most important, to use the powers of the state to increase the social wage in the hope that the unions would respond by moderating wage claims and, where possible, discouraging the resort to strikes.[88]

The AES left justified the social contract on the basis that co-operation between the unions and the Wilson governments of the 1960s had been undermined by the unwillingness of those governments to address the underlying causes of industrial conflict—the decline of workers' living standards, lack of economic growth, a lack of investment in social services, a failure to enforce price controls to fight inflation (and thereby reduce wage militancy), and the reluctance to assert greater state control over a British economy led by the unaccountable giant companies of the private sector. In other words, the Labour government had failed to uphold its own side of the bargain, seeking wage restraint from the workforce while giving to it little in return. As discussed in Chapter 6, however, the AES left did not oppose incomes policy in principal: its case for the social contract was that the condition for incomes policy must be an effective strategy for 'fundamental' changes in workers' interests.

### The Rise of Left-Wing Union Leadership

By the end of the 1960s, four of the five largest Labour-affiliated unions were led by figures from the trade-union left.[89] Jack Jones and Hugh Scanlon, as leaders of Britain's two largest unions, together formed the basis for the dominance of a new left-wing block vote inside the Labour Party. It appeared to many that the unions may no longer function as the reliable 'praetorian guards' against the Labour left as they had in previous decades, a possibility which represented a major reason for optimism across the AES left (see Chapter 6).

Yet it was evident almost from the outset that the new left-wing union leaders would not represent a fundamentally different attitude or mode of practice in their relations with Labour leaders. This was illustrated by the nature of their opposition to *In Place of Strife* in 1969, an early test of their left-wing radicalism, and arguably an early indication of the manner in which they would later come to relate to the Labour leadership. Wickham-Jones argues that the union and Labour government relationship had deteriorated to the point that, by 1970, 'the government was barely on speaking terms with the unions'.[90] However, at no point during the dispute was an organisational break ever on the agenda between the left-wing union leaders and the Labour Party. As Jack Jones reminded Labour's critics: 'For trade unionists to talk of breaking with Labour, or opting out of paying the political levy, is to cut our own throats while giving our Tory opponents a blood transfusion'.[91] As Minkin argues, the restraint that had always characterised union leaders in their relations with the party was never abandoned during the disagreements over *In Place of Strife*, and none of the 'intra-Party sanctions which the union leadership might have applied was used'.[92] The rebellion of the left-wing union leaders was 're-markably diplomatic'; and upon their victory over the White Paper, 'they hurried to bury the signs of the discord', declaring their support for Labour and agreeing to *raise* their unions' affiliation fees to the party.[93] 'Within months of the General Election defeat', writes Minkin, 'Jack Jones was feeling his way towards a new accommodation with the Wilson leadership'.[94] Despite what on the surface may have appeared as a highly ideological new union leadership,

> what was remarkable was the extent to which this generation of union leaders continued to abide by the 'rules' of the union-Party relationship. The ideological thrust of their activities was limited by a trade union perspective.[95]

*In Place of Strife* did prove to be a miscalculation by the Labour leadership, since it underestimated the strength of union aversion to punitive anti-union measures, as well as the pre-existing mood of disillusionment by the perceived failures of the first Wilson governments. However, itself keen to strengthen official union structures in the face of growing unofficial industrial action at shopfloor level, the TUC agreed to adopt rule changes to strengthen its ability to contain unofficial union action.[96] During the 1970s Labour government, this swift de-radicalisation of the left-wing union leaders was at its zenith during the phases of wage restraint. Despite the large fall in workers' living standards between 1975 and 1977, 'the TUC evolved a "nod and wink" understanding with the Government that in spite of its formal opposition to a wage limit it would not seek to mobilise the Movement against Government policy'.[97] For Jones, 'the election of a Labour Government [was] more important than a substantial wage claim'.[98] The radicalism of Jones and Scanlon was contained by their overriding loyalty to the Labour government.[99]

Jones and Scanlon continued to perform, if in modified form, the conventional trade-union role of restraining left-wing voices within the Labour Party. Once dubbed by the media as the 'terrible twins' of the union left, they 'were now as defensive of the Parliamentary leadership as they had once been critical'.[100] This was symbolised by the famous row between Jones and the veteran Labour-left politician Ian Mikardo at the Tribune rally during the 1975 Labour Conference, as Mikardo's criticisms of Labour's income policy provoked public fury from the union leader.[101] As Jones later recalled, 'we were almost more concerned to keep a Labour Government in power than was the Labour Government itself'.[102] Indeed,

> in terms of direct access and consultations, formal and informal, they [the TUC] had done better from this Labour Government than from any previous peacetime administration.[103]

As Jones and Scanlon agreed to wage restraints ('voluntary' but reinforced by sanctions) in 1975, Jones stated that 'if the TUC wrote off the social contract on account of the [April 1975] budget they would in effect be writing off the Labour government'.[104] Whatever impression may have been had about the social contract as it was devised with Labour in opposition, its practical reality had become wage restraint enforced by left-wing union leaders committed to protecting the Labour leadership from left-wing dissent.

In a sense, the lead and co-operation given by Jones and Scanlon to Labour's pay policy validated Labour's claim that it was better placed to 'work with the unions' than were the Conservatives. In the four years before the 'winter of discontent', the number of days lost to strikes were lower than they had been for a decade, while between 1975 and 1978 real wages fell by an average annual rate of 13%.[105] As Hay writes, 'It was not since 1931-2 that workers had suffered such a reduction in real wages.'[106] Yet the restraining influence of union leaders, at a time of falling wages, proved transitory. The explosion of rank-and-file militancy in the winter of 1978–1979, against Labour government policy, marked the end of the social contract, its demise representing 'the final exhaustion of a last ditch attempt to manage the contradictions, tensions, and failures of a post-war settlement that had been visibly disintegrating throughout the 1970s'.[107]

This turning point was also seen in the sphere of electoral popularity. In the months leading up to the 'winter of discontent', there was little to separate the two parties in the opinion polls and 'Callaghan himself was consistently preferred to Thatcher'.[108] As late as November 1978, Labour was five points ahead of the Conservatives in the polls. Three months later it was behind by 20 points.[109] It was Labour's stark inability to bring industrial peace to the country which discredited it as a party for government. Labour's claim that it was best placed to control union militancy appeared decisively and finally discredited (and graphically underlined by repeated media depictions of uncollected bin bags and stories of unburied human corpses). That Labour's domestic politics in this period had been so heavily centred around its self-professed capacity to deliver class peace helped ensure that it would also be judged primarily on such terms.[110] As long as the party presented organised labour as something to be contained in the interests of the existing economy, it was poorly placed to change or even challenge the widely held public view of industrial militancy as a negative phenomenon to be curtailed. Thus Labour lost the 1979 election on the same terms that it had itself set, and, with the 'winter of discontent', 'Labour, and Callaghan in particular, had lost their reputation for being able to "handle" the unions'.[111]

Indeed, it was significant that the 'winter of discontent' occurred *after* the retirement of the two left-wing union leaders who had been the bastions of the social contract. As Cronin points out:

> By 1978 both Jones and Scanlon were preparing to retire and their replacements, Moss Evans and Terry Duffy respectively, were to play very different roles. Neither had a background on the left and so neither could command automatic support from that quarter; and both still needed to prove themselves to their own members. Thus, although their politics were on the whole more centrist, they were far less willing or able to deliver the support of their unions or of the TUC overall for the policies of the government.[112]

With this shift in the leaderships of two of Britain's most powerful unions, union discipline in support of Labour's pay policy was weakened: 'By mid-1978, therefore, support for continued pay restraint was waning. The annual Trades Union Congress formally rejected incomes policy and so, too, did the Labour Party conference.'[113] When the Callaghan government nevertheless imposed its five per cent limit on pay increases ('Phase IV' of its pay policy), it could no longer rely on the stalwart support of those union leaders who had made commitment to the maintenance of the Labour government their overriding objective. The union leaders whose elections a decade prior had represented a major cause for optimism to union militants and the AES left, proved to be more reliable allies of wage restraint than the union centrists who came to replace them.[114]

## CONCLUSION: THE ROLE OF THE AES LEFT?

While it is true that the left-wing union leaders served to protect the Labour government from left-wing dissent, there was limited fundamental disagreement between the politics of Jones and Scanlon and that of the Labour left. The Labour left may have opposed incomes policy in the circumstances in which it was implemented but it did not oppose it on principle, and the Labour Minister Peter Shore was broadly right in his claim that 'On the left it was absolutely clear to anyone who thought about it that you had to have an incomes policy'.[115] Incomes policy was not new to a Labour socialism which saw the 'planning of incomes' by a Labour government as a legitimate and indispensable component of socialist planning more broadly—'the planned growth of incomes', as the left-wing union leader and Labour minister Frank Cousins had once called it.[116] As Chapter 6 will show, the idea of a 'socialist incomes policy' to regulate wage demands found much credence within the bulk of the Labour left during the AES period. Though Jones and Scanlon were pivotal to the Labour government's implementation of its pay policy, the ideological basis for its legitimisation had also been laid by left-wing figures more closely associated with the theoretical development of the AES.

The AES left's inability or unwillingness to look beyond a left-wing politics whose horizons were limited to the confines of the existing economic system was related to the limited repertoire of ideas constituting its socialist outlook and its requirement to devise a viable economic programme for a Labour government. Mainstream AES figures like Stuart Holland advanced a critique of Labour's reformist heritage and expressed a desire to establish a type of 'revolutionary' anti-capitalist strategy that could be pursued by Labour upon its election. As the next chapter discusses, it was a significant development of the 1970s that the rhetoric of 'revolutionary transformation' had gained a high degree of prevalence among Labour socialists, as they tried to make sense of, and relate to, what appeared to be a highly dynamic and unpredictable political and economic climate. AES discussions frequently gave the impression of a political strategy seeking to overcome the restrictive parameters of prior Labour reformism.

However, these attempts were themselves constrained by the established parameters of Labour socialism. This was well encapsulated by Holland's slogan 'revolutionary reforms', which, as discussed later, sought to insert a programme of socialist transformation (however defined) into a reformist framework. This attempt to reconcile arguably irreconcilable phenomena was a prominent feature of the AES. The AES wanted economic planning, but it did not look far beyond an economy dominated by private ownership and market competition. It espoused socialist internationalism, but it also believed that a left-wing strategy should uphold Britain's economic interests and reassert its position in the competitive global market. Finally, as discussed in Chapter 6, AES advocates sought to advance workers' interests through industrial democracy and workers' control, and some even saw such measures as a means to intensify class conflict, as a form of 'transitional strategy' to engender working-class socialist radicalisation; but the AES also endorsed a social contract for better relations between capital and labour. As one major CPGB proponent of the AES put it in 2015, the AES 'never resolved a contradiction at the heart of it: was it designed to make the capitalist economy work better, or was it designed to destabilise it?'[117] The following chapter will consider how this basic unclarity affected the AES's view of itself as a socialist strategy.

## NOTES

1. Tony Benn, 'Preface', p. 1. Reproduced by kind permission of the Fabian Society.
2. Labour Party Young Socialists, *Programme for Britain*, p. 21. Reproduced by kind permission of the Labour Party.
3. Fishman, '1951–1960'.
4. Warde, *Consensus and Beyond*, p. 44. See also Thompson, *Political Economy and Labour Party*, p. 169.
5. Crosland, *The Future of Socialism*, p. 97.
6. Thompson, *Political Economy and Labour Party*, p. 168.
7. Crosland cited in Minkin, *The Contentious Alliance*, p. 92.
8. Ibid.
9. Ibid.
10. Allen, *Militant Trade Unionism*, Merlin Press, pp. 104–5.

11. Ibid., p. 105.
12. Coates, *Crisis of Labour*, p. 5.
13. Ibid., p. 7.
14. Ross and Jenson, 'Post-War Class Struggle and the Crisis of Left Politics', p. 24.
15. Abrams and Rose, *Must Labour Lose?*
16. Bell, *The End of Ideology*, pp. 254–5. See also Nisbet, 'The Decline and Fall of Social Class'.
17. Cited in Titmuss, 'Social Welfare and Art of Giving', p. 85.
18. As Minkin has observed with regard to post-war Britain: 'The assumption was that economic success, political moderation, industrial accommodation, and access to Government by the unions would be permanent features of future British politics.' (*The Contentious Alliance*, p. xiv.)
19. Wickham-Jones, *Economic Strategy and the Labour Party*, p. 38.
20. Ibid.
21. Panitch, 'Socialist Renewal and the Labour Party', p. 339. See also Looker, 'A Golden Past?', p. 38.
22. Seyd, *The Rise and Fall of the Labour Left*, p. 76. For an in-depth account of Labour's management of internal dissent during and after revisionist dominance, see Shaw, *Discipline and Discord in the Labour Party*.
23. House of Commons Debate, *Hansard*, 3 November 1959, vol. 612, cc. 860–985.
24. Minkin, *The Contentious Alliance*, pp. 77, 106.
25. Ibid., p. 107.
26. Wickham-Jones, *Economic Strategy and the Labour Party*, p. 51.
27. For example, Norman, 'Signposts for the 60's'.
28. Minkin, *The Contentious Alliance*, p. 107.
29. Seyd, *The Rise and Fall of the Labour Left*, p. 41.
30. Ibid, p. 40. As Seyd explains, Labour membership figures were inflated by the fact that they were based on the affiliation fees paid to the national Labour Party by the CLPs. Since Labour had a fixed minimum membership on which the CLPs affiliated to the Labour Party (800 between 1957 and 1962, and 1000 between 1963 and 1979), Labour's published membership figures were an overestimate of the actual membership.
31. Forester, *The Labour Party and the Working Class*, p. 79.
32. Pimlott, 'Are CLPs Necessary?', p. 11.
33. Whiteley, *The Labour Party in Crisis*, p. 61.
34. Hindess, *The Decline of Working Class Politics*.
35. Pimlott, 'Are CLPs Necessary?', p. 11.
36. Cited in Seyd, *The Rise and Fall of the Labour Left*, p. 43.
37. Seyd, *The Rise and Fall of the Labour Left*, p. 43.
38. Burton-Cartledge, 'Marching Separately, Seldom Together'.
39. Crossman, 'Introduction', pp. 41–2.

40. Miliband, *Capitalist Democracy*, p. 67.
41. Panitch, 'Socialist Renewal and the Labour Party', p. 335.
42. Seyd, *The Rise and Fall of the Labour Left*, p. 97.
43. Bearman, 'Anatomy of the Bennite Left'.
44. Seyd, *The Rise and Fall of the Labour Left*, pp. 92–3.
45. Ibid., p. 82.
46. Ibid., p. 94.
47. Ibid.
48. Franklin, *The Decline of Class Voting in Britain*, p. 1.
49. Crewe et al., 'Partisan Dealignment in Britain 1964–1974', p. 183; Evans, 'Class and Vote', p. 331.
50. Pulzer, *Political Representation and Elections in Britain*, p. 89.
51. Alford, 'Class Voting in Anglo-American Political Systems', pp. 69–70.
52. Butler and Stokes, *Political Change in Britain*, p. 67.
53. For example, McKenzie and Silver, *Angels in Marble*.
54. Lipset, *Political Man*, p. 444.
55. Franklin, *The Decline of Class Voting in Britain*, p. 153. See also Crewe et al., 'Partisan Dealignment in Britain 1964–1974'; Evans et al., 'Modelling Trends in the Class/Party Relationship 1964–87'.
56. Driver, *Understanding British Political Parties*, p. 19.
57. Well-known left-wing intellectuals like Eric Hobsbawm, Stuart Hall, Andre Gorz and Ernesto Laclau each wrote obituaries for working-class politics (at least for its 'traditional' forms) in the late 1970s and 1980s (see Chapter 7). Political science accounts included: Butler and Stokes, *Political Change in Britain*; Crewe et al., 'Partisan Dealignment in Britain 1964–1974'; Franklin, *The Decline of Class Voting in Britain*; and Rose and McAllister, *Voters Begin to Choose*, 1986. Prominent opposition to the decline thesis was voiced by Heath and his colleagues, who argued that 'trendless fluctuation' rather than steady decline best characterised contemporary dips in levels of class voting (Heath et al., *How Britain Votes*, p. 35).
58. Butler and Stokes, *Political Change in Britain*, p. 193.
59. Crewe et al., 'Partisan Dealignment in Britain 1964–1974', p. 183.
60. Ibid.
61. Leys, *Politics in Britain*, p. 7.
62. Coates, *Crisis of Labour*, p. 37.
63. Ibid.
64. Ibid., p. 38.
65. Ibid., p. 39.
66. Minkin, *The Contentious Alliance*, p. 113.
67. Wickham-Jones, *Economic Strategy and the Labour Party*, pp. 48–9.
68. Minkin, *The Contentious Alliance*, p. 114.
69. Diamond, *The Crosland Legacy*, p. 112.
70. McIlroy, 'Notes on the Communist Party and Industrial Politics', p. 243.

71. Laybourn, *A History of British Trade Unionism*, pp. 162–8. For a polemical account, see Ellen, 'Labour and Strike-Breaking 1945–1951'.
72. Seyd, *The Rise and Fall of the Labour Left*, p. 20.
73. Allen, *Militant Trade Unionism*, p. 51.
74. Office for National Statistics, *Labour disputes in the UK: 2018*.
75. Minkin, *The Contentious Alliance*, p. 95.
76. Cited in Panitch, *Social Democracy and Industrial Democracy*, p. 142.
77. Minkin, *The Contentious Alliance*, p. 91.
78. Ibid., p. 111. See also Darlington and Lyddon, *Glorious Summer*, p. 7.
79. Cronin, *New Labour's Pasts*, p. 102.
80. Hyman, *Industrial Relations*, p. 165. His italics.
81. Hall, 'The Great Moving Right Show', p. 24.
82. Jacques, 'Thatcherism', p. 49.
83. Labour Party, *Let Us Work Together*.
84. Labour Party, *Britain Will Win with Labour*.
85. Labour Party, *Labour's Call to the People*, p. 22.
86. House of Commons Debate, *Hansard*, 15 December 1970, vol. 808, cc. 1126–2470. From the left, Barbara Castle likewise referred to the ballot procedures in Heath's legislation as a 'charter for militants' (despite having advocated ballots in her White Paper *In Place of Strife*)—see Darlington and Lyddon, *Glorious Summer*, p. 20.
87. Cronin, *New Labour's Pasts*, pp. 9–10.
88. Ibid., p. 168.
89. Hugh Scanlon (the Amalgamated Engineering Union, elected in 1967), Lawrence Daly (the National Union of Miners, in 1968), Richard Seabrook (the Union of Shop, Distributive and Allied Workers, in 1968), and Jack Jones (Transport and General Workers' Union, in 1968).
90. Wickham-Jones, *Economic Strategy and the Labour Party*, pp. 49–50.
91. Cited in Panitch, *Social Democracy and Industrial Militancy*, p. 157.
92. Minkin, *The Contentious Alliance*, p. 118.
93. Ibid.
94. Ibid.
95. Ibid., p. 124.
96. Cronin, *New Labour's Pasts*, p. 106; Thorpe, 'The Labour Party and the Trade Unions', p. 140.
97. Minkin, *The Contentious Alliance*, p. 126.
98. Cited in Minkin, *The Contentious Alliance*, p. 179. This echoed the post-war miners' leader Sam Watson's remark that it was better to 'advocate a reduction of wages' than to see the defeat of a Labour government (cited in Panitch, *Social Democracy and Industrial Militancy*, p. 31).
99. Jack Jones also indicated a willingness to extend this fellowship to Conservative Prime Ministers. As he wrote in his memoirs: 'No Prime Minister either before or since could compare with Ted Heath in the efforts he made

to establish a spirit of camaraderie with trade union leaders and to offer an attractive package which might satisfy large numbers of work people'. (Jack Jones cited in Taylor, *The TUC*, p. 197.)

100. Minkin, *The Contentious Alliance*, p. 164.
101. Holmes, *The Labour Government, 1974–79*, pp. 66–7.
102. Cited in Minkin, *The Contentious Alliance*, p. 179.
103. Minkin, *The Contentious Alliance*, p. 178.
104. Cited in Cronin, *New Labour's Pasts*, p. 171.
105. Hay, 'Narrating the Crisis', p. 259.
106. Ibid.
107. Ibid., pp. 260–1.
108. Cronin, *New Labour's Pasts*, p. 189.
109. Thorpe, *A History of the British Labour Party*, p. 205.
110. Thorpe, 'The Labour Party and the Trade Unions', p. 145.
111. Thorpe, *A History of the British Labour Party*, p. 198.
112. Cronin, *New Labour's Pasts*, p. 189.
113. Ibid.
114. This is not to argue that the new union leaders opposed the pay policy on principle. More likely, as Hay has argued, they 'were simply being sanguine about their own prospects of imposing this upon their members – and reluctant, perhaps, to become scapegoats for what they saw as an inevitable failure'. (Hay, 'The Winter of Discontent Thirty Years On', p. 548.)
115. Cited in Cronin, *New Labour's Pasts*, p. 105.
116. Panitch, *Social Democracy and Industrial Militancy*, p. 80. See also Thorpe, 'The Labour Party and the Trade Unions', p. 136.
117. Author's interview with Bob Rowthorn, Cambridge, 10 June 2015.

# CHAPTER 3

# Reform or Revolution: The AES as Socialist Strategy

## INTRODUCTION

This chapter considers the ways in which the major proponents of the AES understood it as a programme for socialist transition, how they perceived that this transition would occur, and how they positioned themselves against other radical strategies for socialist transition. An underlying enquiry is how the major intellectual supporters of the AES addressed the reform/revolution question in socialist theory. As Perry Anderson noted in the 1960s, the two models that dominated the history of the socialist movement were the 'parliamentary and insurrectionary roads to socialism',[1] the former model often characterised as reformist, the latter as revolutionary. This chapter will show that many of the prominent advocates of the AES went to significant lengths to attempt to bridge the gap between reform and revolution in their theories, to espouse revolutionary aims, reject a purely parliamentary road, while also dismissing the 'insurrectionist' politics of those to their left.

Formulated at the point of ideological correspondence between the Labour left and the Communist Party of Great Britain (CPGB), the AES received support from broad sections of the British left and the ways in which this support was explained and justified therefore varied. For analytical purposes, the supporters of the AES will be divided into two groups here, since it is possible to identify two differing but overlapping views of the AES as a strategy for socialist transition. In the first group were those

© The Author(s) 2020
B. Tufekci, *The Socialist Ideas of the British Left's Alternative Economic Strategy,*
https://doi.org/10.1007/978-3-030-34998-1_3

with greater association with the political traditions of the Labour Party: individuals like Stuart Holland and Tony Benn, and groups like the Labour Co-ordinating Committee (LCC) and the Tribune Group. This group will be referred to as the Labour left. The second group involved those with somewhat less proximity to Labour's political traditions, whose rhetoric was often more radical and whose theoretical underpinnings tended to a greater degree to employ the language of Marxism: figures from the CPGB, former Trotskyists like Geoffrey Hodgson, New Left figures like Michael Barratt Brown and related individuals like Ken Coates from the Institute for Workers Control (IWC), and those associated with the Conference of Socialist Economists (CSE). This group will be referred to as the radical proponents of the AES. It should be noted that this typology does not necessarily relate to party or organisational allegiance—there was, after all, universal agreement that the strategy's implementation would be the work of the Labour Party and many of the strategy's radical proponents were Labour members or would have considered themselves as belonging to the 'Labour left' (Barratt Brown, Coates, Hodgson). Nor does it imply, of course, that close collaboration between the two groups did not frequently occur—prominent Labour-left figures contributed to the work of the IWC, for example, and the London CSE Group and members of the LCC co-wrote a book on the strategy.[2]

The classification relates to theoretical differences, but here too, as this chapter will argue, the distinction is by no means strict or sharply defined. Both groups saw the AES as a strategy for socialist transformation. They both argued that the strategy's implementation would not in itself create socialism but that the challenges and struggles to which it would give rise could lead the way to a socialist Britain. Both approaches posited the British state as an important arena for these struggles, although they saw working-class support, initiative or pressure as decisive also. Both groups saw Labour as the strategy's main political agent, which would legislate socialist reforms with a sufficient parliamentary majority and mass support among the British public. Both argued that such reforms would not be merely ends in themselves: their purpose would be to create possibilities for further, increasingly radical socialist change, whether by increasing the public's appetite for such change or by shifting the balance of social power to the working class, as pledged in every Labour Party general-election manifesto between 1974 and 1983.

The basis for identifying a difference between the two groups' understanding of the relationship between the AES and socialist transition lies in the emphasis that they each gave to the *socially destabilising* consequences of the implementation of the strategy. Several radical proponents of the AES argued that their support was based on their expectation that the strategy would deepen capitalist contradictions and intensify class struggle. The AES would face strong resistance from the capitalist class and large sections of the establishment, and the mass mobilisation that would need to accompany this opposition could bring with it revolutionary implications. The Labour left's position, in contrast, tended to place less emphasis on the political advantages of social destabilisation. This difference was highlighted by the strategy's radical proponents Bob Rowthorn and Geoffrey Hodgson, who criticised figures among the Labour left for expecting the AES's fairly harmonious procession within the existing state and socioeconomic framework, and for underplaying the role of mass mobilisation in defence of the strategy.

However, this chapter will argue that, on the central problem of reform/revolution, the difference between the two groups was not as marked as it may have appeared at the level of rhetoric. Both groups sought to reconcile 'reformist' and 'revolutionary' socialist strategies, and it would be mistaken to regard the Labour left as at one end of the reform-revolution/state-masses spectrum with the radical proponents at the other. A large degree of convergence of positions existed in the way that the course of the strategy's implementation was perceived. Differences in theoretical argument and justification were present, but they did not tend to represent vital disagreements on either policy choices or the means for their implementation. The attempt to resolve the reform/revolution question occurred in differing ways, but, ultimately, similar conclusions were reached.

## A Strategy for Socialist Transformation

The AES was presented by its leading proponents as a starting point for further socialist change that would lead to a socialist transformation. While the implementation of the AES would not in itself amount to socialism, its reforms, implemented within the present system, would initiate further left-wing challenges to a capitalist society whose economic foundations would be undermined. Stuart Holland, a dominant Labour-left theorist of the strategy, tied its programme of reforms with a revolutionary intent in the following way:

progress to socialism would be an on-going process, but one in which the critical centres of capitalist power and class were transformed by a socialist government, backed by the trade unions. It is a key premise of this analysis that such transformation can be achieved through democratic processes...On the other hand, such democratic reforms must be effectively revolutionary in character. In other words, they must reverse the present dominance of capitalist modes of production and capitalist motivation into a dominance of democratically controlled socialism. They must transform capitalist society rather than try ineffectively to alleviate its implicit injustice.[3]

That such a transformation would succeed the AES reforms was seen as their logical implication. Across the board, though with theoretical variations, the prominent advocates of the AES argued that the strategy would not be containable within the boundaries of the prevailing economic framework. As the CPGB's Sam Aaronovitch argued, the proposed reforms could not be 'inserted into the old system like a new fuse in an old fuse-box'; any attempt to implement them 'must alter the way the system works and open it up to even more fundamental changes'.[4] The LCC made a similar point: there should be 'no illusions about the radical break in the working of the economy' that the AES entailed[5]; the AES was not only an economic strategy but 'also a political strategy with radical implications'.[6] The purpose of the AES was to end 'the essence of the capitalist mode of production', as Michael Meacher put it, not to consolidate and protect it.[7]

Among the strategy's radical proponents, there was a greater tendency to employ Marxist language to assert the revolutionary implications of the strategy. According to Bob Rowthorn, a Cambridge economist and member of the CPGB, the AES was 'not a recipe for social peace and capitalist prosperity' but for 'mounting class struggle and a growing challenge to the authority of big capital'.[8] Although the AES constituted a limited programme that was '*democratic* rather than revolutionary in character', if implemented it 'would lead to a radical shift in the balance of power in favour of the working class and its allies'.[9] In response to criticisms that the AES was reformist, Rowthorn argued that it had revolutionary implications due to the mass mobilisation it would require to defend it from right-wing resistance. Its implementation would launch 'a revolutionary *process* characterised by intense conflict and struggle'.[10]

Hodgson, another left-wing theorist who played a prominent role in defending the strategy against its Marxist opponents and often on their terms, saw in the AES an opportunity for a revolutionary diversion in the political consciousness of the labour movement. Since the AES had some roots in the trade unions and the Labour movement, 'it was a means by which revolutionary socialists can reach the ear of literally thousands of workers and inject important ideas of their own'.[11] Reformism was indeed a dangerous avenue, Hodgson argued, but, like Rowthorn, he pointed out that calls for reforms need not be reformist:

> ...Lenin's slogan of 'Peace, bread and land' could have had reformist connotations. The real antidote to reformism is not criticism from the sideline but active involvement in real struggles so that they may be diverted in a revolutionary direction.[12]

An effective strategy to regenerate Britain's economy on the basis of workers' control was 'likely to face the stiff, and even violent, resistance of the capitalists', and the working-class mobilisation that would necessarily need to confront this resistance would represent an opportunity for workers' radicalisation.[13] Thus the AES would have 'a revolutionary purpose, as a politicising and mobilising agent'.[14]

This was related to a view among radical supporters of the AES, as discussed in Chapter 6, that the strategy would create a situation of 'dual power' or 'dual control' in industry. The argument was that the strategy's increase of working-class strength would make it increasingly difficult for capitalist society to contain workers' demands, thereby creating something of a revolutionary crisis of power in the country. In an early exposition of the strategy, Michael Barratt Brown pursued this argument in quite radical terms:

> What we may expect in the 1970's is a long series of struggles energised both by revolutionary and counter-revolutionary potential, ranging far beyond the confines of the British nation state, in which the political economy of labour...builds and reinforces its own unassailable bases, with international links, over against the political economy of international capital. A period of uneasy truce might lead to a moment of violent confrontation.[15]

A socialist Labour government, with trade-union pressure, would push for reforms that capitalist society could less and less accommodate. In this way 'the conflicts between the giant concentrations of capital and the national labour movements will be more frankly recognised'.[16] The war between the two major classes would thereby intensify to a point at which it would become insoluble within a capitalist framework. That situation could not be reached, however, before the project of reforming capitalism had stood exposed as exhausted, through a strategy of left-wing reforms that would push the boundaries of the system. Barratt Brown cited Marx's evaluation of the British Parliament's 1847 Factory Act as a victory for 'the political economy of labour over the political economy of capital'.[17] A left-wing Labour government could likewise open the way for the final triumph of the 'political economy of labour' through its radical-reforming programme.

While such assertions, in Marxist language, of the revolutionary implications of the AES were associated more closely with its radical proponents, the 'mainstream' Labour left also frequently presented the strategy's implementation as a means to 'begin to unlock the potential' for a socialist transformation.[18] Holland—who also pointed to Marx's analysis of the Factory Acts as an example of capitalism's retreat before pressures to 'alleviate the worst vicissitudes of the system'[19]—saw a vital difference between reforms as such and 'revolutionary reforms'.[20] While the former had characterised most of the reforming legislation of hitherto Labour governments, the AES constituted revolutionary reforms aiming to transform irreversibly the 'basis on which economic, social and political power is organized within society'.[21] Although 'insurrectionist' methods must be rejected, revolutionary reforms could not be gradual, partial, purely pragmatic or solely state-driven—they must transform the existing 'mode of production'.[22] As argued in Chapter 4, Holland's understanding of terms like 'transformation', 'revolution' and 'modes of production' differed significantly from their use in Marxism—for Holland, this new mode of production would entail 'a new and more balanced mix in the so-called mixed economy'.[23] Nevertheless, the language of revolution was prevalent in his work. Like Barratt Brown, Holland was striving to outline a Labour-left strategy distinct from prior Labour reformism. This was not 'old revisionism in new clothes'.[24]

For Benn, meanwhile, there was a radicalising element in the relationship between the existing policies of the AES and the challenges presented by their implementation. The key ingredient for this radicalisation was the democratic momentum with which the AES was to be accompanied. Anything that was democratic had 'to emerge from discussions' and could not be 'handed down from the top and imposed whoever likes it or not'.[25] Benn raised the prospect that this democratic influence would compel a left-wing Labour government to adopt increasingly radical positions. A policy for full employment, for example, which in itself may not have been especially radical, would force a left-wing Labour government to 'more radical solutions simply to make [the] policy work'.[26] If that government failed to adopt these solutions and therefore failed to reduce unemployment as pledged, this 'would be noticed and rejected by the majority of the movement, and the public would lose faith in our capacity to do anything about it'.[27] Labour's 'unfulfilled function', therefore, was to formulate demands that would raise people's expectations and create 'pressures that would be released very rapidly' upon Labour's election to power.[28]

The 'Bennite' left's frequent assertion that mass mobilisation and democratic input were required for the strategy's success implied that its long-term goals were not limited to its immediate policies. This democratic element suggested that the AES contained a degree of open-endedness which rendered unpredictable its political outcomes. It was perhaps this which helped raise the hopes in the AES of those, like Barratt Brown, Rowthorn and Hodgson, who expressed sympathies with revolutionary variants of socialism but at the same time an optimism about the strategy's potentially radical consequences. This was a basis for the common ground shared by the strategy's radical supporters and those aligned more closely with the Bennite Labour left. If a left-wing Labour government could pursue a fundamental change in the balance of social power in favour of the working class, it could widen the scope for socialist radicalisation.

Indeed, it was the fact that the AES was not an 'ultra-left' programme unable to offer immediate and 'practical' solutions that was seen as its strength, by both the Labour-left and radical proponents of the strategy. The AES was presented as a pragmatic programme of viable reforms addressing the immediate concerns of the British public. Hence, it was suggested, its capacity to win mass support, something that groups to its left could not do. As the London CSE Group and the LCC put it, 'without a programme which responds to people's basic concerns with job security, the cost of living, housing availability and the level of pensions and child benefits, socialist appeals will be regarded with justifiable suspicion'.[29] In an IWC pamphlet, Peter Hain and Simon Hebditch argued that socialists needed to fight on issues 'in the heart and minds of working people', rather than embark 'on a grand design with impeccable theoretical credentials but no relevance to day-to-day life'.[30] Socialists must start where they are, not where they would like to be.[31]

Radical proponents of the AES acknowledged that this implied the need for a certain degree of programmatic moderation. However, they argued, the campaign to implement such a programme would provide a route to programmatic radicalisation. According to the CPGB's Ben Fine and Laurence Harris, the AES would bridge the gap between readily acceptable demands, such as full employment, and those with far more radical connotations, such as nationalisation without compensation. Thus, not only could the strategy win broad support in the short term, it could also provide 'the basis on which to radicalise that support in the longer term'.[32] It would encourage people to overcome their view of economic policy '*as a technical and politically neutral problem of getting the economy right*' and begin to think in terms of social power and society's organisation.[33] Benn opposed nationalisation without compensation[34] but, as we saw, he made a similar point with regard to the radicalising potential of an apparently moderate demand like full employment: the process of its implementation could push Labour towards increasingly radical measures. As the CPGB's Bert Ramelson also put it, the AES had indicated how 'universally desirable aims'—job creation, education, etc.—could be achieved and 'in the course of their realisation move us nearer to the socialist objective'.[35]

Alongside this call for policies to attract mass support in the short term, was the idea that a commitment to a socialist future should not be a requirement for supporting the strategy. According to Sam Aaronovitch, the AES

> does not and should not require those who support it to be committed to a socialist reconstruction of Britain. If we are not clear on this we shall abandon one of its main sources of strength, namely that it is a 'common programme' being constructed by many groups and interests.[36]

This part of Aaronovitch's argument was criticised in the CPGB journal *Marxism Today* on the basis that it could suggest the dilution of the strategy 'to the level of the lowest common political denominator in the hope of winning mass support'. Instead, socialists should aim to win the labour movement to the AES on the basis that it presented 'the real possibility of establishing a beachhead from which the advance to socialism can be made'.[37] However, political diversity and non-socialist participation were arguably unavoidable features of a strategy devised to appeal to broad sections of the British population based on their existing level of political consciousness—with the caveat, of course, that the AES would radicalise those sections once their support had been given. For the CPGB, a broad political alliance was necessary because the prospects for revolutionary politics in the immediate term were unfavourable. As Rowthorn argued, the Labour left would 'be forced into alliance with less radical elements in the movement, such as Foot, Silkin and Shore, and will also need to establish a working relationship with the so-called "moderates" like Healey and Hattersley'.[38]

Yet this is not to underplay the AES's marked tendency to justify itself in revolutionary terms. Indeed, Rowthorn and other CPGB figures raised the prospect of a coup by the British army: the AES contained implications so revolutionary that it could provoke military intervention, an 'ultimately decisive' issue which, according to Rowthorn, the Labour left was guilty of dangerously neglecting.[39] Though the CPGB opposed 'insurrectionist' methods, it often did so less on principle than as inapplicable to contemporary Britain, mainly along the lines that the strength and deep-rootedness of its parliamentary traditions prevented the acceptability of those kinds of socialist strategies that may have been legitimate and appropriate in different contexts. This had been the CPGB's official approach since its 1951 programme *The British Road to Socialism* (*BRS*). As the party's national organiser wrote in a 1978 article defending the latest (fifth) edition of the *BRS* published the previous year, the CPGB recognised 'that insurrectionary models from past eras and different conditions are totally inappropriate'.[40] Revolutionary change in Britain would be achieved through 'a lengthy (but not gradual) process of struggle' involving a broad democratic alliance of the left 'extending democratic control over all areas of life', but where the intervention of revolutionaries (the CPGB) would be crucial as a radicalising ingredient.[41]

Barring emphases on the role to be played by the CPGB, Holland's position here was similar. Capitalism's violent overthrow 'may in some countries be the only means of progress, but in others is simply a painful means of changing the form of exploitation'.[42] Britain's political institutions were vitally different from those of countries where nominally democratic forms were in reality 'the facade of absolutism'. Most of the British electorate saw in these institutions 'a machinery of restraints...important for the defence of their own civil liberties'.[43] Armed uprisings for socialism had only worked in countries with weaker democratic traditions; hence the 'Bolsheviks succeeded, but the Spartacists [in Germany] failed'.[44] It is worth noting, however, that Holland did not rule out workers' violence as a tactic: opposing political violence in the current British context was not to say that it was illegitimate for workers to 'take arms in future if threatened by a fascist government in Britain'.[45] Nevertheless, as things stood, the insurrectionist path was riskier 'than concerted pressure for revolutionary change within democratic structures'.[46]

It is because the AES contained this prominent self-justification as a revolutionary strategy that it was perhaps problematic to characterise it as simply yet another form of left-wing reformism. Although proponents of the AES opposed 'insurrectionism', their frequent emphases on mass mobilisation, radical democracy and social transformation seemed to indicate a kind of leftism to which the Labour Party had grown unaccustomed in its own ranks, at least since the 1930s. Partly as a result of this, as was shown in Chapter 1, a number of academic accounts have interpreted the AES as a significant shift away from post-war Labour thinking: as a 'violent break', a fundamental challenge to capitalist ethos and practice, or as an 'extremely radical' strategy whose theoretical foundations had more in common with Marxism than Keynesianism. However, a few factors need to be considered in relation to such characterisations. It is necessary to consider the way in which the prominent supporters of the AES understood the problem of socialist transition.

## THE PROBLEM OF SOCIALIST TRANSITION

As highlighted, a feature of Labour-left and radical support for the AES was its attempt to resolve the reform/revolution issue without departing from what it saw as the strategy's radical essence. Brian Sedgemore, Tribune Labour MP and a prominent advocate of the AES, argued that the 'great debate about reform and revolution' should see the socialist on the side of the latter—the 'revolution that socialists seek to bring about is the overthrow of capitalism'. However, such 'fundamental change' would 'be achieved peacefully through the democratic process'.[47] By the latter was meant parliament and the existing institutions of government, albeit reformed by a socialist Labour government. As we saw, Holland's *Socialist Challenge* also talked in such terms: the AES must be 'effectively revolutionary', but it must be achieved by 'democratic processes'. The meaning of 'democratic processes' was made clear in a shorter, introductory version of that book published in the same year: 'reforms legislated in parliament'.[48]

Left-wing figures with greater distance from the Tribune Group, such as Geoffrey Hodgson and Bob Rowthorn, criticised the view of socialist transition that they saw as prevalent in the Labour Party. Rowthorn argued that Labour-left figures like Stuart Holland and Brian Sedgemore gave 'a rather harmonious impression' of the AES and understated 'the degree of resistance it would face and the conflict to which it would give rise'.[49] Hodgson argued that the Tribune Group had largely neglected extra-parliamentary action—the main focus of its activity was the attempt to get the AES 'adopted as an item of legislation and policy within Parliament and the Cabinet'.[50] Such an approach risked restricting the AES to

> an alternative set of policies to be adopted *within* the existing structures of power, *with* the existing relationship of forces between classes and groups in capitalist society, *with* the existing bourgeois hegemony, and *with* the working class as a subordinate class in political, social and economic terms. To risk a caricature of this position: the object is simply to replace Denis Healy as Chancellor with a member of the Tribune Group.[51]

For Hodgson, such a conception of the AES was 'classically reformist' because it saw political power as concentrated in Parliament and the state as 'neutral between social classes'. If the AES retained this 'predominantly reformist flavour', it was destined to 'failure, oblivion or bloody defeat'.[52] 'Insurrectionism' should be rejected, but so too should the reformist attempt to effect change through parliament alone—neither strategy had been effective in advanced capitalist countries.[53]

There was, however, an interesting twist in Hodgson's argument: the problematic reformism of the AES was located not in its actual policies but in the way that their implementation was being understood. The strategy's reformist advocates were failing to appreciate the incompatibility of their proposals with reformism, the fact that the AES could not be implemented 'within the existing structures of power'.[54] Thus there was a contradiction within the AES: it was 'packaged as reformist' but it contained 'implicit and unspelt revolutionary implications'.[55] As discussed above, CPGB figures like Rowthorn, Bert Ramelson, Ben Fine and Lawrence Harris argued in similar terms: the revolutionary potential of the AES was located in the *struggle* to implement it.

Such arguments at times appeared to bear a similarity to those of Trotsky's transitional programme in the 1930s, insofar as both approaches saw a campaign for left-wing reforms as a means to stimulate workers' action and expose to them the limitations to what they could achieve within a capitalist framework. Hodgson drew this parallel with Trotsky explicitly, arguing in his polemics with hostile Trotskyist groups that Trotsky would have likely given critical support to the AES because he had given critical support to Henri de Man's social-democratic policies in Belgium in the 1930s. In response to a Militant Tendency pamphlet criticising the AES,[56] Hodgson charged Militant with a sectarian 'maximalism'—raising the maximum demand of socialist planning without engaging with the existing left-wing strategy of the labour movement, thereby offering 'a rather crude version of Trotskyism to the Labour left'.[57] Without explicit references to Trotsky, Peter Hain and Simon Hebditch of the LCC also called for 'a series of transitional demands' to link the everyday concerns of workers with the project of socialist transformation.[58] Although there was 'no real reason' to pose 'revolutionary' and 'reformist' strategies as contradictory in modern Britain, the significance of particular proposals and campaigns was how they were framed and interpreted by the left: 'It is the political perspective within which these struggles are waged, rather than the actual demands themselves, which makes them revolutionary'.[59] According to the CSE, meanwhile, the AES represented 'a transitional strategy, capable of mobilising working class struggle around immediate issues within an overall and coherent framework of advance towards socialism'.[60]

There was a similarity with Trotsky's position here insofar as he had insisted that the correctness of demands and tactics should be decided not at the level of abstract principle but in the light of overall strategic considerations. However, Trotsky's strategic considerations were distinct from those of left-wing figures like Hodgson and Hain. Contrary to their strong defence of AES policies, Trotsky's concern was to win workers *away* from left-wing social-democratic demands. For example, Trotsky argued that Henri de Man's government 'would be a step forward [not because it would play] any progressive role in the replacement of capitalism by socialism, but [because] the experiment of a social-democratic government would be of progressive importance in the revolutionary development of the proletariat'.[61] Workers needed real-life experience of a left-reformist government so that they could lose, what Trotsky called, their 'illusions' in such governments, illusions which, he argued, Marxists should not share.[62] The aim was to discredit a social-democratic route which existed to 'deceive' the working class, but to do so in a way that would not encourage left-wing passivity by a mere dismissal of social-democratic politics. Left-wing proponents of the AES stood in a rather different socialist tradition, since they upheld the AES itself. For Hodgson, the AES offered 'realistic policies for beginning the socialist transformation',[63] and Labour's 1973 party programme was a 'radical, even revolutionary, document'.[64]

Indeed, as Chapter 6 will examine further, support for independent working-class initiative and agency was in fact heavily qualified in the AES.

In the first place, such support existed within a theoretical framework which premised the success of the AES on its successful legislation in parliament. This was not a basis for fundamental disagreement between the strategy's Labour-left and radical proponents. Rowthorn's party had long accepted the parliamentary road to socialism and Hodgson, like Holland, saw parliamentary legitimation of socialist policies as crucial. The British public saw parliament as 'the legitimate arena for resolving conflict and making fundamental decisions'; therefore a radical movement had to win a majority in parliament if it wanted support in the country as a whole.[65] Hodgson argued that this parliamentary majority was not by itself sufficient—also indispensable were 'extra-parliamentary activities, such as demonstrations and campaigns, and localised institutions of popular power'[66]—but he presented parliament as the dominant location for political legitimation, the institution towards which extra-parliamentary activity should therefore ultimately orient itself and, to some extent at least, be channelled into. He called for the introduction of democracy into the workplace and into 'control of the economic system' and reproached the parliamentarists who often 'belittled and ignored' such reform. However, he posed such democratic forms merely as an 'important supplement' to parliamentary power.[67] The latter came first in Hodgson's account, as it did in the strategy of the Labour left. His view that workers' control and regional bases of democratic power must be important *appendages* of parliamentary power did not, as discussed in Chapter 6, differ fundamentally from Holland's proposals for industrial democracy.

There was also a more elementary reason for the need to qualify workers' agency and decision-making. As discussed further in later chapters, such matters needed to be considered against another, indeed more immediate and powerful concern: economic growth and the revitalisation of British industry, which was presented by all the prominent advocates of the AES as the essential prerequisite for implementing the progressive social policies of the strategy. Furthermore, economic growth was advanced as a solution to class conflict: low growth increased 'the struggle between different social groups for scarce resources', as Holland's *Out of Crisis* put it, and strong growth was among the 'conditions for consensus'.[68] As discussed in Chapter 6, the Labour left had a strong tendency to view class conflict as the unfortunate and divisive consequence of right-wing government policies, dictatorial management in the workplace and industrial inefficiency and decline, and it expected industrial relations to substantially improve upon the introduction of economic expansion, planning and industrial democracy by a Labour government.

This was clearly a very different justification for the AES from that put forward by the strategy's more radical advocates. Indeed, it was an opposite view: that a virtue of the AES was that it would ease, not intensify, class tensions. Yet the radical advocates did not disagree that solving Britain's economic crisis was the priority and the foundation for the strategy's left-wing policies. For Rowthorn, the AES rested on 'the assumption that Britain is a declining industrial power whose problems are primarily due to structural weaknesses in the domestic economy'.[69] As a result, 'by tackling these structural weaknesses, Britain's situation could be greatly improved…and the material base could be created for higher wages and improved social services'.[70] The same point was made by the London CSE Group: the AES's 'essential basis' was 'a policy for planned economic expansion', without which there was little prospect of reducing unemployment, increasing living standards and improving public services.[71]

This emphasis on solving the economic crisis highlighted a serious tension between the economic and political goals of the radical advocates of the AES.[72] Their greater tendency to argue that the AES would play a revolutionary role by intensifying class conflict contained two core propositions: (i) since the implementation of the AES would be strongly resisted by the employers and the right-wing establishment, mass working-class support would need to be mobilised in its defence; and (ii) the strategy would 'render explicit the political assumptions and choices normally hidden in capital's circulation'[73]—i.e. it would help more clearly expose the class interests underlying the capitalist economy, thereby raising the socialist consciousness of the labour movement.

Yet, if the immediate aim of the AES was to solve the British economic crisis by restructuring the existing economy (via parliamentary legislation), the implication was that progressive solutions could be found within a (reformed) capitalist economy. But if capitalism could be made to work better for the working class, it might be expected that this would subdue rather than intensify class conflict and decrease the urgency and indeed the relevance of a socialist project. If a restructured capitalist economy could provide the goods for the working-class beyond a short-term and unstable basis—continued economic growth, rising living standards, full employment—a large part of the theoretical justification for social revolution would collapse and left-wing reformism could be seen, with good reason, as the logical course.[74] The revolutionary rhetoric of the radical AES proponents would thereby appear largely extraneous, and their theoretical differences with the Labour left rather superficial. The AES would represent no significant qualitative break with the belief underlying the reformist socialism of an Eduard Bernstein or, indeed, an Anthony Crosland: that the existing economic system, once appropriately adjusted, could begin to meet the aspirations of the working class and thereby evolve into something other than capitalism.

Again, AES proponents attempted to justify this feature of the strategy in Marxist terms. Hodgson, for example, cited Lenin's view in 1918 that 'state capitalism would be a *step forward* as compared with the present state of affairs' in Soviet Russia.[75] Upholding the socialist potential of markets, Holland also included the Soviet government's New Economic Policy as evidence that virtually all socialist revolutions have had to maintain the market over long periods (see Chapter 4 below).[76] Yet these parallels were confronted by the problem of social context. For Lenin, Bolshevik state capitalism was a temporary retreat until workers' revolutions in Europe ended Russia's isolation and created conditions more favourable for socialising production. Whatever the consistency of this position, its theoretical justification centred around the class content of the state by which it would be regulated. In the same article from which Hodgson quoted, Lenin argued that the state capitalism of a 'Junker-bourgeois' Germany was fundamentally different from the state capitalism of a '*Soviet* state, that is, a proletarian state'.[77] The latter's aim was to create 'the conditions necessary for socialism' and socialism was 'inconceivable unless the proletariat is the ruler of the state'.[78] This was not so for Hodgson or Holland. Indeed, Hodgson rejected the notion of a strict qualitative difference between a 'proletarian' and 'bourgeois' democratic state—since there was no 'Chinese Wall' between them, the 'Leninist idea of "smashing" the entire "bourgeois state"' was unacceptable, and the theoretical distinction between the two kinds of states was apparently not very important.[79]

In Marxist theory, however, this was a crucial distinction. Indeed, it was at the crux of the reform/revolution problem for Marxists: whether socialist change was possible in the absence of workers' political power, i.e. state power. Marx and Engels' *Communist Manifesto* had set the 'immediate aim' as the 'formation of the proletariat into a class, overthrow of bourgeois supremacy, conquest of political power by the proletariat'.[80] In a famous letter to Joseph Weydemeyer in 1852, Marx stated that the distinctiveness of his theory did not lie in his 'discovery' of classes or the class struggle but (partly) in his identification of workers' state power as the necessary political means to the transition to a classless society.[81] This political power was the precondition for socialist changes in the economic realm: reflecting on the Paris Commune almost two decades later, Marx argued that its 'true secret' was that, as a workers' government, it was 'the political form at last discovered under which to work out the economic emancipation of labour'.[82] The Paris Commune had proved that 'the working class cannot simply lay hold of the ready-made state machinery, and wield it for its own purposes'.[83]

This was also the approach of the dominant figures of 'classical' Marxism in the early twentieth century. For Lenin, workers' 'fundamental economic interests' could not be satisfied without the replacement of 'the dictatorship of the bourgeoisie by the dictatorship of the proletariat'.[84] According to Preobrazhensky, the Marxist economist, capitalist production arose and developed within the womb of feudalism, but the socialist system could only begin 'its chronology with the seizure of power by the proletariat'.[85] The Marxist philosopher Georg Lukacs made a similar point: the 'enormous difference' between capitalism and socialism was that, while the former developed under feudal conditions,

> it would be a utopian fantasy to imagine that anything tending towards socialism could arise within capitalism apart from, on the one hand, the *objective economic premises that make it a possibility* which, however, can only be *transformed* into the true elements of a socialist system of production after and in consequence of the collapse of capitalism; and, on the other hand, the development of the proletariat as a class.[86]

From outside Bolshevism, Rosa Luxemburg also rejected the possibility of establishing socialism without a revolution for '*the conquest of political power by the proletariat*'.[87] In her classic discussion of the reform/revolution problem, she argued that support for reforms to improve workers' conditions was common to both reformist and revolutionary politics. For reformists, however, these reforms 'gradually reduce capitalist exploitation' and 'remove from capitalist society its capitalist character'—that is, they begin to realise 'the desired social change' objectively.[88] Marxists, in contrast, saw parliamentary and trade-union activity not as a means to enact socialism under capitalism but as useful insofar as they raised the socialist consciousness of workers and increased their organisation as a class—i.e. prepared them for the seizure of state power.[89]

As discussed, advocates of the AES endowed the strategy with revolutionary potential and sought a position between reformist and revolutionary socialism. However, their understanding of socialist transition did not represent a fundamental break with the traditions of reformism as defined by the Marxist positions identified above. Where the latter saw workers' state power as a prerequisite for socialist changes in the economic realm, Labour-left and radical proponents of the AES approached socialist transition very differently. Having rejected 'insurrectionism', they believed that socialist aims could be accomplished in a society led by the reformed state institutions of the present, if also supplemented by politically empowered trade unions and new institutions for greater democracy in the workplace. This in turn entailed an inherent tension between their justification of the AES as a strategy for socialist transformation and their aim to revive the existing economy under conditions of capitalist domination. As the following three chapters will aim to show, this basic tension pervaded the AES left's attempts to forge an economic strategy that was a programme both for an immediately viable industrial regeneration via a left-wing Labour government atop the existing institutions of the British state, and a strategy for a fundamental social transformation in the interests of the working class.

## THE LABOUR PARTY

In the AES, the strategy to work via the existing state granted an integral role to the Labour Party, which would be the main political agent of the socialist transition, as a socialist party of government with a mass base in the organised working class. As with prior Labour-left initiatives, the socialist strategy of the AES hinged on the socialist transformation of Labour and its ability to win sufficient electoral support to enact radical policies in power. Although the AES was openly critical of the right-wing Labour leadership, and supporters of the AES struggled against the right for greater power within the party, Labour-left support for the AES contained a deep loyalty to Labour and a strong criticism of leftists who rejected the party. It demanded left unity around Labour and sought to maintain the loyalty of industrial militants and left-wing activists in what was, as the previous chapter outlined, a period of widespread disillusionment with the party. As the Labour-leftist Eric Heffer warned in *The Class Struggle in Parliament*, the party's left-wing opponents were 'in practice being divisive and giv[ing] great comfort to those who are enemies of socialist advance'.[90] As Michael

Foot recalled of the 1970s, 'We were not prepared, any of us, to risk the alternative; opening the gate to the Tory enemy, through resignations or the destruction of the [Labour] government'.[91]

However, sections of the Labour left also sought to demonstrate a significant degree of open-mindedness to groups and individuals to their left. Benn opposed the Labour leadership's campaign in the 1980s against the party's Militant Tendency 'entrists' and argued that attacks on left-wing radicals would 'threaten the radical tradition itself'.[92] Although Labour's origins lied more in Jesus than Marx, the latter should be listed among the greatest of those who had 'contributed by their courage, and their intellect, to the advancement of humanity', and socialism could only advance if it accepted 'the full and rich diversity of our separate traditions and [was] ready to discuss the success and failures of our own experience in socialist ideas and practice'.[93] Indeed, Benn advanced the idea that Marxism should be recognised as a world faith and 'welcomed into a dialogue with other world faiths, including Christian and other beliefs'.[94] Somewhat in keeping with this religious theme, he argued in 1983 that socialist 'sects' should not be 'witch-hunted' but treated as 'ideological pressure groups', since they were an indication of the growth of interest in socialist politics.[95]

Related to this was the suggestion that Labour should change its attitude towards such left-wing groups to increase their incorporation into its sphere of influence. Hain and Hebditch laid a heavy stress on this point, arguing that the extra-Labour left should be taken seriously in order for Labour to better harness it. The unacceptance by some Labour members that 'committed socialists' could remain outside the Labour Party was 'based upon a somewhat self-righteous complacency' that could only weaken the labour movement.[96] The 'major priority' for Labour was to form 'working links between the Party and the rank and file socialist movement outside' with the aim of a 'realignment of the left around a rejuvenated Labour Party'.[97] Hain and Hebditch were encouraged by the fact that Labour's apparent shift to left in the 1970s had led to a 'switch back to Labour'.[98] Labour's main challenge was to transform itself so that it could 'harness' the 'energies of the "alternative" groups' for an industrial and electoral strategy with mass support against 'the existing capitalist system'.[99]

Such arguments appeared to offer some validity to the critique that Labour's leftward shift in the 1970s may have represented, as Leo Panitch put it, a process of reconstructing its viability as a 'mediating agenc[y] for the consensual reproduction of capitalism and the containment of industrial militancy and radical structural reform'.[100] That Labour-leftism enabled

Labour to better manage social discontent was a central idea in the Milibandian analysis of which Panitch was an influential exponent, despite the
sympathetic and at times positive angle from which it eventually came to
appraise the Labour left of the 1970s and 1980s.[101] As Ralph Miliband
argued, Labour's periodic expressions of commitment to radical left-wing
aims did not 'make it less but more useful in the preservation of the existing social order', since this allowed social discontent to be channelled into
the safe bounds of Labour's parliamentarist politics.[102] Leftward shifts in
Labour's policy and rhetoric were means by which it sought to maintain its
relevance to key sections of its base in periods of increased social discontent
and instability. It was argued that the Labour left played a significant role
in this regard, helping to keep 'alive the myth of a transformable Labour
Party', the belief that Labour could enact radical socialist policies.[103] In the
early 1970s, Miliband's co-thinker John Saville suggested that the Labour
left, 'storing up...the greater part of the reserves of the Left within the
labour movement as a whole', was 'the major stumbling block in the way
of a serious reassessment of the means towards a socialist future'.[104]

This interpretation has been strongly dismissed as an unfounded 'func-
tionalism' in Wickham-Jones's study of the AES.[105] Of course, there is
little evidence of any conspiracy among the Labour left in this period, any
self-conscious, 'Machiavellian' attempt by Benn and his supporters to move
Labour leftward so as to undermine left-wing radicalism outside it. There
was a genuine conviction among Benn's supporters that, whatever its faults,
Labour was the only party through which socialist politics could be effectively practiced in Britain, at least for now. Ken Coates insisted on this latter
point strongly, arguing that Labour's socialist potential could not be dismissed, since there were no viable political alternatives, and particularly in
the light of historical experience, which showed that socialist groups did
not prosper in Britain outside of Labour.[106] The factors in Labour's favour
seemed undeniable to its left-wing supporters; or rather, the obstacles to
socialist politics independent of Labour seemed insurmountable. And an
effect of this belief was the tactical conviction that Labour must attempt to
draw the wider socialist movement under its umbrella. It was in this sense
that the Milibandian argument had validity, insofar as the greater openness
of sections of the Labour left to co-operation with the left outside Labour
had the effect of incorporating, and therefore to an extent discouraging,
extra-Labour socialist organisation.

As with their attempts to reconcile reformism with revolutionary aims,
some radical proponents of the AES sought to justify their support for

Labour with references to Marxist theory. Lenin was often cited by figures in the CPGB, particularly his well-known work *'Left Wing' Communism*, which had argued against the 'left-communist' opposition to tactical engagement with the Labour Party. According to Andrews, Lenin's advice henceforth became a main source for the unclarity among British Communists regarding their approach to Labour: the CPGB 'was never clear whether it was in competition with [it] or was part of the same movement'.[107] Although the *BRS* had in 1951 formalised the CPGB's commitment to the parliamentary road, Lenin was not discarded by the party, and his opposition to 'ultra-leftism' was invoked by CPGB supporters against Marxist criticisms of their 'reformist' politics.[108] Indeed, the apparent ambiguity in Lenin's prescriptions proved so far-reaching that they could be employed by Eric Hobsbawm to criticise the 'extremism' of the Labour left's by then increasingly rearguard defence of the AES in the mid-1980s.[109]

Whatever its ambiguity, however, there was an underlying principle in Lenin's approach which distinguished it from radical-left support for Labour in the AES period. While Lenin's analysis had rejected a blanket dismissal of Labour (whose formation represented the first step 'towards a conscious class policy and towards a socialist workers' party'),[110] it had seen it as a 'thoroughly bourgeois party' whose role was to 'systematically dupe' the working class.[111] Lenin's opposition to the left-communist view concerned the tactics needed to shift workers' political loyalties; as in Trotsky's approach, the aim was to deplete Labourism of its working-class support by winning workers' allegiance to revolutionary politics. Furthermore, Lenin's emphasis on the 'vanguard' of the working class was important in this sense. Defined as the most militant and politically conscious workers, its role was, in Lenin's view, of key strategic importance for a viable intervention in the Labour Party, since it was only through this vanguard that revolutionary politics could be contrasted at a mass level to reformism.[112] This suggested the need to secure support for Marxist politics among potentially leading sections of the working class as a preliminary to the further advance of socialist politics within the population at large and the wider labour movement.[113] In *'Left Wing' Communism*, Lenin was clear that this was a condition for effective work in the Labour Party, without which 'not even the first step towards victory can be made'.[114]

In comparison, left-wing support for the AES called for political broadness, a set of policies devised to win wide-ranging support among the British electorate at the next general election. The CPGB's strategy in this period rejected what one supporter characterised as a conception of 'the role of the party...in exclusivist, vanguardist terms'.[115] Socialist leadership was 'the prerogative of the left as a whole' and the task was 'the development of a united left capable of coming to terms with the strategic problems that confront it'.[116] Although an 'independent organisation of revolutionaries' was essential to this broad-left strategy, the role of the CPGB should be to enter, with Labour and the unions, into a 'Broad Democratic Alliance' of which it would be a co-operative if also radicalising element.[117] As the party's national organiser argued, the 'objective of left unity' would be a key aspect of this alliance. Couched in an interpretation of Gramsci that had found much favour within the Western European official Communist movement in this period, the stated aim was to show that the left had 'the capacity to become an alternative ruling force at every level' of society—by putting forward 'realistic and sophisticated policies' as a left-wing alternative to the status quo.[118]

This differed from Lenin's perhaps more modest suggestion of the initial need to establish an independent socialist working-class leadership that would be able to intervene in the wider labour movement and attract wider support. Thus, the AES raised the question of what would be the leading and organising political agent of its process of socialist transition. Across the board of AES support, the Labour Party was viewed as the primary political body for this task, since it was the only mass political organisation of the British working class. Naturally, this meant an increased level of left-wing concern with the internal balance of political power inside the Labour Party, and intra-party struggle was a determining feature of the Labour left in this period.[119] The campaign to 'democratise' the Labour Party—i.e. to increase the internal power of its activists—was the corollary of the AES. If the AES depended on Labour's agency, a major hurdle was the dominance of the right at the level of the Labour leadership.

## Conclusion

In a *New Left Review* article in 1976, Raymond Williams identified two kinds of socialist strategy on the radical left.[120] On the one hand was the strategy of those self-proclaimed 'revolutionary' groups, which understood campaigns for reforms within a 'politics of response', where the aim was to put the system under strain to engender its crisis and breakdown, but where, Williams argued, there was no coherent strategy in which political demands could converge 'in the actual (as distinct from the theoretically assumed) organization of social forces'.[121] On the other hand was a strategy superficially similar to the former, and which also adhered to the 'politics of response', but which saw the need to mobilise

> need and demand, in existing and where necessary new organizations, to the point where one struggle connects with and implies another, and where there is then a process of putting the central system under strains which can lead to transformation, since the converging demands can be met by no less.[122]

This latter strategy, which Williams favoured, described well the perception of the AES by many of its prominent advocates. As this chapter has attempted to show, there was a significant degree of convergence, between the Labour-left and radical supporters of the AES, on the idea that the purpose of the strategy was to transform the existing social order by mobilising mass support and encouraging its radicalisation. Both groups made attempts to resolve the longstanding reform/revolution problem while employing, though to varying degrees, the language of Marxism. The difference between the two groups rested on the level of emphasis they gave to the notion that the AES was a means to intensify class conflict—Williams' 'politics of response'—with the radical proponents of the strategy highlighting this virtue in their polemics with Marxist critics, and the Labour left laying more stress on the agency of a Labour government and parliamentary legislation.

However, as this chapter suggested, and as later chapters will examine in greater detail, fundamental disagreement between the two groups on the central questions of socialist transition tended to be limited: on the crucial need for mass support and extending democratic power to the economy to overcome the difficulties that the strategy would face; on the vital importance of the Labour Party and parliament; on the need to work within and through the existing state; on the idea that the policies of the AES would be implemented in a reformed capitalist economy, with Britain's economic regeneration representing the basis for the strategy's progressive aims. The latter position, this chapter suggested, risked rendering the AES incoherent as a strategy for socialist transformation. The next chapter will examine further how the proponents of the AES understood capitalism and its transformation.

## NOTES

1. Anderson, 'Problems of Socialist Strategy', p. 223.
2. London CSE Group and the LCC, *The Alternative Economic Strategy.*
3. Holland, *The Socialist Challenge*, pp. 37–8.
4. Aaronovitch, *The Road from Thatcherism*, p. 108.
5. Labour Co-ordinating Committee, *There Is an Alternative*, p. 4.
6. London CSE Group and the LCC, *The Alternative Economic Strategy*, p. 133.
7. Meacher, *Socialism with a Human Face*, pp. xiii–xiv.
8. Rowthorn, 'The Alternative Economic Strategy'.
9. Rowthorn, 'The Politics of the Alternative Economic Strategy', p. 4. His italics.
10. Rowthorn, 'The Alternative Economic Strategy'. His italics.
11. Hodgson, 'Britain's Crisis and the Road to International Socialism'.
12. Ibid.
13. Ibid.
14. Hodgson, *Socialist Economic Strategy*, p. 29.
15. Barratt Brown, *From Labourism to Socialism*, p. 22.
16. Ibid., p. 23.
17. Ibid., p. 12.
18. Hain, *The Democratic Alternative*, p. 74. See also LCC, *The Realignment of the Right*, p. 30.
19. Holland, *The Socialist Challenge*, p. 155
20. Ibid., pp.154–62.
21. Ibid., p. 158.
22. Ibid., pp. 158–9.
23. Ibid, p. 149.
24. Ibid., p. 162.
25. Benn, *Parliament, People and Power*, p. 85.
26. Ibid., p. 80.
27. Ibid., p. 81.
28. Ibid., p. 83.
29. London CSE Group and the LCC, *The Alternative Economic Strategy*, p. 5.
30. Hain and Hebditch, *Radicals and Socialism*, p. 10.
31. Ibid. See also Meacher, *Socialism with a Human Face*, p. 167.
32. Fine et al., *Class Politics*, p. 22.
33. Ibid., p. 22. Their italics.
34. Foote, 'Interview with Tony Benn', pp. 17–33.
35. Ramelson, 'Gospel According to Sam', p. 39.
36. Aaronovitch, *The Road from Thatcherism*, p. 108.
37. Dix, review of Sam Aaronovitch's *The Road from Thatcherism*, p. 32.
38. Rowthorn, 'The Politics of the Alternative Strategy', p. 5.

39. Ibid., pp. 8–10. See also Harrison, 'The Politics of the Alternative Strategy'.
40. Cook, 'The British Road to Socialism and the Communist Party', p. 370
41. Ibid., p. 371.
42. Holland, *The Socialist Challenge*, p. 162.
43. Ibid., p. 163.
44. Ibid.
45. Ibid., pp. 163–4.
46. Ibid., p. 164.
47. Sedgemore, *The How and Why of Socialism*, pp. 80–81.
48. Holland, *Strategy for Socialism*, p. 78.
49. Rowthorn, 'The Alternative Economic Strategy'.
50. Hodgson, *Socialist Economic Strategy*, p. 26.
51. Ibid. His italics.
52. Ibid.
53. See Hodgson, *The Democratic Economy*, pp. 47–64 for his discussion of reformism and 'Leninism'.
54. Hodgson, *Socialist Economic Strategy*, p. 27.
55. Ibid.
56. Glyn, *Capitalist Crisis*.
57. Hodgson, *'Militant' and the Alternative Economic Strategy*, p. 14.
58. Hain and Hebditch, *Radicals and Socialism*, pp. 9–10.
59. Ibid., p. 10.
60. London CSE Group, 'Crisis, the Labour Movement and the Alternative Economic Strategy'.
61. Trotsky, 'Revisionism and Planning'.
62. Ibid.
63. Hodgson, 'Socialist Economic Strategy: A Reply to Donald Swartz', p. 129.
64. Hodgson, *Labour at the Crossroads*, p. 86.
65. Hodgson, *The Democratic Economy*, p. 54.
66. Ibid.
67. Ibid., p. 52.
68. Holland (ed.), *Out of Crisis*, pp. 101, 103–4.
69. Rowthorn, 'The Alternative Economic Strategy'.
70. Ibid.
71. London CSE Group and the LCC, *The Alternative Economic Strategy*, p. 35.
72. See Williams, 'Review Article'; Swartz, 'The Eclipse of Politics'.
73. London CSE Group, 'Crisis, the Labour Movement and the Alternative Economic Strategy', p. 88.
74. Yaffe, 'The Crisis of Profitability'.
75. Hodgson, 'Britain's Crisis and the Road to International Socialism'.
76. Holland, *The Socialist Challenge*, p. 165.

77. Lenin, '"Left-wing" Childishness'. His italics.
78. Ibid.
79. Hodgson, *The Democratic Economy*, p. 55.
80. Marx and Engels, 'Manifesto of the Communist Party', p. 484.
81. Marx, 'Class Struggle and the Mode of Production', p. 220.
82. Marx, 'The Civil War in France', pp. 634–5.
83. Marx and Engels, Preface to the 1972 German edition of the Communist Manifesto.
84. Lenin, *What Is to Be Done?* pp. 87–8, fn. 1.
85. Preobrazhensky, *The New Economics*, p. 79.
86. Lukacs, *History and Class Consciousness*, p. 283. His italics.
87. Luxemburg, *Reform or Revolution and Other Writings*, p. 31. Her italics.
88. Ibid., p. 32.
89. Ibid., pp. 32–3.
90. Heffer, *Class Struggle in Parliament*, p. 226.
91. Cited in Mark Wickham-Jones, *Economic Strategy and the Labour Party*, p. 152.
92. Benn, *Fighting Back*, p. 73.
93. Ibid., pp. 58, 61.
94. Ibid., p. 61.
95. Ibid., p. 21.
96. Hain and Hebditch, *Radicals and Socialism*, p. 1.
97. Ibid., p. 20.
98. Ibid., pp. 10–1.
99. Ibid., p. 18.
100. Panitch, 'Socialist Renewal and the Labour Party', p. 322.
101. Tufekci, '"Politics of Containment"'.
102. Miliband, *Parliamentary Socialism*, p. 376.
103. Miliband, 'Moving On', pp. 128, 133.
104. Saville, 'Britain: Prospects for the Seventies', p. 210.
105. Wickham-Jones, *Economic Strategy and the Labour Party*, pp. 194–6.
106. Coates, 'Socialists and the Labour Party'.
107. Andrews, *Endgames and New Times*, p. 76.
108. Jack Conrad, *In the Enemy Camp*, p. 40.
109. Hobsbawm, 'The Retreat into Extremism', pp. 87–99.
110. Lenin, 'Meeting of the International Socialist Bureau'.
111. Lenin, 'Report of the Second Congress of the Communist International'.
112. Communist International, *Manifesto of the Second World Congress*.
113. For a left-wing critique of Labourism along these lines, see Ryan, 'Labour or the Red Front', pp. 7–28.
114. Lenin, *'Left-Wing' Communism*.
115. Roberts, 'The CP, the SWP and the Strategy for Socialism in Britain', pp. 22–4.

116. Ibid.
117. Ibid.
118. Cook, 'The British Road to Socialism and the Communist Party', p. 373.
119. See Seyd, *Rise and Fall of the Labour Left*.
120. Reproduced in Williams, Raymond, *Problems in Materialism and Culture*, pp. 233–51.
121. Ibid., p. 248.
122. Ibid.

# CHAPTER 4

# Planning the Market: The AES and Capitalism

## INTRODUCTION

As shown in Chapter 1, several academics have described the AES as a radical left-wing departure from Keynesian social democracy. They have pointed to Labour's adoption of much of Stuart Holland's economic ideas as evidence of the extent to which its programme broke with post-war Labour revisionism. This chapter discusses the extent and nature of this break and examines the anti-capitalist alternative of the AES. It focuses heavily on Holland, who is widely acknowledged as the strategy's dominant economic theorist. As the author of numerous books, articles and essays on economic topics related to the AES, Holland's body of work provides an abundance of information to understand the anti-capitalism of the strategy supported by its diverse left-wing proponents. This chapter aims to provide a detailed critical analysis of Holland's anti-capitalist economic theory, and then to consider the ways in which some of the other left-wing advocates of the AES approached some of the key questions Holland raised.

The first part of the chapter will briefly discuss Keynes and the relationship between Keynesianism and post-war Labour politics—why Keynesianism appealed to Labour and why, by the early 1970s, it became increasingly doubted. This will lead to a discussion of Holland's break with Keynes. It will be argued that Holland did not 'jettison' Keynesianism but demanded its supplementation with greater state intervention in the market economy. At the same time, however, Holland's approach did not uphold the

© The Author(s) 2020
B. Tufekci, *The Socialist Ideas of the British
Left's Alternative Economic Strategy*,
https://doi.org/10.1007/978-3-030-34998-1_4

state as his Labour-left predecessors had. Contrary to common depictions, Holland was far from hostile to market economy and private enterprise. His approach contained an interesting deviation from prior Labour leftism: his highly positive assessment of the potential of markets and private firms placed him far more in line with post-war revisionism than a 'Clause 4 socialism' for extensive nationalisation and planning.

The final part of the chapter will then briefly review the economic approaches of some of those figures the previous chapter categorised as 'radical' proponents of the AES, individuals who had a greater tendency than Holland to depict the AES as a means to mobilise workers, mount class conflict and intensify opposition to capitalism. It will argue that the assumptions underlying their economic proposals did not differ fundamentally from Holland's. Their disapproval of capitalism did not lead them to propose a society without capital or markets—at least not in the short or medium term, and, as we will see, probably not in the long term either. Although frequently noted for its radical demands for greater state control, perhaps the more interesting feature of the socialism of the AES was that it did not look very far beyond the existing organisation of the British economy. AES approaches contained a distinct lack of confidence in non-market solutions to Britain's economic crisis, therefore embodying, in a sense, a significant moderation of Labour-left thinking since the 1950s.

## KEYNES AND THE LABOUR PARTY

Just as Holland's theory emerged with the loss of confidence in one orthodoxy—Keynesianism itself—the historical and intellectual basis for Keynes's analysis was the apparent discrediting of another: 'laissez-faire', classical political economy. First published during the Great Depression, a world capitalist crisis on an unprecedented scale, Keynes's *The General Theory of Employment, Interest and Money* was certain it was violating past assumptions. As he told George Bernard Shaw, the book would 'largely revolutionize…the way the world thinks about economic problems'.[1] Believing in the world-shaping value of ideas—famously stating that practical men who believed themselves free from intellectual influence were 'usually the slaves of some defunct economist'[2]—Keynes sought to revise the theoretical precepts he thought responsible for the existing capitalist disorder. This is, as argued below, something he had in common with his successors on the British left. The AES, launched in yet another period of global capitalist crisis, had similar aspirations: it pointed to the strengths as well as the inadequacies of the currently dominant—this time round, Keynesian—principles guiding, at least until the monetarism of the late 1970s, the economic policies of capitalist governments.

Of course, *The General Theory* did not invent state intervention in the capitalist economy, and laissez-faire assumptions had in practice already been undermined by the interwar economic crisis. Britain's response to the crisis was what Beer called the 'Managed Economy' of the 1930s' National Government, which helped lay the political groundwork for the post-war move towards Keynesian methods.[3] While Labour placed greater emphasis on economic planning in this period, the Conservative Party, whose Ministers dominated the National Government, also contained a 'reassertion of state power over the operation of the economic system as a whole'.[4] In fact, as Jones and Keating point out, 'expanding the role of the state was by the 1930s part of a political consensus', the product of a political dialogue since the 1920s to which both Labour and the Conservatives contributed.[5] So the affront to the classical assumptions Keynes identified did not begin with him but in the 'real world' of economic crisis and state responses. What *The General Theory* is often credited with is the explicit theoretical outlining of a policy orientation that would come to characterise post-war government approaches to economic policy throughout the advanced capitalist world.

Put simply, Keynes disagreed that capitalism worked best when left entirely to its own automatic devices. He saw economic orthodoxy as presupposing that all goods produced would necessarily be sold, because all income (profits, wages, savings) must ultimately be spent on consumption or investment. It was wrongly assumed, Keynes argued, that the market forces governing investment and consumption would produce an equilibrium whereby deficiencies of demand in one market would be counterbalanced by excesses in another: aggregate supply and demand would necessarily equal in free market conditions; neither gluts nor shortages would occur at the macroeconomic level. Full employment was also assured, as an economy undistorted by trade unions and state interference would not contain tendencies to 'involuntary' unemployment.

This was rejected by Keynes: a lack of aggregate demand was a common feature of the market economy, the latter lacked a suitable automatic mechanism to correct it, and government intervention was therefore required to raise demand when the nation's economic resources were underemployed. For Keynes, writing amid devastating levels of mass unemployment, joblessness was not caused primarily by workers' indolence or even their reluctance to accept necessary wage cuts, but by the economy's inability to maintain sufficient investment by maintaining required levels of effective demand. The solution was to manage demand through the control of the interest rate and, if necessary, by government spending, accruing state debts if needed. Keynes was optimistic that slumps could be abolished through demand management by state economists.[6] The 'Keynesian revolution' was the apparent discovery of technical solutions to the deeply contradictory nature of economic growth under capitalism.

Keynes's theory looked like an opposition to hitherto essential claims in defence of the capitalist economy. In a sense, it was. Marx's predictions of overproduction, growing unemployment and declining investment due to crises in profitability were all acknowledged by Keynes.[7] However, *The General Theory* did not credit Marxism itself, which it dismissed as deriving 'ultimately from Ricardo' and the 'classical hypotheses' Keynes was seeking to confute.[8] There was indeed a basic and unbridgeable distance between the two theories. Keynes was not attacking capitalism but its direction by mistaken theories, even if he did tentatively ally his book with 'an anti-Marxian socialism'.[9] Hence his contrasting of Marx with the market socialist Silvio Gesell: posterity would 'learn more from the spirit of Gesell than from that of Marx' because whereas the latter wanted to abolish market competition, Gesell wanted to 'unfetter' it.[10] One should not 'respond to anti-Communist rubbish with anti-capitalist rubbish', as the Labour Party was, in Keynes's eyes, guilty of doing.[11]

Nor, indeed, was Keynes's theory a rejection of the *promise* (as opposed to the implements, or the lack thereof) of liberal political economy. He was not so much interested in 'finding logical flaws' in the classical analysis as 'pointing out that its tacit assumptions are seldom or never satisfied'. With central controls for aggregate output to correspond as closely as possible to full employment, however, classical theory would come 'into its own again', and 'private self-interest' would continue to 'determine what in particular is produced, in what proportions the factors of production will be combined to produce it, and how the value of the final product will be distributed between them'.[12] Apart from these controls, 'there is no more reason to socialise economic life than there was before'.[13]

In the post-war period, Keynes's theory challenged but also appealed to Labour's state-oriented interpretation of socialism. In the 1950s the revisionists on the party's right posed Keynesianism as the alternative to what they saw as an outdated Labour socialism of public ownership and state planning, and leading revisionists like Anthony Crosland believed that socialist objectives could be met without further socialisation.[14] The latter, enshrined by the 1918 Clause 4 as 'the common ownership of the means of production, distribution and exchange', implied, for the Labour left at least, a commitment to broad public ownership.[15] While this commitment may not have guided the practice of Labour governments—whose nationalisations did not tend to extend beyond 'natural monopoly' utilities and failing firms or sectors—for the revisionists it was nevertheless an electoral liability, a misleading statement easily falsified by the Conservative enemy to suggest the overextension of the state.[16]

Yet, despite some criticism from the Labour left, Keynesianism could also be saleable to the party because it spoke to Labour's traditions of state socialism.[17] It was with this in mind that Crosland framed his arguments. Since Keynesianism granted a vital role to state intervention, it was really the party in power that would be in charge. Indeed, in Crosland's theory governmental power was decisive irrespective of the economic system: 'whatever the modes of economic production, economic power will, in fact, belong to the owners of political power'.[18] Keynesianism meant that the government could 'exert any influence it likes on income-distribution, and it can also determine within broad limits the division of total output between consumption, investment, exports and social expenditure'.[19] Thus, as Shaw writes, Keynesian social democracy represented something of a rapprochement between the left's egalitarian and welfare aspirations and the capitalist mixed economy.[20] An important ideological basis for this reconciliation in logic was the revisionist assertion that Keynesian methods provided a way to accomplish socialist ends via state power. In this way, revisionism could be posed as in large measure consistent with Labour's principles, albeit also as a refutation of the idea that those principles rested upon extensive state ownership.

## DISILLUSION WITH KEYNESIANISM

If an element of consistency with its traditions was needed for Labour's acceptance of Keynesian revisionism, so too was the relative economic prosperity and social stability of post-war Britain. As mentioned in Chapter 2, the Labour left's focus in the 1950s was Britain's Cold War militarism and foreign policy; although it expressed opposition to Keynesianism, it tended to do so with general slogans rather than detailed alternatives.[21] With sustained economic growth, low unemployment, the welfare state and relative harmony in industrial relations combined with steady wage increases, systematic Labour-left challenges to Keynesianism had reason to be limited.

Yet, as Foote notes, revisionism's success could only be temporary, since it was founded on 'the solution of the old problem of boom and slump which had bedevilled the economy before the war'.[22] By the 1970s, with economic crisis, rising labour militancy and the British economy's structural weakness increasingly apparent, loss of confidence in Keynesian methods provided encouragement for alternative ideas from the left.

This loss of confidence affected the perspectives of the Labour right, too, however, i.e. those in the party most closely associated with the Keynesian consensus. With the experience of the 1960s Labour government—during which real wages fell, strikes rose and the party lost on a predominantly revisionist manifesto a general election which saw an exodus of its working-class support—revisionist self-confidence and optimism was markedly lower than it had been. Although Crosland remained attached to the revisionist course he had prescribed in *The Future of Socialism* in 1956, rejecting the early AES analyses in his 1974 book *Socialism Now*, there was also a greater tone of uncertainty in the second book than in the first, perhaps in the light of the mood of 'pessimism, lack of clarity, a flight into chiliasm' that he identified as at odds with the 'hopeful and purposive optimism [of] twenty years ago'.[23] There was indeed no 'panacea for crisis-free growth', Crosland stated.[24] In his 1972 book *What Matters Now*, Roy Jenkins displayed a somewhat greater degree of revisionist self-criticism: 'In the 1950s, many of us thought that the inequalities would diminish as society became more prosperous. It is now clear that this view was at best simplified, and at worst just wrong.'[25] In general, as discussed in Chapter 2, there was a greater openness in the party (and the unions) to the idea that a change was needed in Labour's approach, and to a re-evaluation of the politics of the two preceding decades. It was out of this climate that the Labour left's economic strategy emerged.

## Holland's Socialist Challenge

Holland's break with Keynes had something in common with Keynes's break with laissez-faire. Keynes had abandoned laissez-faire 'not enthusiastically, not from contempt for that good old doctrine, but because, whether we like it or not, the conditions for its success have disappeared'.[26] Similarly, Holland evaluated Keynesianism not so much as something that should have been opposed from the start as a matter of socialist analysis and principle, but mainly as an economic theory that could no longer produce desirable outcomes on its own. Keynesianism had to be questioned not primarily because it was wrong but because it had become partly outdated.

It is true that Holland mentioned the illusions which had led Labour into the Keynesian camp after the Second World War. He argued that, contrary to post-war Labour assumptions, Keynesian state intervention was less a policy for 'a limited form of state socialism than an extensive formula for state capitalism'.[27] Holland also seemed aware that Keynes, far from being a man of the left, sought to 're-establish the conditions in which [liberal capitalist] principles could come into their own'.[28] However, the crux of Holland's case against Keynesianism was that economic developments had rendered its prescriptions inadequate for economic stability and growth. The contemporary economy of monopoly and multinational power had partially invalidated Keynesianism. But, like Keynes, Holland did not call for the old orthodoxy to be discarded in total—just as Keynes had seen liberal economy as viable only with a certain amount of state direction, Holland suggested that Keynesian demand management could be effective only if bolstered by a greater role for public enterprise. Indeed, there was

> nothing wrong in principle with Keynesian demand management techniques in a market economy composed of the small, national firms of the old competitive model. What is wrong is the failure of demand management instruments to ensure a focused investment response in an economy in which the market has increasingly been eclipsed by the rise of mesoeconomic power and multinational capital.[29]

Holland therefore accepted a key premise of Keynesian revisionism: that, since in a competitive and national market economy individual firms lacked the leverage to dictate economic outcomes at the 'macro' or 'aggregate' level, such outcomes could be determined by the government through its management of demand. The 'commanding heights' of the economy could thereby be controlled. Where Holland differed from Keynesianism was in his argument that this ability had become undermined by the rise of global companies large and powerful enough to evade previously appropriate government measures. Thus, there was 'nothing wrong in principle' with Keynesianism. Holland's concern was that capitalism had to an extent outgrown it. His use of verbs like 'restore' and 're-establish'—regarding, respectively, 'economic sovereignty' and 'government capacity to manage the British economy'[30]—was a feature of his belief that Britain needed to regain something it had once had but had since lost.

To a large extent, Keynesian theory had failed 'to relate to the real-world market economy as it has evolved since the mid-twentieth century'.[31] The 1930s' crisis was mainly one of insufficient demand, which could be solved by 'straightforward reflation'.[32] Hence the validity of Keynesian demand management—'there seemed to be a clear and decisive alternative to the slump syndrome'.[33] In the 1930s capital remained predominantly national in scope and scale, so state policies to raise demand or protect trade had more chance of success. Additionally, firms had a greater tendency to respond to fiscal and monetary government stimulus because their 'investment horizon' was shorter; now firms' investment portfolios extended beyond the 'budget cycle of the government', causing a loss of government control of longer-term investments.[34] Keynesian demand management remained relevant to controlling consumer demand and creating 'an appropriate demand climate for small- and medium-sized firms of the conventional competitive model'.[35] But the rise of the multinational monopolies meant that it was no longer enough. Realising that the more indirect fiscal and monetary measures of Keynesianism in response to the inter-war depression had failed to stave off crisis in the 'new mode of production', Holland went further in his recommendations.

The 'new mode of production' was an economy dominated by multinational monopolies. The latter had given rise to a 'mesoeconomic' power, a new intermediate structure within the old micro-macro model. There had been a sharp increase, since about 1950, of large multinational firms with the power to escape the macroeconomic control of governments. These companies had established 'a new mode of production, distribution and exchange in the heartland of the British economy'.[36] Due to their monopoly power and multinational presence, they had an unprecedented ability to determine prices, employment, wages, national investment and international trade. Moreover, they were often 'multi-company companies'—several enterprises were owned by a single company and, as a result, what may have appeared as a competitive market to the consumer was in fact a 'super firm' dominating consumers through takeovers and mergers which raised its ability to set prices. 'Consumer sovereignty' had thereby been replaced by 'producer sovereignty', which was a key cause of inflation.[37] The old conditions for the successful application of Keynesianism—price competition, national markets, and investment horizons shorter than the scope of governments' budgets—were now met by less than half the firms operating in the country.[38]

Hence the 'divorce' of the 'conventional micro-macro synthesis' of Keynesian theory and the consequent loss of government control over key economic processes.[39] Whereas the competitive firm of the past may have been too small to influence macroeconomic aggregates like national investment, trade and employment, the rise of the giant companies of the mesoeconomy 'substantially qualified the legitimation of liberal capitalism embodied in Keynes's synthesis of the old competitive model with his new demand management economics'.[40] What concerned Holland, therefore, was that private firms had taken over decision-making implements previously under government control. If governments were to regain their grip, they needed to assert themselves over this new mesoeconomy—now with stronger stuff than only demand management.

Yet it is misleading to suggest that Holland's concern was to 'jettison' or sideline Keynesianism, as the academic literature has tended to do. Holland saw the utilisation of the reflationary power of Keynesian policy as indispensable to the AES's ambitions for social reform, since he regarded such reform as unattainable without a strong economic recovery that reflationary policies were key to providing. 'Supplementing Keynes' did not mean a demotion of Keynesianism. In fact, at a time of monetarist ascent, it meant the opposite—demanding that Keynesianism be returned to its rightful place at the centre of policy-making to resuscitate the British economy. As Holland warned his monetarist opponents, Keynesianism needed to be 'transcended, not rejected, on both the ownership and control aspects of supply and on the redistribution of demand'.[41] 'On key issues Keynes is still right and the monetarists have been wrong',[42] and Keynesianism remained vital for demand-control: in this sense, 'If we are not all Keynesians now, then we certainly ought to be.'[43] The rejection of Keynesianism was part of the right's 'manichaean explanations of the crisis', as he argued in the late 1970s.[44]

## HOLLAND'S ANTI-CAPITALISM

Cronin has written that, while Labour's relationship to socialism has long been debated, there can be little doubt of the 'core antipathy to capitalism' that it traditionally possessed, whether based on ideas about capitalism's injustice and inefficiency or its 'competitive individualism' and 'culture of consumption'.[45] In Holland's case this antipathy did not involve calling for the abolition of capital or the market. Holland talked of 'harnessing' the power of capital and the market, not ending and transcending it. In the case of regional development, for example, the problem was not that the market could not 'be made to work', but that it could not 'be relied upon to work without state intervention to mobilise investment and location in economically and socially desired directions'.[46] His policy for company transparency—'opening the books'—was also related to this: the idea was that powerful monopolies were concealing the true extent of their profits, costs and investments, thereby obstructing appropriate measures of public regulation.[47] In this sense, Holland's anti-capitalism seemed to amount to policies for a 'better regulated' capitalism, although he certainly did not see it in such terms. Holland believed that, through this improved intervention, capitalism could be brought under social control and thereby come to lose its capitalist character.

Yet, like the revisionists before him, and aware of the prevailing unpopularity of nationalised industry and the bureaucratic command economies of the Soviet bloc, Holland depicted the market as an indispensable feature of a modern, progressive society. He made 'explicit the fact that harnessing the market mechanism to a process of socialist planning countervails the claim that any extension of public ownership and strategic planning will result in a central state bureaucracy of the Stalinist type'.[48] He opposed arguments that the maintenance of the market was an obstacle to socialist transformation. Pointing to the Russian experience of the New Economic Policy (NEP) in the 1920s, he argued that 'virtually all socialist revolutions' have had to 'maintain a market sector over substantial periods'.[49] But whereas Lenin had supported the NEP as a short-term retreat for a war-torn Soviet economy confronting food shortages, rural backwardness and international isolation,[50] Holland saw the market as compatible with socialist society. He endorsed the French left-wing economist Charles Bettelheim's claim that the market was not inherently capitalist, and argued against the belief that 'because the market system exploits the working class under capitalism, it must be abolished with the transition to socialism'.[51] Socialist anti-market views 'prevented the identification of feasible strategies for socialist transformation'.[52]

With a close resemblance to Crosland, Holland argued that the particular features of the economy—if it was dominated by markets or planning—were 'secondary to the nature of state power': whether the market was maintained, the crucial question concerned whose interests the state apparently standing above the economy served.[53] Although Lenin had taken a somewhat similar line in justifying the NEP—that despite Soviet 'state capitalism' workers remained in power because they had state power—he had posed the reintroduction of the market as an unfortunate exigency: the temporary retreat to market forms was intended to salvage the socialist revolution in circumstances unfavourable to it.[54] For Holland, in contrast, the 'revolutionary reforms' called for a 'new and more balanced mix in the so-called mixed economy'[55]—that is, they called for the maintenance of the market.

In this sense, Holland did not look far beyond the market for a superior means to generate growth and allocate economic resources. Although he believed his theory was influenced by Marx, he did not share the latter's belief that generalised commodity production and market competition were specific to capitalism and to be superseded by socialist society.[56] Instead, in principle like Keynes, Holland believed that the market should be subjected to a degree of social control to work more desirably and for more people; in this regard, he differed from Keynes only in policy prescriptions, not underlying intentions. The socialisation he called for went beyond Keynes in the extent of its reach, but the basic assumption of Keynesianism remained intact in its purpose: market enterprise was the basic engine for efficiency and growth; a viable alternative to it did not really exist for a country like Britain; and the point of public policy should be to harness the market's energy more effectively so as to reap its fruits more fully. Far from obstructing socialism, the market could be at its heart if its mechanisms were controlled in accordance with socialist aims. What would this social control of the market involve?

## Holland's Planned Market

If the market was to be at the heart of the new socialist society, the state was to be closer to the heart of the market. In the remixed economy Holland favoured, state intervention would differ from that of previous Labour governments but also that espoused by prior Labour-leftism. It would go beyond the limited and ineffective interventions of the 1960s Labour government, but its view of socialisation would also diverge fundamentally from the traditional left-wing rejection of private enterprise in favour of nationalisation.

To simplify somewhat, prior Labour-leftism had tended to depict increasing state/public/community economic power as a matter of *encroaching* on the powers and activities of private production. In other words, it had tended to pose a private-public dichotomy in which socialism meant the extension of the (variously defined) public over the private. As Tomlinson puts it, the belief was that

> public ownership would be the defining characteristic of the future socialist society, because it would simultaneously deprive the capitalists of their power and make possible the end of production guided by the search for profits.[57]

As mentioned above, it was this element at the core of Labour-leftism that Crosland's revisionism challenged, and which the Labour left continued to assert in the 1950s, however ineffectually. As the left-winger John Strachey argued in 1956, to lose 'sight of social ownership of the means of production' would be to 'subside into the role of well-intentioned amiable, rootless, drifting social reformers',[58] echoing Stafford Cripps's argument two decades earlier that private ownership of the means of production was 'inimical, indeed fatal, to a just and fair distribution of wealth'.[59] While this is not to claim that private capital had not featured at all in this Labour-leftism, its equation of socialism with public ownership had seen progress to a socialist society as necessarily involving a large *diminution* of private enterprise. Labour left-wingers in the 1930s had seen an industry's public ownership as incompatible with 'the continuance of any representation of shareholders or owners of capital in its controls', since 'socialisation of any industry involves the complete disappearance of private ownership from that industry'.[60] The basis for this equation of socialism with public ownership was explained by Bevan in 1944:

> This party did not come into existence demanding socialism, demanding the state ownership of property, simply because there was some special merit in it. This party believes in the public ownership of industry because we think only in that way can society be intelligently and progressively organised. If private enterprise can deliver [a progressive society and an expanding standard of life], there will not be any argument for Socialism and no reason for it.[61]

Holland's position contained an interesting deviation from this Labour-left perspective. Unlike Bevan, Holland did see an 'argument for socialism' which did not involve an extensive supplantation of private enterprise, and he certainly did not share Cripps's belief that private ownership was 'inimical' to socialism. Despite the common characterisation of the AES as upholding the superiority of public over private enterprise, Holland did not counterpose the two in the same way his Labour-left predecessors often had. Accompanying his view that the state should harness private capital and the market was the idea that this public-private relationship should become complementary rather than dichotomous and conflictual. That is, his acceptance that the market would be the generator of growth and innovation led logically to his belief that the role of the state would be to harness but also help to *thrive* the market and private enterprise.

## ENTREPRENEURIAL STATE

Sometimes presented in radical language, this perspective was broadly consonant with Labour's official position during its AES period. In 1973, Labour published a Green Paper outlining plans for a National Enterprise Board (NEB) to exert, within five years, 'a controlling interest over a large slice of the economy', i.e. between twenty and twenty-five companies.[62] The Industry Act 1975 facilitated the establishment of the NEB and defined its general purpose as the 'the development or assistance of the economy', 'the provision, maintenance or safeguarding of productive employment', and 'the promotion…of industrial efficiency and international competitiveness'.[63] Labour's aim in this period was to present its state-interventionism via the language of public-private partnership. As its 1974 White Paper *The Regeneration of British Industry* argued, for too long the government-industry relationship had been too remote and based on 'regulation to prevent the activities of industry, or the abuse of its powers, damaging the interests of other sectors of the community'.[64] It now needed to be a relationship of 'partners in the pursuit of the objectives which spell success for industry and prosperity for this country', which called for 'a closer, clearer and more positive relationship between Government and industry'.[65]

*The State as Entrepreneur*, a 1972 book edited by Holland, provided a detailed exposition of this 'positive' approach to the public-private relationship, drawing a strong distinction between its recommendations and a 'traditional public ownership pattern'.[66] On the one hand, it took the familiar left-wing position that Labour governments should no longer be content to nationalise 'traditional or declining' sectors such as steel, transport, fuel, communications and banking—such sectors could sustain growth but they could not initiate it, because the demand for their products was initiated in the more dynamic sectors of modern manufacturing, which were 'the real commanding heights of modern market economies'.[67] Yet this was less a call to extend nationalisation than for a qualitatively different approach to public intervention: the state must now place itself in a position within the market from which it could *promote* private enterprise as well as mobilise it in accordance with social and political ends.

The inspiration for Holland's model of state intervention was the Italian Institute for Industrial Reconstruction (IRI), the public holding company founded in 1933 by the Mussolini regime to raise its control of bank credit after the Wall Street Crash had devastated the Italian economy.[68] Needless to say, *The State as Entrepreneur* did not see the IRI as inherently fascist. The IRI was launched under fascism but its 'birth owed nothing to the fascist conception of the corporatist state...[I]t functioned very much as an anti-body to corporatism'.[69] Overall, the book's evaluation of the IRI was positive and enthusiastic. The IRI demonstrated that state enterprise could be 'as efficient and dynamic as leading private enterprise groups, yet still directly [serve] the ends of government economic policy and the interests of society as a whole'.[70] It also showed that nationalisation of entire economic sectors or even total state ownership of individual firms was unneeded: one of its 'main gains' was its mobilisation of investment 'without state ownership of a large proportion of the companies in the sector concerned, or of the total shareholding of those companies in which IRI holds shares'.[71]

In adopting this intervention formula, the British government would own a partial yet controlling share in 'sector-leading companies or companies with the potential for such sector leadership'.[72] By taking advantage of the 'follow-my-leader' effect in oligopolistic markets—whereby the leading firms in a sector tended to guide the sector as a whole—the state's control of leading firms would allow it to lead the sectors of the economy in general. Thus, it was the reality of oligopolistic power which would facilitate this strategy. The oligopolistic structures frequently 'lamented in other contexts' could favour a state prepared to intervene directly in firms in a position of sector leadership:

> Granted that less than 51% of the shares of a company may be sufficient to secure control (or share it in the event of a joint venture), and granted also that the influence of a dominant (oligopolistic) company on investment patterns is not limited to its nominal proportion of the output of the sector concerned, state ownership of less than half the shares in a company or companies with less than half the output of the sector could enable it to influence not only the investment behaviour of the company in which it had a holding but also other companies within the sector.[73]

The idea that the concentration of capitalist production advantaged social-ist transformation was, of course, not new; it had featured, albeit with major variations, in the theories of a range of left-wing traditions, from Marxism to early Fabianism. However, this idea had tended to accompany a belief in the superiority of planning over private ownership and market competition—a belief that the increased concentration of capitalist production improved the prospect of a future society of state or 'common' ownership and plan-ning. In contrast, Holland's position did not emphasise the superiority of planning. Planning was only a 'partial means' to 'fulfilling…economic and social ends'.[74] In fact, the 'constraint of market forces' on planning was a virtue because it enabled cost- and price-competitiveness, thus ensuring 'maximisation of efficiency and welfare effects from both state and private enterprise in the sectors concerned'.[75] As Holland put it decades later:

> A central point about state shareholding on the IRI model was that while the main holding company would be 100% owned, the holdings in individual companies could be much less and even minority. This was not 'old style' nationalisation but the case for selective state shareholding.[76]

Contrary to prior positions on the Labour left, therefore, the success of the IRI system would *presuppose* a large *lack* of public ownership: after all, if the state firms were monopolies, there would be no private firms to take their lead and follow their example. As such, state firms must 'to a certain extent amount to a *primus inter pares* in relation to private firms'.[77]

This 'first among equals' relationship, in which state shareholding improved the performance of markets, would also imply the maintenance of market competition, what Marx called 'nothing other than the inner *nature of capital*, its essential character'.[78] Market concentration did not provide an opportunity to move to an economy without market competition, but to reinvigorate the latter by countering market concentration. A key concern here was large firms lowering prices, which operated 'as abuses of com-petition, rather than the reverse'.[79] A state agency for competition was needed, but it would 'complement state entrepreneurship in the mainte-nance of competition', since state entrepreneurship itself would be a means to bolster market competition.[80] This theme of complementation—of the market by the state—underlay Holland's approach. Overcoming market failure should not mean the state substituting itself for the market but pro-viding 'conditions within which the market mechanism can be made to work in an economically efficient and socially just manner'.[81] Far from abolish private control of the 'advanced technology frontier', the IRI-type state 'should complement rather than substitute private enterprise initiative in technical progress and innovation within a planning framework'.[82]

But if state enterprise was not only to complement but also lead sectors otherwise constituted by private firms guided first and foremost by the discipline of the market, it would itself need to be at the cutting edge of market efficiency. Although helped by the measure of favour afforded to it by the IRI-type regime, its basic function—to play the role of oligopolistic sector-leader—ultimately required it to set an example to its private competitors by its own business efficiency. Indeed, Holland saw the state firm's market efficiency as the basis of its efficacy. For example, to be able to prompt the relocation of private investment by shifting its own investment to underdeveloped regions, the state firm would need to be 'as efficient in cost terms as other firms with which it is in competition'.[83] Otherwise the private competitors would not voluntarily follow suit to raise investment in these local economies, because they would not fear a major loss of profits to their inefficient state competitor if they did not. In other words, the state could act as a genuine spur to private investment only through its own entrepreneurial prowess in the market.

How would the state firm ensure its efficiency with respect to its private competitors? To a large extent, it would do so by conducting itself as they did. The state firm's competitiveness depended on the quality of its 'entrepreneurship and entrepreneurs'.[84] It also required that its entrepreneurs felt 'free from continual bureaucratic interruption' by the state, so that they may 'identify with the success of the enterprise itself'.[85] Traditional modes of nationalisation placed a stranglehold on market efficiency. According to Christopher Layton's chapter in *The State as Entrepreneur*, the monopolistic features of 'British-style nationalised sectors' tended to impede 'a climate of efficiency and...a spirit of enterprising management'.[86] He compared this to public intervention elsewhere in Western Europe, where public-enterprise competition with private firms allowed prices and profits to be 'determined by the discipline of the market'.[87] Hence the need for public-enterprise efficiency, the criterion of which was, of course, profitability: the aim to 'maximise efficiency can only be pursued systematically if profits are the yardstick of this efficiency.'[88]

Therefore, *The State as Entrepreneur* had few illusions that its proposals would evade profit as the motive force of production. Although it talked far more of 'efficiency' and 'entrepreneurship', it was aware that encouraging efficiency in a market environment meant ensuring profitability. But, of course, as discussed further below, profit would cease to be an end in itself. The government's 'overall strategic control' would allow it to harness management 'initiative and entrepreneurship...to public rather than private ends'.[89] Layton argued in similar terms: management efficiency would be 'measured by profitability', but its goals would be 'determined by wider social and economic needs'.[90] In other words, profit would motivate but not necessarily determine the ends of economic activity—if not so much 'profit before the people', then 'profit for the people'.

## REVISIONIST PARALLELS

Holland was aware that Britain's adoption of the IRI model would not mark a radical break with international trends in government policy, including the policies of the 1960s Labour government. He explained that IRI-type state intervention had occurred in France, Canada, Australia, Sweden and West Germany, and his concern seemed to be that Britain should keep abreast with progressive developments elsewhere in the capitalist world, rather than relapse into outdated free-market dogma.[91] By 1966 he had realised 'that the need to align the oligopoly power of leading firms to national planning objectives had become central to all French planning', along with planning measures in Belgium and Italy.[92] He certainly saw the Labour government's establishment of the Industrial Reorganisation Corporation (IRC) in 1966 as a positive development. The problem with the IRC was its minimal impact on the British economy. Nevertheless, it was a step in the right direction, and, in some respects, it had been 'converging more closely towards both the principle and practice of the IRI formula at the time when the incoming Conservative Government in 1970 announced its disbandment'.[93]

Indeed, Holland's stance on public intervention very much reflected Labour thinking *before* its purported break with revisionism was formalised with its 1973 party programme. The 1970 Labour manifesto described the IRC as a 'valuable and flexible [instrument] of public enterprise for furthering industrial policies'.[94] Harold Wilson, for whom Holland worked as adviser in the 1960s and under whose government the IRC was formed, told the party's 1971 annual conference that Labour in power would 'establish a State Holding Agency on the lines of the IRC—but written large this time, and with clearer power to ensure that where society invests in private industry, society will stake a claim in the profits'.[95] Far from an irregular intervention from the party's 'hard left', Holland's public enterprise proposals were in step with ideas in the mainstream of the party's leadership.

In fact, it was figures from the old revisionist right who had initiated the state enterprise proposals, welcoming the concept as a 'sweeter-sounding alternative to "nationalisation"'.[96] *Industry and Society*, a Labour Party, Crosland-inspired document published in 1957, had called for selective state shareholding instead of new nationalisations, which the Conservative *Spectator* magazine greeted as having 'very little to do with the traditional objectives of public ownership' and representing 'a substantial retreat from doctrinaire Socialism' (adding that 'Labour's proposals as a whole…will not do much harm. They should on that account be warmly welcomed – though not, presumably, by the lunatic fringe of the Labour Party').[97] As Holland wrote in 2010,

> the case first was endorsed by the Right of the Party, in the case of Bill Rodgers and Roy Jenkins…[who] had endorsed it in his 1972 *What Matters Now*,[98] before they both reneged on it when it was adopted by the NEC.[99]

This confirms Hatfield's account, which argues that many on the party's left were at first 'highly dubious', suspecting that the initiative for a state holding agency was 'a device concocted by the social democrats to deflect the party from its commitments to nationalisation'.[100]

Indeed, this aversion to nationalisation had underpinned the proposed amendments to Labour's Clause 4 under Hugh Gaitskell, which were opposed by the Labour left and eventually abandoned by the party leadership. The draft twelve-point 'declaration of aims' submitted by the Gaitskell leadership to Labour's NEC in March 1960, as a proposed addition to Labour's constitution alongside Clause 4, had declared 'that both public and private enterprise have a place in the economy', and that 'further expansion of common ownership should be decided from time to time in the light of these objectives, and according to circumstances with due regard for the views of the workers and consumers concerned'.[101] As with Holland's approach, the constitutional proposals stood for a limited nationalisation to co-ordinate the widescale private ownership that would remain—'an expansion of common ownership substantial enough to give the community power over the commanding heights of the economy'.[102]

In *The Socialist Challenge*, Holland acknowledged his influence by revisionism. He quoted Crosland's arguments in the 1950s, to challenge

Crosland's later criticisms of AES policy. According to Crosland in *The Future of Socialism* (published in 1956):

> the method should be to take over not whole industries, but individual firms, leaving others still in private hands: or to set up new government-owned plants to compete with existing firms. This is the 'competitive public enterprise' approach. It need not rule out occasionally nationalizing whole industries where the arguments for doing so seem overwhelming; but it should have preference wherever possible.[103]

Holland had valid reason to highlight Crosland's inconsistency, since he had upheld a state-intervention model in principle identical to Holland's. 'With a bit of foresight, Mr Crosland might have claimed credit for the leaven in Labour's new public enterprise proposals', Holland wrote in *The Socialist Challenge*,[104] later suggesting that Crosland could be considered the 'godfather' of his proposals.[105] This is not to deny that Holland's public enterprise proposals went further than Crosland's, but to point to a large element of political continuity. Both figures shared an opposition, differing only by its degree, to the old Labour-left socialism of broad nationalisation. Like Crosland, Holland believed that a market economy made up mainly of private firms could be directed for socialist purposes.

## HOLLAND'S SOCIALISM

In a 2010 article upholding his earlier positions, Holland made no mention of what had been a core claim of the AES at the time of its formulation: that it was a strategy not only for the rejuvenation but also the socialist transformation of the British economy. Attempting to 'demythologise' New Labour depictions of the AES, Holland focused on upholding the technical-economic aspects of the strategy. The AES was not '"Old Labour" looking back' but had sought to countervail trends in globalisation to 'avoid de-industrialisation and the loss of effective taxation through transfer pricing and other techniques adopted by multinational capital'.[106] Holland did not refer to the strategy's socialist ambitions, which of course had far less purchase in 2010 than they had had in 1973. His aim seemed simply to be to debunk the caricature of Labour's 1973–1983 project as one 'for "outdated nationalisation" or civil servants running industry or a variant on Gosplan'.[107] The AES was in fact a strategy 'based on emerging "best practice" in continental Western Europe, and Japan'—that is, a strategy based on better-functioning capitalist economies abroad.[108] As this chapter so far has indicated, Holland was right to dismiss the inaccurate recollections of his 'Third Way' party successors.

However, at the time of its formulation, Holland had not presented the AES merely as a mildly unorthodox strategy for technical reforms in the capitalist economy. Although *The Socialist Challenge* upheld the IRI model, it also made very high claims for the AES, among which was that it would carry out 'revolutionary reforms' leading British society into a new 'mode of production' and new 'social relations' in industry.[109] The 'crucial difference' between a socialist and a capitalist strategy was whether the state 'serves rather than hinders the extent to which working people can exercise control over the conditions and results of their own activity'.[110] But how would the AES go beyond 'capitalist planning'?

For Holland, continental examples of public enterprise pointed in the right direction but did not go far enough. They took place in a 'mainly state capitalist framework' in which they reinforced rather than transformed capitalism.[111] Implemented in this context, governments were reluctant to 'maximise the potential' of state enterprise because it was an 'implicit challenge to competing private enterprise'—large and profitable private companies could only accept so much state intrusion into market territories they saw as their own.[112] This meant that prior cases of state holding company had been for 'salvaging bankrupt enterprise' or reinforcing the 'competitive position of private enterprise which was failing the nation through underinvestment, the location of insufficient jobs in the regions and so on'[113]—in other words, a model of public enterprise whose potential was constrained by its prioritisation of the demands of capitalist production.

Overcoming this predicament was to raise the question of social control, which Holland sought to define in class terms. In *Beyond Capitalist Planning*, he stated that the important question for 'class power' was not only 'who owns but also who controls the means of production, distribution, and exchange'.[114] According to Franco Archibugi, a contributor to the book, socialist planning would distinguish itself from capitalist planning only insofar as it overcame capitalist 'mystification of exchange value' and its 'fetishism of commodities'.[115] In place of these phenomena, 'socialist indicators' would need to be installed, which expressed social welfare and social needs.[116] Holland agreed:

If the dominance of social and public criteria for the use of resources was established within enterprise in such a socialized mode of production and distribution, the finance for key projects and services through the economy could be democratically negotiated through the planning process on social use value rather than the private exchange value of capitalist enterprise.[117]

Therefore, an extended and democratised version of IRI-type intervention could mean overcoming the defining feature of the capitalist economy: production for market exchange. The economy would cease to operate on capitalist criteria and begin to produce for use value rather than exchange value. With the democratic negotiation of finance for economic projects, state involvement would 'represent finance for enterprise rather than capital in the classic sense'.[118] A socialist transformation would 'demand changes in the terms on which investment was undertaken, for whose use, in which markets, with *social* criteria substituting for private criteria, and public benefit for private profit'.[119] This position was based on Holland's view, discussed above, that the influence of the market was secondary to that of the existing state. That is, whether the economy was market-driven or planned, the more important factor in determining the nature of production was the 'nature of state power'.[120]

The idea that state control (via Holland's proposals) was just as important as state ownership (the expropriation of private owners) could be interpreted as a radical reformulation of the conventional nationalisation model, and Holland certainly presented it as such, as an alternative to the bureaucratic 'state capitalism' of existing nationalised industry. However, it also served to justify a moderate position on public ownership relative to that of prior Labour-leftism. In emphasising 'control' over 'ownership', among Holland's intentions was to bolster his view that enterprise could be controlled without its ownership necessarily being taken from the hands of private individuals.

An interesting feature of this perspective was an elevated view of the role of ideology in market functions, especially the ideology of the state: if the state could have this kind of indirect primacy over the market, the ideas influencing the state could determine market outcomes. Thus Holland supported Bettelheim's emphasis on the importance of ideology in ensuring that state power aided a social transformation in favour of workers.[121] This position was repeated in *Beyond Capitalist Planning*, in which Holland argued that the 'dominance of capital's power' depended 'substantially on the continued hold of liberal competitive capitalism in an era of monopoly capitalism',[122] which required a strategy to expose ideological free-market 'myths' and 'legitimize new public intervention for socialized development through democratic planning'.[123]

This perspective was broadly in line with the Eurocommunist current to which Holland and much of the British left were, by the late 1970s, increasingly drawn.[124] A 1980 Labour pamphlet by the Labour NEC's Western Europe sub-committee, contributed to by Holland, pointed to the closer ties now possible between Labour and the reformed parties of 'official' Communism (particularly those in Italy, France and Spain), with their further distancing from the Soviet Union model and their acceptance of the values of political pluralism, civil liberties and parliamentary democracy.[125] In addition, Eurocommunism meant the endorsement of a mixed economy, pointing to its shift from Stalinist political economy. According to the pamphlet, the Italian Communist Party (PCI)

> emphatically rejects the idea of a totally state-controlled and bureaucratically planned economy. Indeed, it accepts the continued survival of a flourishing private sector in the foreseeable future.[126]

The pamphlet cited Giorgio Napolitano, then a leading PCI spokesman (and decades later president of Italy), as upholding 'the role of private initiative, and even large-scale private industry, [and] the function of profit and the market economy'.[127] Similarly to Holland, he envisioned private firms' co-operation with a socialist government as a means to 'democratic control of the uses of the "surplus"'.[128] As Wood wrote, Eurocommunism was marked by a tendency to depart from old Marxist emphases on relations of production and class conflict, and '[establish] not only the autonomy but the *dominance* of the political, and then of ideology.'[129] In Holland's case, this manifested as a fairly subjectivist view of the social significance of the market, expressing, as with the Eurocommunists, a confidence that its purpose and outcomes could be socialised if the right political ideas were mobilised to motivate its state regulation.

In an essay published soon after Labour's 1979 defeat, Holland provided a useful explanation of ideology's ability to re-form capital and the market after its own image. What prevailed in Britain was a contradictory economic ideology presenting an inverted view of economic reality, where the economy was falsely depicted as subordinate to democratic politics and the state, and the Labour government's key failure had been its inability to challenge this prevailing ideology.[130] The socialist alternative meant reversing the 'main axis of power in the heartland of the system', whereby Labour would integrate its ideology into the centre of the political process.[131] In this way, the newly hegemonic socialist ideology would be at the core of the existing system. Capital and the state would become subordinate to the new prevailing ideology, which would lead to the '[effective *transformation* of] capital itself': with socialist ideology 'integrated with the political process', it would, with a socialist Labour Party in power, 'reflect the interests of labour in transforming the ownership and control of capital in society'.[132] Capital would serve labour not so much by the latter's direct control of the former, but by the Labour Party engendering an ideological framework by which the economy, though pervaded by private firms, would come under greater public direction. Hence Holland's rejection of the view, prevalent among Marxists, that capital remained capitalist whether it was owned by private individuals or controlled by the existing state—the lines along which several 'far-left' critics rejected the AES as demanding a transfer of capital's ownership rather than an end to capitalism itself.[133]

In a sense, however, Marx's criticisms of state-centred socialist approaches had more direct relevance to Holland's Labour-left predecessors than to Holland himself, although this in itself shed further light on his theory. For example, insofar as a bulk of Marx's attacks on state-led socialist initiatives were aimed at a Lassallean policy for state-aided workers' co-operatives 'on such a scale *that the socialist organization of the total labour will arise from them*',[134] they did not apply easily to Holland's views. As the Labour historian G. D. H. Cole pointed out, Lassalle had called on the existing state to give workers 'the capital and credit that would allow them to dispense with capitalist employers and to reserve for themselves the whole product of their collective production'.[135] Holland, in contrast, neither called for an economy of workers' co-operatives nor dispensing with capitalist employers. He did not want to eliminate capitalists while maintaining capital—he wanted to maintain both, and to make 'markets work in the public interest and [gain] accountability for public money in the private sector'.[136] In comparison with Lassallean socialism—which Engels called 'very moderate'[137]—Holland's socialism was, in this sense at least, far less drastic in its anti-capitalism. What set Holland's perspective apart was its relative lack of confidence in a modern British economy without a very large role for private enterprise.

## 'COMPULSORY' PLANNING?

In practical terms, finally, this standpoint informed what is often regarded as a key feature of the AES's radicalism: the 'compulsory' nature of its proposed planning agreements, i.e. an obligation on firms to comply with a left-wing Labour government. With this perception of radicalism, it is seen as a significant retreat or betrayal that the 1970s Labour government did not implement planning agreements and the NEB as they were initially conceived.[138] However, while Harold Wilson and James Callaghan were indeed strongly averse to a compulsory agreements system, Holland had himself significantly qualified the compulsory nature of his planning proposals. In fact, *The Socialist Challenge* had not really emphasised state compulsion at all, but had called essentially for an indicative planning system—such as that of the Labour Government's National Plan in the 1960s—that would now be *reinforced* by greater imperative powers against firms 'failing the nation' (by not expanding investment, creating jobs, etc.).[139] That is, it called for state compulsion as a last resort.

Indeed, looking back, Holland regrets that the AES was portrayed as a strategy for wide-ranging state control via compulsory agreements, as 'such headlines as "the top twenty-five" companies caricatured [selective state shareholding] as dogmatic regress to old-style nationalisation'.[140] Contrary to the media misrepresentation, he had seen a case for state compulsion 'only in that if leading firms wanted public grants or contracts they would be obliged to negotiate a planning agreement on how they used them'.[141] According to Holland, the press misrepresentation of Labour's proposals was understandable given Tony Benn's tendency to reference state compulsion. He had remonstrated with Benn that 'his use of the term "compulsory planning agreements" made the policy sound like *Gosplan*', which was entirely mistaken, 'since what we were offering was not a totally planned economy but a means of harnessing oligopoly power on the lines of European planning models'.[142]

Holland's recollections are broadly accurate: his 'planning agreements' had not meant taking direct charge of capital but setting out a strategic economic framework to which companies would be encouraged to adhere. The government would indicate to firms what its overall objectives were, and firms would advise the government as to their intended actions in the light of these objectives.[143] Thereafter, the planning agreements system would 'operate as a systemized bargaining process between the government and the giant private and public corporations'.[144] This arrangement remained tripartite—action negotiated between state, industry and the unions—albeit a tripartism promising greater leverage to those previously at the junior end of the negotiating table. But Holland was clear that planning agreements did not mean company management being 'messed around on a continuous basis'.[145] In fact, 'greater public power' needed to be combined with a 'wide degree of continued management freedom'.[146] As in the case of public enterprise, the purpose of state intervention was not to dictate the actions of companies, but to use the state's increased leverage within the market to influence company decisions through negotiation.

## Holland's Radical Allies

The previous chapter identified a potentially contradictory duality of aims in the approaches of the strategy's radical proponents: the view that the AES was a strategy for economic growth as well as for intensifying class conflict, one for alleviating the economic crisis and one for encouraging workers' resistance to capitalism. It was suggested that this represented an incompatibility between economic policies and political aims, because a coherent socialist strategy could not aim to at once reinvigorate and destabilise the capitalist system.

Holland's approach was less affected by this tension because the aim to 'intensify class conflict' was not a prominent feature of his theory. Far from a strategy to heighten any social conflict, Holland was clear that the AES intended to provide a sustainable solution to what he saw as a crisis in public policy—the inability of governments to implement policies in the 'public interest'. Although the economic crisis was an opportunity for a radical economic restructuring in favour of 'modes of socialised development', class tensions were undesirable for Holland, since social conflict obstructed left-wing policy-making (see Chapter 6 below).[147]

However, other proponents of the AES were less clear on this question. They voiced the idea that the AES was a means to intensify anti-capitalist resistance, but to what extent were their economic proposals compatible with this idea? The rest of this chapter will consider this question in relation to some of the figures identified in the previous chapter.

### *Geoffrey Hodgson*

Hodgson was a close representative of this ideological tension. As discussed in the previous chapter, he posed the AES as a possible transitional strategy akin to that theorised by Trotsky in the 1930s, and as a prelude to far more radical socialist changes, changes to be spurred by the increased anti-capitalist radicalisation of Labour's working-class supporters, engendering something of a revolutionary crisis in the British economy.

In its policy proposals, however, Hodgson's approach did not differ fundamentally from Holland's. Indeed, Hodgson was arguably more forthright in his support for markets, linking extensive state planning directly to authoritarian government or economic inefficiency. He argued that there was no 'genuinely democratic socialist society in which more than 50 per cent nationalisation actually works'.[148] Central planning could be effective in sectors producing relatively homogeneous goods and where quality was less relevant or more easily controlled (e.g. coal). But in sectors where quality was paramount (e.g. agriculture), where innovation had to be stimulated continuously (electronics), and where consumer demand was difficult to determine with accuracy ('most consumer goods'), central planning was inferior to the market, and, furthermore, it would 'remain *inferior whatever the feasible level of democracy in a future socialist society*'.[149]

Although Hodgson cited Soviet failures, the object of his criticism was not solely planning of the bureaucratic and over-centralised type but planning itself, specifically the socialist idea that planning could replace the market as the source of economic efficiency and innovation: 'In some quarters it is difficult to say this, but it must be said: in certain sectors of the economy there is no substitute for *competition* and a *market*.'[150] By 'certain sectors', Hodgson meant 60% of GDP, 40% of which would be under public ownership. The existing split of '20–80, public-private', endorsed by sections of the Labour right, was inadequate.[151] His preferred 40–60 split, which he argued Labour's state ownership in the top 25 firms would produce, would represent a more appropriate public-private mix.[152] Hodson recognised the incompatibility of this position with a Clause 4 socialism for broad nationalisation. Twelve years prior to Tony Blair's revision of Clause 4 in 1995, he called for its rewriting to include a declaration of support for markets and a mixed economy.[153] He proposed 'economic pluralism', as he also did in his 1984 work *The Democratic Economy*.[154] And, like Holland, he believed that a market could function along 'non-capitalist' lines, via a 'market collectivism' made up partly of co-operatives inspired by the Yugoslav workers' self-management system of the 1950s and 1960s[155]— support for which, as discussed in Chapter 6 below, was a feature of the AES's disquiet with non-market socialist models.

It also cannot be said that Hodgson 'jettisoned' Keynesianism. He presented capitalism's departure from Keynesianism as a product of the strength of Britain's deeply ingrained liberal-economic traditions, and certainly as a regression. He agreed with Holland that Keynesian demand management needed to be bolstered rather than abandoned. This called not for 'policies "minus Keynes" but "Keynes plus" policies'.[156] Contrary to monetarist claims, Keynesianism had not proved itself useless. Keynesian demand management was '*necessary* but not *sufficient* for economic buoyancy in advanced capitalism'.[157]

Of course, Hodgson's analysis contained more than calls for Keynesianism supplemented with an extended public sector. Hodgson repeated Holland's proposals for political and economic democratisation and a transformation of economic 'social relations'. What these meant in practice will be further discussed in Chapter 6. However, Hodgson's analysis contained the inconsistency pointed to in the previous chapter, between theoretical content and stated political aims. Although Hodgson saw a planned economy as objectively inferior to a 'mixed' economy, he also concluded both *The Democratic Economy* and *Labour at the Crossroads* with the argument that the AES would set in motion a 'socialist transformation'. In the latter book, he argued that 'the development of a public sector working *alongside* the private sector will show in practice the advantages of public ownership' and thus 'help to build up the necessary mass popular movement for socialist change'.[158] Hence the interesting problem in Hodgson's analysis: if a planned economy was ruled out from the outset in favour a mixed economy, where should the mass left-wing radicalisation produced by the AES lead? According at least to two of its major theorists, it should not lead to planning replacing an economy of capital and market competition.

### Bob Rowthorn and the Communist Party

Rowthorn, looking back at his support for the AES, explained this problem in direct and lucid terms:

> The AES never resolved a contradiction at its heart: was it designed to make the capitalist economy work better, or was it designed to destabilise it? In the latter, you propose changes that people think are good, they don't work, and that provokes opposition from the capitalists. The revolutionary view would be that you then say: 'We've got to go further because they're blocking these changes'. I think that would be the view of someone like Bert Ramelson; it

probably would not have been the view of someone like Sam Aaronovitch, for example. I think Aaronovitch—and most of the Economic Committee of the Communist Party—were basically reformists. We wanted to make the system work better. I know I wrote things which suggested the opposite. But I think basically we wanted the system to work better to generate higher incomes and more jobs.[159]

In the early 1980s, Rowthorn had upheld the AES as a strategy to challenge 'the undisputed authority of capital' and thereby 'destabilise the political situation and lead to demands for further change'.[160] The AES was 'the first stage in a revolutionary *process* characterised by intense conflict and struggle'.[161] Yet, as he has since acknowledged, there were contradictions between such statements and the policy content of his approach, which did not diverge fundamentally from the 'Keynes plus' orientation of Holland and Hodgson.[162] As with Holland, Keynesian reflation to 'raise output and create more employment' was central to Rowthorn's position, and was mentioned first in his list of AES proposals.[163] His analysis recognised that the 'AES accepts the "mixed" economy', and pointed out that 'the economy would remain primarily capitalist in nature, for most production would still be in the hands of private firms whose aim is to make profits'.[164] Although the AES would effect a 'radical shift in favour of the working class and its allies', this would occur, as in Holland's 'new mix in the "mixed" economy', by altering 'the mix radically in favour of the working class'.[165]

The Communist Party of Great Britain (CPGB) showed a similar decline of left-wing confidence in public ownership in this period. The 1977 edition of its party programme, *The British Road to Socialism* (*BRS*), combined a call for a 'strategy for socialist revolution' with a relatively moderate approach to nationalisation.[166] The 1951 edition of the *BRS* had demanded the nationalisation of '[all] large-scale industry and transport, the banks, monopoly-owned wholesale and retail trading concerns, as well as large landed property'.[167] The 1977 edition, by contrast, did call for 'a phased nationalisation' that would eventually encompass 'all monopolies and other large concerns in productive industry, finance and distribution'.[168] However, reflecting a rather different mood from that which had existed in the early 1950s, its immediate nationalisation demands were limited to state takeovers of 'the key firms among the top firms which dominate the economy'.[169]

Rowthorn suggested correctly that this cautious approach to nationalisation was more prominent among CPGB 'modernisers' like Sam

Aaronovitch and others in the party's Economic Committee. In his book *The Road from Thatcherism*, Aaronovitch presented AES policies as very much within the repertoire of social democracy, despite adhering to the standard left-wing narrative that the AES would 'prepare the ground for more far-reaching changes'.[170] As with Rowthorn, demand management was key among his recommendations: the need to raise demand was 'a characteristic emphasis of all supporters of the AES from whatever angle they approach it'.[171] Large private firms would play an important role in this economic expansion, and the profit motive would remain in an AES economy.[172] Like Holland, Aaronovitch looked to models of capitalist development abroad for policy inspiration. Countries like Sweden showed that 'an efficient capitalist economy can have virtual full employment, a low rate of inflation, and yet also have levels of public spending far greater than the UK even before Thatcher'.[173]

Bert Ramelson, characterised by Rowthorn as representing a more revolutionary current in CPGB politics, was perhaps somewhat outside the inner core of British Eurocommunism, since his politics continued to take inspiration from the Soviet model at a time when influential sections of his party had grown increasingly distant from it.[174] Yet, as the party's industrial organiser, Ramelson was certainly not outside the party's core. Indeed, in the 1970s he was Chair of the CPGB's Economic Committee, which included not only economists from the party's right but also influential figures from within the structures of British trade-unionism.[175]

Thus, Ramelson's support for the AES subscribed to a framework not fundamentally different from that of the party's modernisers, calling for 'viable' economic reforms not only to raise workers' living standards but also to rejuvenate the British economy. In line with his party's 1977 programme, he expressed the hope that Britain would one day be a 'socialist planned society'.[176] But this did not mean that nothing could be done in the present 'to alleviate the lot of our people, to reduce unemployment, stabilise prices and restore and expand the social services'.[177] This demanded a strategy to expand industrial investment, control foreign trade and 'compel those large firms and multinationals which remained in private hands to enter into binding planning agreements on aspects such as investment, siting of industries, forward manpower planning, export projects, etc.'[178] Unlike Holland and Hodgson, an open celebration of markets was absent from Ramelson's approach. Yet the policies he proposed did not go dramatically beyond the immediate horizons of the AES. At least in the short and medium term, the aim was to control the market for socially desirable ends.

## Conclusion

This chapter aimed to qualify common depictions of the AES—concerning its break with Keynesianism and its positions on markets, private capital and the state. Focusing on the strategy's main economic theorist, it argued that the political economy of the AES did not mark a fundamental break with the moderate, Keynesian-revisionist ideas that had dominated postwar Labour politics. Keynesian demand management remained central to the AES, as did private capital and the market. Adjectives like 'fundamental' or 'extremely radical' to describe the AES's break from 'capitalist principles' and 'Keynesian social democracy' are, therefore, unjustifiably strong and give a distorted portrayal of what figures like Holland, Hodgson and prominent CPGB figures like Rowthorn and Aaronovitch were seeking to accomplish.

As this chapter also discussed, Holland's approach to socialism differed significantly from that of his Labour-left predecessors, representing, in a sense, a moderation in Labour-left thinking since the 1950s. Holland lacked the traditional Labour-left confidence in planning replacing the market as the generator of economic efficiency, innovation and growth. Due to what he saw as the loss of state control over the macroeconomy since the 1950s, he proposed mechanisms by which the market and private capital could be better harnessed by government. Reflecting a growing left-wing disillusion both with 'old-style' British nationalisation and the command economies of the Soviet Bloc, Holland saw a market economy constituted mainly by private owners as the most viable model for a modern British economy.

Finally, the chapter addressed a tension highlighted in the previous chapter—whether the AES would aim to revitalise or destabilise British capitalism. As Rowthorn pointed out in 2015, this contradiction, at the heart of several prominent AES analyses, was not satisfactorily resolved. For Hodgson, the AES was a 'Keynes plus' strategy, and planning more than half of the economy's output was neither viable nor desirable. For CPGB figures like Rowthorn and Aaronovitch, the AES would resolve the economic crisis via a mixed economy. Somewhat to their left, Bert Ramelson, who expressed little enthusiasm for markets, nevertheless did not look beyond a strategy which prioritised industrial investment and economic growth. As such, it was not clear how a strategy for the improved performance of the existing (albeit reformed) economic system could at the same time be a strategy to encourage the overthrow of that system. Although AES proponents sought to endow their strategy with revolutionary implications, the AES was characterised by a profound unease and pessimism about fundamental alternatives to the existing economic order. As discussed in the following chapter, this pessimism also featured the AES's retreat into the politics of economic protectionism.

## NOTES

1. Cited in Stewart, *Keynes and After*, p. 65.
2. Cited in Andrews, *Keynes and the British Humanist Tradition*, p. 22.
3. Beer, *Modern British Politics*, p. 278.
4. Ibid., p. 277.
5. Jones and Keating, *Labour and the British State*, p. 66.
6. Keynes, *The General Theory*, p. 322.
7. Mattick, 'Marx and Keynes'.
8. Keynes, *The General Theory*, p. xviii.
9. Ibid., p. 355.
10. Ibid.
11. Cited in Foote, *The Labour Party's Political Thought*, p. 140.
12. Keynes, *The General Theory*, p. 238.
13. Ibid., pp. 378–9.
14. Shaw, *The Labour Party Since 1945*, p. 51.
15. Fielding and McHugh, 'The Progressive Dilemma,' p. 143.
16. Shaw, *The Labour Party Since 1945*, p. 62.
17. For a review of Labour-left criticisms of Keynesianism in the post-war period, see Thompson, *Political Economy and the Labour Party*, pp. 158–64. This is not to suggest, of course, that Labour had not contained left-wing alternatives to state socialism—guild socialism and even syndicalism played an important part in interwar Labour debate, for example. See Foote, *The Labour Party's Political Thought*, for a discussion of these alternative currents in Labour ideology.
18. Cited in Shaw, *The Labour Party Since 1945*, p. 53.
19. Ibid., p. 54.
20. Shaw, *The Labour Party Since 1945*, p. 55.
21. Seyd, *The Rise and Fall of the Labour Left*, p. 13.
22. Foote, *The Labour Party's Political Thought*, p. 232.
23. Crosland, *Socialism Now and Other Essays*, p. 53.
24. Ibid., p. 58.
25. Cited in Warde, *Consensus and Beyond*, p. 128.
26. Cited in Foote, *The Labour Party's Political Thought*, p. 142.
27. Holland, *The Socialist Challenge*, p. 22.
28. Ibid.
29. Ibid., p. 187.
30. Ibid., pp. 151, 177.
31. Holland, *The Market Economy*, p. 24.
32. Holland, *Out of Crisis*, p. 26.

33. Ibid., p. 27.
34. Holland, *The Socialist Challenge*, p. 238.
35. Ibid., pp. 14–5.
36. Ibid., p. 51.
37. Archibugi et al., 'The International Crisis', p. 169.
38. Ibid.
39. Holland, *The Market Economy*, p. 24.
40. Holland, *The Socialist Challenge*, pp. 50–1.
41. House of Commons Debate, *Hansard*, 22 May 1979, vol. 967, cc. 874–1012.
42. Holland, *Out of Crisis*, p. 41.
43. Holland, 'State Entrepreneurship', p. 39.
44. Holland, 'Introduction', pp. 1–2.
45. Cronin, *New Labour's Pasts*, p. 55.
46. Holland, 'State Entrepreneurship', p. 25. See also Holland, *The Regional Problem*.
47. Holland, *The Socialist Challenge*, p. 200.
48. Ibid., p. 164.
49. Ibid., p. 165.
50. Lenin, 'The New Economic Policy'.
51. Holland, *The Socialist Challenge*, p. 143.
52. Ibid.
53. Ibid., pp. 166–7.
54. Lenin, 'The New Economic Policy'.
55. Holland, *The Socialist Challenge*, p. 149.
56. See Holland, *The Global Economy*, pp. 379–91, where he seeks to bridge the economic theories of Marx and Keynes.
57. Tomlinson, 'Labour and the Economy', pp. 52–3.
58. Cited in Thompson, 'Supply Side Socialism', p. 48.
59. Cited in Ellison, *Egalitarian Thought*, p. 31.
60. Cole and Mellor, *Workers' Control*, p. 5.
61. House of Commons Debate, *Hansard*, 23 June 1944, vol. 401, cc. 491–582.
62. Cited in Sassoon, *One Hundred Years of Socialism*, p. 514.
63. Industry Act 1975, c. 68, p. 2. Available at http://www.legislation.gov.uk/ukpga/1975/68/pdfs/ukpga_19750068_en.pdf (accessed January 2018).
64. Labour Party, *The Regeneration of British Industry*, p. 1.
65. Ibid.
66. Holland, 'State Entrepreneurship', p. 19.
67. Holland, 'Introduction', p. 3.
68. For Holland's analysis of the establishment and development of the IRI, see Holland, 'The National Context'.
69. Johnson, 'Relations with Government', p. 202.
70. Holland, 'Introduction', p. 1.

71. Holland, 'State Entrepreneurship', p. 43.
72. Ibid., p. 20.
73. Ibid.
74. Holland, 'The National Context', p. 91.
75. Holland, 'State Entrepreneurship', p. 26.
76. Holland, 'Demythologising "Old Labour"', p. 23.
77. Holland, 'State Entrepreneurship', p. 26.
78. Marx, *Grundrisse*, p. 414. His italics.
79. Holland, 'State Entrepreneurship', pp. 35–6.
80. Ibid., p. 38.
81. Holland, 'Introduction', p. 6.
82. Ibid., p. 8.
83. Holland, 'State Entrepreneurship', p. 25.
84. Ibid., p. 44.
85. Ibid.
86. Layton, 'State Entrepreneurship', p. 46.
87. Ibid., p. 47.
88. Ibid., p. 50.
89. Holland, 'State Entrepreneurship', p. 44.
90. Layton, 'State Entrepreneurship', p. 53.
91. Holland, 'Adoption and Adaptation', pp. 242–65.
92. Holland, 'Alternative European and Economic Strategies', pp. 105–6.
93. Holland, 'Adoption and Adaptation', p. 246.
94. Labour Party, *Now Britain's Strong*.
95. Cited in Hatfield, *The House the Left Built*, p. 80.
96. Forester, 'Neutralising the Industrial Strategy', p. 77.
97. *The Spectator*, 'Industry and Society', 18 July 1957, p. 4.
98. Jenkins's book included a version of a speech he gave that was drafted by Holland. See Forester, 'Neutralising the Industrial Strategy', p. 77.
99. Holland, 'Demythologising "Old Labour"', p. 26.
100. Hatfield, *The House the Left Built*, p. 81.
101. Cited in Miliband, 'Postscript', p. 96.
102. Ibid.
103. Cited in Holland, *The Socialist Challenge*, p. 24.
104. Ibid.
105. Wickham-Jones, 'The New Left', p. 38.
106. Holland, 'Demythologising "Old Labour"', p. 27.
107. Ibid., p. 26.
108. Ibid., p. 18.
109. Holland, *The Socialist Challenge*, pp. 158–62.
110. Ibid., p. 153.
111. Ibid., pp. 181–2.
112. Ibid., p. 181.

113. Ibid.
114. Holland, 'Introduction', p. 3.
115. Archibugi, 'Capitalist Planning', p. 57.
116. Ibid.
117. Holland, 'Planning Disagreements', p. 157.
118. Ibid.
119. Holland, *Uncommon Market*, p. 124. His italics.
120. Holland, *The Socialist Challenge*, pp. 166–7.
121. Ibid., p. 167.
122. Holland, 'Planning Disagreements', pp. 157.
123. Ibid., p. 158.
124. See Holland, 'The New Communist Economics'; and Labour Party, *The Dilemma of Eurocommunism.*
125. Labour Party, *The Dilemma of Eurocommunism.* As the pamphlet pointed out, Labour invited Italian, French and Spanish Communist delegates to its 1977 annual conference, and in 1978 the NEC's international sub-committee approved a recommendation for 'informal discussions' with the Italian Communist Party (PCI), p. 33.
126. Labour Party, *The Dilemma of Eurocommunism*, p. 21.
127. Ibid., p. 21.
128. Ibid.
129. Wood, *The Retreat from Class*, p. 22. Her italics.
130. Holland, 'Capital, Labour and the State', pp. 217, 232.
131. Ibid., p. 232.
132. Ibid, p. 233. My italics.
133. See, for example: Grafton, 'The Road from Thatcherism'; and Sparks, 'The Reformist Challenge'.
134. The 'Gotha Programme' cited in Marx, *Critique of the Gotha Programme*, p. 24. Italics in original.
135. Cole, *Socialist Thought*, p. 79.
136. Holland, 'Demythologising "Old Labour"', p. 26.
137. Engels, 'Socialism in Germany'.
138. See, for example, Wickham-Jones, *Economic Strategy and the Labour Party*, p. 138; and, more recently, Medhurst, *That Option No Longer Exists*, p. 77.
139. Holland, *The Socialist Challenge*, pp. 230–1.
140. Holland, 'Alternative European and Economic Strategies', p. 110.
141. Ibid.
142. Ibid.
143. Holland, *The Socialist Challenge*, p. 231.
144. Ibid.
145. Ibid., p. 230.
146. Ibid.
147. Holland, *Out of Crisis*, p. 42.

148. Hodgson, *Labour at the Crossroads*, p. 205.
149. Ibid., p. 206. His italics.
150. Ibid. His italics.
151. Ibid, p. 207.
152. Ibid., p. 203.
153. Author's interview with Geoffrey Hodgson, 1 June 2015. See also *Guardian*, 'Labour Breaks Taboo on Ownership', 28 November 1983; and Hodgson, 'When I Tried to Rewrite Labour's Clause Four'.
154. Hodgson, *The Democratic Economy*, p. 109.
155. Ibid., pp. 176–7.
156. Hodgson, *Labour at the Crossroads*, p. 168.
157. Ibid. His italics.
158. Ibid., p. 226. His italics.
159. Author's interview with Bob Rowthorn, 10 June 2015.
160. Rowthorn, *Capitalism, Conflict and Inflation*, p. 145.
161. Rowthorn, 'The Alternative Economic Strategy'. His italics.
162. 'The AES probably wasn't [a radical break from Keynesianism]. It accepted a mixed economy and then said, "We want to go into a less mixed economy". But I don't think we had a clear view of the longer-term future.' (Author's interview with Bob Rowthorn, 10 June 2015.)
163. Rowthorn, 'The Politics of the Alternative Strategy', p. 4.
164. Ibid.
165. Ibid.
166. CPGB, *The British Road to Socialism*, 1977.
167. CPGB, *The British Road to Socialism*, 1951.
168. CPGB, *The British Road to Socialism*, 1977.
169. Ibid.
170. Aaronovitch, *The Road from Thatcherism*, p. 124.
171. Ibid., p. 31.
172. Ibid., pp. 35, 42.
173. Ibid., p. 41.
174. Whereas Aaronovitch looked to the Scandinavian model, Ramelson contrasted capitalism to the 'socialist world' of the Soviet bloc, where, he argued, the problems of inflation and mass unemployment had been largely solved (Ramelson, *Bury the Social Contract*, p. 19).
175. Andrews, 2004, *Endgames and New Times*, p. 127.
176. Ramelson, *Bury the Social Contract*, p. 21.
177. Ibid.
178. Ibid., p. 32.

# CHAPTER 5

# A Britain Oppressed: The AES and the Nation

## INTRODUCTION

As discussed in Chapter 3, Alternative Economic Strategy (AES) theorists sought to distinguish themselves from both the reformist and 'insurrectionist' roads to socialism, offering a position they saw as reconciling a revolutionary aim with a programme of 'viable' reforms. Similar attempts at reconciliation also pervaded AES approaches to Britain's economic decline. AES proponents prioritised Britain's global economic interests, but they also sought to uphold a socialist internationalism by justifying their protectionist policies through a dialogue with Marxist theory.

However, a nation-oriented outlook provided the framework within which the AES situated itself. In contrast to the present period, in which support for EU integration is posed as a key marker of progressive politics by many on the British left, the AES was hostile to Britain's loss of national sovereignty and depicted Britain as a country oppressed, subjugated by foreign interests and under the control of a self-serving national elite selling out the nation to powers abroad. Such lines of logic featured prominently in AES positions on international trade and the European Economic Community (EEC). Underlying the socialism of the AES was a national focus that saw the re-prioritisation of Britain's economic interests as an urgent necessity and called for Britain's democratisation to reduce the influence of a powerful national minority it saw as harming the country's standing in the global economy.

© The Author(s) 2020
B. Tufekci, *The Socialist Ideas of the British Left's Alternative Economic Strategy*,
https://doi.org/10.1007/978-3-030-34998-1_5

101

Hassan and Shaw argue that 'the long internationalist tradition' in Labour's politics was 'instinctively suspicious of the language of patriotism' and the 'principle that the citizen owed a supreme allegiance to the nation state'.[1] While the discussion here will qualify any such characterisation of the AES, its nation-oriented approach was indeed distinct from the nationalist politics of the right. The former differed from the latter by its language, its political justifications and its emphasis on the working class. By depicting Britain as an oppressed nation, some AES proponents sought to include it among other nations they saw as engaged in left-led independence struggles against foreign domination, such as those in the 'third world'. Although the theme of national subjugation also played a prominent role in the nationalisms of the British right, the latter's overt jingoism or fervent militarism were mostly absent from AES rhetoric. Moreover, unlike the right, AES proponents rejected charges of nationalism, expressed support for a socialist internationalism and saw AES-type strategies abroad as a means to international solidarity and a socialist foreign policy. Overall, AES supporters appeared sincere in their belief that British economic protection could have a socialist content, and they often advanced ideas at odds with their portrayal as left-wing 'Little Englanders' demanding a version of autarky and 'siege economy'. However, their ideas were bound by an economic strategy which ranked Britain's industrial revival foremost on its list of priorities, and which frequently looked abroad for its enemies. On these terms, AES analyses did not break with the nation-oriented framework that had characterised Labour's politics since its formation, and British Communism since at least the early 1950s.

This chapter examines AES analyses of the relationship between Britain and the global economy, discussing the strategy's perspectives on import controls and Britain's membership of the EEC, and considering the political implications of its positions. It first discusses the concept of a British decline, placing AES concerns with this decline in their historical context. It then outlines AES responses to this decline, and critically examines the ways in which the AES rationalised its policies for national economic regeneration.

## Protecting the British Economy

The AES's protectionism had two main theoretical premises: (i) reviving Britain's economy in general, and its industrial base in particular, was the most urgent task, and for which British socialists had to offer immediately viable proposals; and (ii) a major obstacle to this revival was the British economy's special vulnerability within the global economy, along with the barriers to domestic investment that the latter represented.

These two premises were accepted by all the prominent advocates of the AES. As mentioned in the previous chapters, the AES placed Britain's industrial decline at the top of its list of concerns, viewing it as a root cause of low wages, inflation, unemployment and Britain's inability to maintain or improve social services like education and healthcare. As Tony Benn, Frances Morrell and Francis Cripps stated in a 1975 pamphlet, the 'heart of the problem' was that

> British manufacturing industry, the primary source of our national income is trapped in a spiral of decline, and after thirty years of low investment is contracting under its own momentum. Britain's economic and industrial crisis springs directly from this devastating trend to contraction whose symptoms are inflation and unemployment.[2]

They added that Britain's economic decline 'must be completely distinguished from the present world recession although it is likely to be accelerated by it'.[3] This highlighted another core emphasis of the AES: Britain's *relative* decline. The AES's high preoccupation with Britain's special disadvantages in the global economy helped provide a link between its first and second premises pointed to above—its concern for Britain's economic recovery and its belief that outside forces prevented this recovery. The idea that Britain's economy fared badly against its competitors abroad helped direct political focus on to the latter.

## Britain's Long Decline

Fears about Britain's decline cut across the left-right divide in the 1970s and 1980s, and they had a long lineage in British politics.[4] Once the industrial, imperial and military powerhouse of the world, Britain's international dominance had peaked in the middle decades of the nineteenth century. Britain was the engine of the 'great boom' between the 1850s and early 1870s, the first global capitalist boom, which saw a great increase in world industrial productivity and output.[5] Spreading the industrial revolution from its British birthplace, the boom created the economic basis for Britain's relative decline. Within two decades the world had become 'capitalist and a significant minority of "developed" countries became industrial economies'.[6] Capital accumulation on a world scale, and the rapid industrialisation of

Britain's rivals (prominently Germany, Belgium and America), raised new challenges to Britain's global position.

Ironically perhaps, it was British capitalism's commitment to free trade in the mid-1800s which sowed the seeds of its relative decline. Free trade facilitated Britain's export-led economic expansion during the long boom, but it also profited its rivals. As Hobsbawm explains, an unimpeded supply of agricultural products and raw materials advantaged capital abroad, as did its ability to draw upon British industrial equipment and expertise.[7] In steam power, a common measure of industrial strength in the nineteenth century, Britain was matched by Germany by 1870 and outpaced by America.[8] A new global balance of economic power was emerging by the 1880s, and the world leadership of Britain had become increasingly precarious.[9]

By the early twentieth century, British politics expressed an increased concern with the pitfalls of free trade for the British economy. What Gamble calls 'Social Imperialism', a protectionist movement at the turn of the century, 'was the first major political response to the problem of British decline, the first major attempt to change the course of British policy' away from free trade.[10] Right-wing figures like Joseph Chamberlain stressed Britain's need to assert its imperial self-sufficiency, demanding measures to retreat from laissez-faire and secure what was left of the British empire's dominance through policies for economic protection. Germany would 'never rest until she dominates the world...Tariff Reform is our defence', as Chamberlain put it, while supplementing his chauvinist campaign against capitalists abroad with a direct appeal for patriotic support from workers at home:

> Workers cannot live off investments in a foreign country. If that labour is taken from you, you have no recourse except perhaps to learn French or German...[You] cannot go on forever watching with indifference the disappearance of your principal industries.[11]

Parallel ideas also emerged from the British left in the first half of the twentieth century. In 1903, Labour's Philip Snowden had already lamented the long decline of British industry: 'For forty years every one of our staple industries, with the exception of the coal and iron industries, have been declining in relative volume'.[12] During the interwar period, with economic crisis and rising unemployment, arguments for greater national self-sufficiency gained increased purchase within sections of the Labour leadership. In his famous memorandum to the Labour Prime Minister in

January 1930, Oswald Mosley, then a Labour Minister, called for industrial planning and a public works programme of a Keynesian type to solve unemployment, along with import quotas, an end to export-led growth and the development of a fortified home market within the British empire.

The protectionist tendency did not reverse the free-trade orientation of British capitalism; although a degree of protection was afforded to Britain's home and imperial markets during the 1930s crisis and the collapse of the gold standard, 'the bases of liberal orthodoxy were not touched'.[13] After the Second World War, support for protectionism was marginal within the Conservative Party. Some Conservatives opposed British entry into the EEC but not typically with strong protectionist arguments: Enoch Powell, for example, sharply opposed the Common Market but was also among the most vocal proponents of free-market economy.[14] Right-wing enthusiasm for protectionism was confined mainly to the far-right, to individuals like John Tyndall and his colleagues in the National Front (and later the British National Party), for whom protectionism was an essential nationalist policy in the face of national decline, mass immigration and rampant cosmopolitanism.[15]

With that in mind, Gamble argues that the 'cause of protection and the national economy' had 'migrated to the Left'.[16] However, though it was increasingly identified with protectionist ideas in the decades following the Second World War, protectionism was not new on the British left. The Labour left-winger John Strachey had played a major role in drafting Mosley's memorandum,[17] and the manifesto Mosley published in December 1930, restating his ideas, was backed by both Strachey and Aneurin Bevan.[18] The key difference in the 1920s and 1930s was that these ideas were able to be rejected by a Labour leadership committed to liberal-economic orthodoxy. Labour's 1931 general election manifesto repeated the 'tariffs no cure' stance it had put forward in 1923:

> The Labour Party has no confidence in any attempt to bolster up a bankrupt Capitalism by a system of tariffs. Tariffs would artificially increase the cost of living. They would enrich private interests at the expense of the Nation. They would prejudice the prospect of international co-operation. In the circumstances produced by our departure from the gold standard, they have no relevance to economic need. In the face of the millions unemployed in high-tariff America and Germany, they are clearly no cure for unemployment. They would permanently injure our shipping and export trades and conceal our need for greater efficiency in industrial organisation.[19]

With the AES, as shown below, this stance was rejected and reversed. Where the 1931 manifesto believed protectionism would 'conceal' Britain's need for 'greater efficiency in industrial organisation', the AES saw the greater insulation of Britain's economy as a precondition for its industrial revival. What was different in the 1970s, as discussed in Chapter 2, was that the Labour left was in a more favourable position to impress its views upon Labour policy. However, these views carried the torch of previous Labour-left thinking. Like Strachey and Bevan, the AES left saw Britain's economic decline as a special area of concern for British socialists, and it offered nation-centred solutions to the problem.

## Britain's Relative Decline and the AES

Britain's relative economic decline was a dominant concern in all prominent AES analyses. From the Labour left, Peter Hain referred to 'a British crisis' and a Britain that was 'losing the advantages that had accrued to her as the first major industrialised nation',[20] while the Labour Co-ordinating Committee (LCC) argued that British manufacturing was alone in the extent of its 'limited increase in productivity'.[21] For the CPGB economist Bob Rowthorn, Britain had 'lost its former pre-eminence as a leading industrial nation' and was now 'the weakest of all the major capitalist powers',[22] while for Geoffrey Hodgson, there was a 'specific national dimension' to Britain's economic crisis: the global crisis affected all countries, but Britain was 'likely to suffer more than the United States and most of Western Europe'.[23] Michael Barratt Brown referred to Britain's 'special problems': Britain's post-war economy 'may be regarded as peculiar among the developed capitalist states', because other nations achieved far higher levels of economic growth 'without so much inflation or such balance of payments trouble'.[24] In its 1977 programme, the CPGB talked of 'Britain's crisis'—once the leading capitalist power, Britain's crisis was now 'especially deep'[25]—and Labour's 1983 manifesto lamented Britain's loss of markets to its competitors and its failure 'to develop and exploit the new technologies as successfully as other industrial countries'.[26] The CPGB's Bill Warren and Mike Prior summed up this left-wing mood as follows:

> British capital has been on the economic defensive, not only nationally, but also internationally, with Britain's share of world trade declining much more rapidly than that of any other country and with the British market being

persistently threatened by large-scale imports of foreign manufactures which have been both more competitive and of better quality.[27]

Related to this emphasis on a British decline was a concern about the British economy's especially high dependence on the global economy. As the Conference of Socialist Economists (CSE) and the LCC argued, 'To a far greater extent than most capitalist countries Britain is tied into the world economy through UK- and foreign-based companies'.[28] The British economy was 'more closely integrated through trade, more "open", than most industrialised countries', and British production and consumption 'developed in response to world market forces'.[29] British workers' interests were tied to the success of British firms in export markets, and British consumers' interests were tied to the availability and price of imported goods.[30] As a result, the British recession was 'likely to prove deeper and longer-lasting than anywhere else in the developed world'.[31] Labour's 1976 programme, repeating Stuart Holland's case that 'big league firms' were shifting investment away from Britain, expressed a similar concern:

> British companies produce and sell through their subsidiaries and branches located abroad twice as much as total UK exports. Germany and Japan export twice as much from their home base as their companies produce and sell outside their countries. Our competitors invest and produce at home—often for export from their home base; UK companies invest and produce abroad, leaving the UK economy heavily dependent on manufactured imports.[32]

It was, therefore, an apprehension about Britain's special dependence on, and special vulnerability to, economic forces and developments outside its borders that accompanied calls for a greater insulation of Britain's economy. While this is not to claim that the AES sought protectionist policies *only* for Britain—on the contrary, it believed that national governments in general should adopt policies for greater national sovereignty over international trade insofar as the latter proved detrimental to their national economies— it saw economic protection as a matter of particular urgency for the British economy. As the CSE put it:

> the ways Britain is tied into the [world economic] system [are] an important cause of the weakness of British industrial capitalism. The AES must therefore seek ways of restructuring this international dependence...[33]

## European Integration

Concerns about Britain's economic weakness pervaded AES positions on the EEC. As with the import-controls policy discussed below, criticisms of the EEC contained a combination of ideas about democracy, national sovereignty and economic planning with an underlying anxiety about the decline of Britain's status within the global economy. Britain's membership of the EEC was discussed primarily in terms of whether it represented an obstacle to Britain's economic revival.

Opposition to the EEC had had a long history in the Labour Party, whose post-war revisionist leader Hugh Gaitskell had opposed Britain's entry on the grounds that it would end its existence as 'an independent European state', render it 'a province of Europe', and thereby end its role as 'the mother country of a series of independent [Commonwealth] nations'.[34] Nevertheless, Britain's second application to join the EEC, after Charles de Gaulle's veto of Harold Macmillan's bid in 1961, was submitted under Labour in 1967 (again blocked by the French president), whose pre-AES manifestos in 1966 and 1970 endorsed Britain's entry provided it was on terms favourable to the domestic economy.[35] When Britain finally entered the EEC in 1973 under Edward Heath, Labour's February 1974 manifesto denounced the conditions of Britain's membership: they threatened British food consumption from low-cost non-European producers; Britain's tax contribution to EEC finances was unfair; and the proposed monetary union would compel Britain to accept increased unemployment to maintain a fixed parity.[36] If Labour's re-negotiations with the EEC were unsuccessful, the Labour government would consult the British people 'on the advisability of negotiating our withdrawal from the Communities'.[37] Labour's manifesto for the October general election of the same year, written during these re-negotiations, restated Labour's policy to put the matter to the British electorate.[38]

The decisive vote in favour of Britain's EEC membership in the June 1975 referendum was a significant setback for the Labour left. Accepting the referendum result, Labour's 1976 party programme talked mainly of the need for EEC reform, as did its 1979 manifesto, which called for a 'democratic and socialist' EEC along with its enlargement in national membership to reduce 'the dangers of an over-centralised and over-bureaucratic EEC'.[39] With the partial recoupment of the Labour left by the late 1970s, however, and with its continuing association of Britain's EEC membership with an intensifying British economic crisis, the party's 1980 annual conference upheld a British withdrawal.[40] James Callaghan's acceptance of the harsh terms of the IMF loan in 1976, viewed by many on the left as the Labour government yielding its right to determine British economic policy, had also helped strengthen the AES left's hostility to the transnational institution.[41] Thus the 1983 manifesto was less compromising than the previous AES-derived manifestos, declaring EEC membership a 'most serious obstacle' to 'radical, socialist policies for reviving the British economy'.[42] EEC rules conflicted with Labour's strategy for economic growth, full employment, increasing trade, exchange controls, regulating direct overseas investment, and controlling prices and inflation by 'buying food from the best sources of world supply'.[43] An 'amicable and orderly' withdrawal from the EEC was therefore required 'well within the lifetime of the [next] parliament'.[44]

Although Labour's position on the EEC varied during the AES period, therefore, it was consistently guided by practical national-economic considerations. As the 1976 Labour programme put it:

> The Labour Party's attitude towards Britain's membership of the European Community was always based on the belief that membership had to be judged on the practical issue of the balance of advantages and disadvantages that it would bring to the British people.[45]

Labour must press for 'socialist policies' within the EEC, but these would be 'measured against the same yardstick of practicality'.[46] The pros and cons of the EEC should be determined primarily in accordance with the nation's economic interests, its need for industrial growth and productivity.

Stuart Holland's position on the EEC was also led by this practical concern. In 1971, he had tentatively posed Britain's EEC entry as a means to enable greater state direction of the multinational companies that, as discussed in the previous chapter, he saw as defying existing macroeconomic state controls.[47] Like Harold Wilson, for whom the EEC was an 'evolving and dynamic' phenomenon whose future Britain could help determine,[48] Holland saw the EEC as changing and malleable. He argued that EEC principles as set out in the Treaty of Rome, with its formal emphasis on market freedom, did not correspond with the development of the EEC's actual practices. With its Keynesian forecasting framework and its assistance to declining as well as advanced technology sectors, the EEC had 'increasingly evolved towards an economic policy recognisably closer to that of the last Labour government and the present Labour Party than to either nineteenth century liberalism or the neo-liberalism of the present government'.[49]

Indeed, much of Holland's political work in the 1970s focused on alternative economic strategies that could be pursued at joint European level. In 1976, he was a member of a group of experts, formed by the EEC Commission, that produced a report (the 'Maldague report') calling for a joint reflation of demand via increased public spending and credit from surplus to deficit EEC countries.[50] Including Jacques Delors, later the president of the European Commission, one of the group's main proposals was the greater accountability of multinational business, which Holland believed 'could be implemented by joint international action between governments at the Community level'.[51] *Beyond Capitalist Planning*, a 1978 book Holland edited and to which Delors also contributed, likewise combined criticism of EEC monetary integration and supranationalism with a stance that left open the possibility of socialist reform via the EEC.[52]

Holland, therefore, cautioned against the exaggeration of the EEC's importance as an obstacle to socialism 'in relation to the much greater threat posed by multinational capital'.[53] The suggestion, common on the left, that the EEC represented 'cartel Europe' (or a 'capitalist club', according to others) was only partly valid. The EEC Commission was not a 'sabre-toothed tiger ready to cut to shreds the basis of new public ownership and socialist planning', but 'probably the biggest paper tiger outside China'.[54] A determined British government could play the 'EEC game' in any way that it liked. Although EEC member states had to agree in principle to their application of wide-ranging EEC legislation, whether that legislation was enforced depended on the active co-operation of the individual states.[55] The EEC merely disguised the *real* existential conflict between nation states and the multinational firms: EEC institutions were 'emperor's clothes veiling the old reality of the nation state and its conflict with the new Leviathan of multinational power'.[56]

For Holland, therefore, the problem was not EEC membership as such but the British government's failure to assert and uphold Britain's economic interests. The terms of entry accepted by the Conservatives disadvantaged Britain by ending its preference for Commonwealth imports and accepting the costly exchanges of the Common Agricultural Policy (CAP).[57] Much more could have been achieved at much lower cost had Britain looked to the example of France, whose state planners had managed to prevent a large outflow of capital abroad, or to the Italians, who had assisted their small- and medium-sized firms threatened by EEC entry.[58] The issue was less the institutions of the EEC than the political ideas by which they were guided, ideas on which there was a damaging lack of consensus among European left parties.[59] Indeed, two decades of the EEC had shown 'many socialist members at Strasbourg more clearly in the role of abandoning demands for transition to socialism', since for many of them 'waiting for a supranational Community…has replaced the more difficult task of working for socialism'.[60] And 'working for socialism' entailed, for Holland, not only opposition to this supranationalism but, with it, a vigorous assertion of national interests. If socialists were to utilise the EEC, their power would lie 'in a socialist application of the Gaullist veto over those policies which threaten "important national interests"'.[61]

Other Labour-left proponents of the AES shared this basic nation-centred concern, although their positions were often far more categorical. According to Hodgson in the early 1980s, the EEC would reduce Britain to 'an impoverished and deindustrialised region on the periphery of an industrial heartland stretching from the Ruhr to the Seine and lying south of the English channel'.[62] Britain was unfairly treated by its membership of the EEC, which had damaged the British economy by causing 'a net outflow of funds from Britain when richer countries have experienced a net inflow, and holds up no prospect of resolving Britain's underlying economic problems'.[63] According to Peter Hain, whether British withdrawal must be 'pursued as a matter of absolute priority [was] open to question', but the EEC was 'self-evidently a block on socialists' progress internationally as well as domestically' and ultimate withdrawal 'must be the objective'.[64] Britain had lost access to its cheaper food markets and had become 'committed to subsidizing the less efficient agricultures of other EEC countries'.[65] Tony Benn, meanwhile, as discussed below, pursued this idea a little further, at least rhetorically, referring to Britain as a colonial subject of EEC institutions.

For the CPGB, the EEC was eroding the right of the British people to 'determine their own affairs' and was 'seriously threatening national control over the economy and natural resources, such as oil and natural gas'.[66] It imposed 'serious limitations on the country's sovereignty' but also caused a trade deficit, higher prices and 'further economic difficulties for Britain'.[67] The alternative strategy offered by the party's 1977 programme stressed Britain's 'national interests'. Britain's survival as 'a manufacturing country' was at stake, as was its 'capacity to decide its own destiny'. An alternative policy 'must safeguard the national interests of the British people, now under attack from international monopoly capital—an attack facilitated by Britain's entry to the Common Market'.[68] As discussed below, this orientation to patriotism had a long history in the CPGB, which saw 'the development of revolutionary struggle' as tied to the defence of Britain's national interests, at a political, economic and even cultural level.

It is true, as Callaghan has pointed out, that Labour-left and Communist thinking on the EEC underwent significant adjustment through the 1980s.[69] In 1980, the CPGB economist Bob Rowthorn had presented the policy for withdrawal as a measure to extend 'the influence of the working class and its allies, and for exerting social control over the direction of the economy'.[70] In 1982, by contrast, he called withdrawal an 'absurd demand' given the large extent of trade between Britain and other EEC countries, and he argued that it was 'thoroughly dangerous…to think that any purely national economic strategy can compensate for the lack of a European perspective'.[71] As discussed in Chapter 7, this revised approach, ascendant within the British left by the late 1980s and dominating it by the end of the following decade, represented the beginnings of a greater openness to the transfer of political and economic authority to international bodies like the EEC and the European Union—thus marking a left-wing shift away from the nation-state orientation that had defined the AES as well as its Labour-left predecessors.

## Import Controls

This national orientation of the AES was perhaps most apparent in its policy for import controls, and it was mainly for this reason that it was arguably the most controversial of all its policies with 'far left' critics of the strategy. With the notable exception of Holland—who expressed opposition to the policy on the basis that it could create inflationary pressures in Britain and that, in any case, multinational companies would 'evade import controls either by transfer pricing or by relocating production abroad'[72]—the prominent advocates of the AES saw import controls as a vital component of their economic strategy.

The import-controls policy was supported by a straightforward economic argument: there was little point in reflating Britain's economy if much of the nation's increased wealth was to leave the country for its competitors abroad, via cheaper imported goods from foreign firms drawing in the increased consumer demand at home. Controls on imported goods were therefore required if reflation was to expand industry and reduce unemployment. 'Spending will not create jobs if it is soaked up by imports', as Labour's 1983 manifesto stated.[73]

Although import controls were advocated in the 1960s, by sections of the left and Keynesian economists like Roy Harrod,[74] Labour's 1973 programme, in which the party first officially adopted the policy orientation of the AES, did not include an import-controls policy; it was proposed by Labour's National Executive Committee (NEC) in its 1975 document *Labour and Industry*, and formally adopted in Labour's programme in 1976.[75] The latter contained the principal AES arguments for import controls. To avoid the balance of payments problems of the 1960s, selective import controls were for a period required on a number of manufactured and semi-manufactured goods 'where this can be done without provoking retaliation against British exports or starting a trade war from which the poorest countries would suffer the most'.[76] In the past, economic recovery had carried with it 'a most serious risk' of increased imports and massive trade deficits. Britain's export success depended ultimately on the health of its manufacturing industry, and the latter required a 'breathing-space for the reconstruction and regeneration which our industrial policies will secure'. As a result, economic recovery must now be export-led: any rapid growth of consumer spending would otherwise 'fall on imported manufactured goods'.[77]

It should be underlined, however, that the 1976 programme did not oppose free trade on principle: it accepted 'the general principle of free trade in manufactured goods between the democratic industrial countries of the world, as embodied in such treaties as GATT and EFTA'.[78] As a 'general rule', free trade was a sound economic principle, but Labour had 'always accepted that there are certain circumstances which demand that exceptions be made'. Free trade was not an end in itself but 'a means to greater efficiency in the interests of working people as consumers'.[79] And since Labour's programme tied the interests of workers to the interests of the national economy, its position was that it was prepared to oppose free trade insofar as it proved detrimental to British industry.

The AES was characterised by this kind of predominantly pragmatic approach to the question of trade, even if several AES proponents presented 'planned trade' as a component of 'socialist planning'. Certainly in the case of Francis Cripps and Wynne Godley, economists at the Cambridge Economic Policy Group (CEPG), the need for import controls was primarily a matter of dry and sober technical calculation and economic modelling, rather than any overriding political principle. They questioned the 'orthodox Keynesian' model which saw fiscal policy and the exchange rate as the principal instruments for its 'targets of policy'—'employment and output, the current balance of payments and the rate of inflation'.[80] Their own model was based on the assumption that Britain was among the 'relatively unsuccessful' (RU) industrialised countries in an unequally stratified global economy also constituted by 'relatively successful' (RS) industrialised countries and non-industrialised countries (LDCs). The central argument, then, was that it would be unlikely for an RU economy like Britain's to reach the conventional targets of Keynesian policy without also imposing controls on its imports.[81] There were only three broad options for the British economy: deflate the economy, devalue the currency or impose import controls, the latter representing the best hope for an economic recovery.[82]

The CEPG economists' lack of emphasis on socialism, along with their technical, 'Keynes plus import controls' approach to Britain's economic crisis, may have appeared to set them apart from the more radical interpretations of import controls. Rowthorn certainly saw it as such, arguing that their strategy was 'so modest that they hardly deserve such a grandiose name [as the AES]'.[83] As discussed, Rowthorn believed that the CPGB's approach to the AES contained a revolutionary purpose which distinguished it from the more moderate approaches on the left.

However, like Cripps and Godley, Rowthorn presented import controls ultimately as a matter of immediate economic necessity, and as quite apart from the question of whether they represented a socialist policy. In a polemical exchange with a Trotskyist critic, Jonathan Bearman, who argued that import controls were a chauvinist policy that would also raise living costs for workers in Britain,[84] Rowthorn suggested that Britain would need to 'pay her way' regardless of the nature of its economic system:

> If British industry is not competitive in world markets, how on earth does [Bearman] think that Britain can pay the imports which British workers require, for the 'cheap shoes from Seoul' which he holds so dear, or the materials and equipment for our factories? Will the rest of the world supply us with these things for nothing? Of course not. Britain must pay her way in the world. This is a harsh fact of life which applies no matter what kind of economic system or what kind of government we have.[85]

The similarity here with the CEPG's position was that, for Rowthorn, the need for trade controls was ultimately a straightforward and practical matter of '[keeping] imports in line with what Britain can afford'.[86]

AES calls for import controls represented, therefore, not so much an objection to free trade as to its *current* consequences for the British economy. Indeed, as mentioned above, among AES objections to the EEC was that it violated Britain's right to free trade: it restricted Britain's ability to trade freely with the Commonwealth economies from which it could buy food products more cheaply than it could via the EEC's Common Agricultural Policy. Although AES advocates claimed to be providing an 'intellectual case against free trade',[87] in the main they were proposing a more strategic approach to trade at the existing juncture, one which would apply selective controls on imports to promote the growth of certain sectors of the British economy while allowing other sectors to remain open to free international competition. After all, trade restrictions had long been a tool for successful capitalist development: as the LCC put it, 'West Germany, Italy, France, Japan and the United States all industrialised behind major tariffs designed to prohibit imports'.[88]

Indeed, in response to right-wing criticisms that import controls would mean a 'siege economy' cutting Britain off from the global economy, AES proponents posed import controls as a potential *spur* to international trade. Import controls would not necessarily decrease but could increase the overall volume of British imports: 'Logically it is quite possible to have import controls and an *increase* in aggregate imports', as Hodgson argued.[89] Elsewhere, in response to left-wing criticism from Andrew Glyn that import controls would increase the price of consumer goods in Britain,[90] Hodgson argued that Glyn confused import controls with import reduction: 'an increased growth rate consequent upon [Britain's economic] regeneration would eventually provide a larger potential market for imports from countries with which we may desire to trade'.[91] Meacher argued along similar lines: the aim was not to decrease the absolute level of imports but to allow the British economy to 'operate at a higher level of activity…for a given quantity of imports'; therefore, countries exporting to Britain would not lose out 'since the volume of UK imports would not fall'.[92]

According to Benn, British unemployment was itself a form of British import control, since unemployed workers could not 'buy much from abroad'.[93] If money was to be invested to expand an industry, it would be 'ludicrous to allow that industry to be destroyed [by imports] while building it up', which would, among other things, export unemployment to other countries, since Britain would still be 'buying less from abroad'.[94] Import restrictions imposed on certain sectors for their regeneration could raise the country's purchasing power and thereby allow it to consume more goods produced abroad, in a way that profited the British economy as well as its international competitors. As Hain suggested, trade planning would 'actually increase world demand', since under current arrangements national economies were simply 'eating into each other's industrial base, causing a collapse nationally and therefore, in aggregate, across the world'.[95] For Meacher, import controls were a temporary measure for 'investment expansion', since 'ultimately the only hope for British industry is to become competitive with foreign industry on equal terms', requiring a 'period of high profits and investment' after which British industry would 'be able to do without import controls'.[96] Labour's 1983 manifesto was also clear that this was not an anti-trade policy:

> Our purpose in trade policy is **not** to reduce trade but to make possible an orderly expansion of imports, paid for by our growing export trade. We will thus be able to replace the present policies of deflation, which **restrict** world trade, by policies of expansion, which **increase** world trade.[97]

In this vein, AES proponents rejected that their import controls represented 'beggar my neighbour' policies likely to trigger a trade war with competing economies. As Rowthorn argued, 'beggar my neighbour' would be a situation in which trade controls were implemented to 'produce a reduction in total imports and to obtain a huge trade surplus for Britain', which was not the aim of the AES, and 'criticisms based on this assumption are beside the point'.[98] According to Hain, if import controls led to Britain's economic reconstruction, other countries could only gain, since 'a sick British economy simply drags everyone else down and contributes to the world slump'.[99] A revitalised British economy was in the interests of capital abroad.

This was also one of the lines along which AES advocates defended against charges of nationalism from the left. Hain suggested that Britain's trade controls could 'evolve into a general international socialist trading pattern' in which other countries would maintain 'reciprocal controls which defended their industrial interests'.[100] Hodgson wrote that socialist import controls ('implemented under capitalism') could be a means to a 'progressive foreign policy of a Left Government'.[101] Such a government may find it 'desirable to increase imports of sugar from Cuba…in solidarity with their revolution', while restricting imports from 'more reactionary countries' like Brazil and South Africa.[102] Labour's 1976 party programme devoted several pages to a new, progressive economic relationship with countries in Africa, Asia and Latin America,[103] while Rowthorn put forward the Communist position for a new 'pattern' of trade, in which more would be purchased from 'the socialist countries and the Third World'.[104] Barratt Brown suggested that aid provision to underdeveloped countries could be incorporated into a 'foreign trade plan' whereby 'both the developed and underdeveloped countries [were] brought into a fruitful scheme of mutual exchanges'.[105] According to Meacher, trade with third-world countries 'would be the best kind of foreign trade for a country like Britain'.[106]

Yet import controls were above all a policy for national economic defence, for an economic regeneration through a process of greater economic protection. The principles of 'planned trade' and 'progressive foreign policy' were supplementary considerations, added on to what were the central and immediate aims of import controls: reversing British capitalism's relative decline and improving its standing vis-à-vis its global competitors. As in the 1930s, sections of the British left saw a greater national economic fortification as the obvious solution to capitalist crisis. The 1970s saw a renewed trend towards restrictive trade actions by states in Western Europe (through the EEC and otherwise), America, Canada and Japan, as well as a resurgence in protectionist thinking among left-leaning economists across Europe.[107] There was a prevalent belief among observers that the world economy was slipping into a new era of protectionism after the trade liberalisations of the post-war period. According to Hodgson, that latter period was now a 'bygone era': 'free trade is almost dead. Since the early 1970s a new wave of protectionism has swept the world.'[108] For Meacher, 'Britain must become more self-reliant and make better use of its own not inconsiderable resources'.[109] The suggestion seemed to be that Britain ought to claim its own 'economic sovereignty' as other countries were doing, rather than return to a 'sovereignty of the market' evidently no longer in Britain's interests.[110]

For Hodgson, it was

> sometimes strange to find the Far Left using the arguments of orthodox economics against Labour Party policy. Even more strange is the implied suggestion that 'free trade' would be *beneficial*, relatively speaking, to Third World countries and the working class.[111]

However, the argument that British protectionism would benefit third-world economies faced the fact that a key AES objective was precisely to divert investment back towards Britain and, at least for the time being, maintain it there. Among Holland's key concerns, for example, was that firms were shifting their investments away from Britain towards third-world economies. In the 'long boom' years of the 1950s, large firms had greater incentive to invest in Western European countries or the United States due to their 'relatively capital intensive activity'.[112] In the 1960s, however, 'big league companies' began increasingly to locate

> their relatively labour intensive plant in…third world countries such as Tai-wan, Singapore, the Philippines, Mexico, and Brazil, which offer them union-free labour at a tenth or twentieth of the cost of UK labour.[113]

Holland acknowledged that it was 'natural if not obligatory' for firms to invest in economies where they would expect to make the largest profits.[114] But he also believed that the British government could '[change] the rules of the game', primarily by promoting 'a higher generation of income here at home'.[115] The implication was not only that the government could create a profitable national economy at a time of global economic downturn, but also that the aim of directing investment from the third world to Britain was part of the socialist alternative. As Holland put it decades later, 'a state holding company or companies could counter globalisation and the attraction of multinational companies to countries with lower labour costs by offsetting low labour costs by higher-value-added innovation'.[116] But if this capital outflow to third-world countries was to be curtailed at a time of global economic recession, it was difficult to see how those countries would not be further disadvantaged by the new protectionist measures of Western states, at least in the short and medium term.

## Britain as an Oppressed Nation

The argument here is not that it was the *intention* of AES-left analyses to demand British development at the expense of other economies. It was merely that, due to the nation-centred perspective within which they were bound, AES analyses could not avoid advancing solutions which gave precedence to British economic interests. This was a perspective contrary to those strands in Marxist politics 'indifferent' to national interests, in the sense of their reluctance to privilege the interests of their nation over those of others. According to Isaac Deutscher, socialist internationalism meant 'understand[ing] the nationalism of the masses, but only in the way in which a doctor understands the weakness or the illness of his patient'.[117] For Lenin, it meant placing above one's own nation 'the interests of all nations, their common liberty and equality'[118]; indeed, '[s]uccessful struggle against exploitation' required a working class 'free of nationalism' and 'absolutely neutral, so to speak, in the fight for supremacy that is going on among the bourgeoisie of the various nations'.[119] Tied to this interpretation of internationalism was the idea that socialists in dominant capitalist nations (or 'imperialist nations') should renounce their allegiance to any project for national development that would pit their nation against other nations, whether other imperialist nations or those oppressed by imperialism. In addition, socialists in the imperialist nations should take the side of the oppressed nations, at the expense of the imperialist nations, whether in wars or other conflicts. While the nationalism of imperialist nations could only be reactionary, therefore, representing a barrier to international working-class unity and global economic progress, the national aspirations of oppressed nations deserved socialist support insofar as they represented struggles against imperialist barriers to their historical development.[120]

An interesting feature of the AES left was that it contained an awareness of these distinctions and employed them to legitimise its own protectionist policies. It did this by depicting Britain as among the oppressed nations of Marxist theory. Appearing almost as an attempt to utilise a theoretical loophole, this depiction was part of the way in which left-wing AES proponents sought to justify their calls for protectionism in socialist and even Marxist terms. The CPGB and the Labour left were united in this respect: as shown above, they both saw Britain as a specially disadvantaged country among the developed economies, and they both believed that the state's duty was to safeguard Britain's economy from rapacious interests abroad. Britain's oppression by foreign forces was also pointed to directly, however. Referring to Britain, the CPGB's Bert Ramelson argued that

> It has never been considered a breach of international solidarity or Marxist integrity to protect a weaker economy from a more powerful predatory capitalism.[121]

By presenting Britain as a prey of stronger capitalist powers abroad, Ramelson sought to reconcile Marxist internationalism with British protectionism.

This attempt at reconciliation—via the depiction of Britain as an oppressed nation—had accompanied the CPGB's formal adoption of reformism after the Second World War. The party's 1924 draft programme had pointed to the British labour movement's corruption by 'social patriotism' via a 'labour aristocracy' committed to Britain's economic privileges.[122] Its 1951 programme, by contrast, called 'for the unity of all true patriots to defend British national interests and independence', against the national traitors in the leaderships of 'the Tory, Liberal and Labour Parties and their spokesmen in the press and on the B.B.C. [who were] betraying the interests of Britain to dollar imperialism'.[123] This was a policy for 'a Britain, free, strong and independent', one which was 'subordinate and subservient to no foreign power, but [stood] in friendly association and equal alliance with all powers that recognise and respect Britain's national interests'.[124] In this Cold War context, the oppressive foreign power that concerned British Communists the most was America. According to the 1951 programme, 'our country' had lost, for the first time in its history, 'its independence and freedom of action in its foreign, economic and military policy' to this foreign power, and Labour and Conservative leaders had become its 'spokesmen'.[125]

As is common in nationalist politics, British Communists sought to uphold not only Britain's economic and political but also cultural independence. In an intriguing text also published in 1951, *The American Threat to British Culture*, they outlined their fears about America's cultural invasion of Britain. Sam Aaronovitch, the text's main contributor, and later a key CPGB advocate of the AES, angrily condemned America for seeking to 'impose its way of life' on Britain, 'caring nothing if it destroys our own national culture'.[126] The import of American books, films, comics and 'dance-music' was helping to persuade Britons 'to fight for the American trusts or watch and not resist their national independence being taken from them'.[127] According to Montagu Slater, another contributor, the American threat meant 'giving up music and putting in its place jazz', and swapping British beer and literature for 'coca-cola and Dashniell Hamnett [sic]'.[128] For Aaronovitch, British writers were now obliged to embrace 'the slum or tough naturalism...of a Hemingway and a J. T. Farrell' and thereby to

'desert their own country'.[129] The solution to this cultural-imperialist subjection was a renewed popular British patriotism. In response to the apparent lapse in ruling-class patriotism—the British elites had 'lost all national
pride' and were 'prepared to sell out a whole nation'—the British masses
should unite 'to popularize and re-discover our cultural heritage and to
unite wide sections in defence of it'.[130]

The CPGB's 1977 programme, although significantly milder in its patriotic tones, continued with this principal theme of foreign domination:

> The illusion of a 'special relationship' with the US, based on a common inter-
> est in holding back the advance of national liberation and socialism, only
> resulted in increased US economic and political domination of Britain. Sim-
> ilarly, when the big monopolies, backed by successive governments, pushed
> for and achieved Britain's entry into the Common Market, this not only
> imposed serious limitations on the country's sovereignty, but resulted in a
> big trade deficit with the Market, higher prices, and further economic diffi-
> culties for Britain.[131]

In the Labour Party, on the other hand, whose official commitment to
the Western alliance distinguished its foreign policy from the CPGB's, the
idea of a subjugated Britain nevertheless found much favour on its left, in
debates around the EEC and import controls but also those around nuclear
disarmament and Britain's role as America's special ally.[132] Holland saw the
'main threats' to a Labour government as 'international agencies such as
the International Monetary Fund, backed by the US government and the
facilities of the CIA, and forced by US multinational capital'.[133] Michael
Meacher wrote of an external dependence that was 'dragging Britain down'
and had turned it into a 'surrender economy' (his take on the accusation
that the AES sought a 'siege economy').[134] However, it was perhaps Tony
Benn who stressed Britain's oppressed status the most explicitly, depicting
the EEC, the IMF and the American state as sources of Britain's colonisa-
tion. As he argued in a lecture in January 1980:

> it cannot be long before the British people realise that in the space of a
> generation this country has been transformed from being the centre of our
> own world-wide empire to being a colony in someone else's empire; heavily
> taxed, externally controlled and governed by a form of indirect rule, on behalf
> of an imperial commission on the continent.[135]

As with the Mosley policies that Benn's Labour-left predecessors had supported in the early 1930s, and the CPGB's approach in the 1950s, Benn's depiction of Britain as a colony of an imperialist EEC was couched in a left-wing populism that sought to appeal to patriotic sentiments within the British public and the British labour movement. The left-wing character of his appeals was represented by a rhetorical hostility to the British 'establishment' and an emphasis on 'the people' and their democracy. When pressed on the consistency of his argument in an interview by the Marxist academic Geoffrey Foote, Benn distinguished between the British establishment and 'the British people', arguing that it was the latter who were under a colonial subjugation. Although the British establishment still performed an 'imperial role' in an 'economic sense', the British people were 'now governed by a complex range of international powers, the Common Market, the IMF, to some extent the Pentagon, the multinationals'.[136] The British people were experiencing a subjection that placed them alongside 'the people of Zimbabwe or the old colonies of the British empire'.[137] With these extraordinary claims about a British oppression in line with that of former African colonies, Benn's socialism advanced the solution of a national struggle: 'there was an element of a national liberation struggle about what we were doing [by struggling for self-government]'.[138]

Benn also related the struggle against oppressive forces abroad to the struggle for greater democracy at home. The undemocratic rise of civil-service power had become increasingly acute with Britain's membership of the EEC, which had greatly increased the dependence of ministers upon civil service expertise.[139] In addition, successive British parliaments had abandoned 'powers borrowed from the electorate' to NATO, the IMF, the multinational corporations and the EEC Commission, as well as to the executive in Britain, the military and the security services.[140] The 'unfinished business' of Britain's democratisation meant that power needed to be returned from these institutions to a strengthened British parliament with greater authority over British government. Benn disagreed that this was a nationalist approach to the state, arguing that it was 'an internationalist view based on the belief that for international labour to prosper, international institutions must reflect the interests of labour and not those of capital'.[141] But as discussed in the next chapter, Benn's support for the interests of labour over capital was premised on his view that an empowered British workforce would be in the interests of the nation as a whole, in the interests of employers as well as workers, since the existing industrial conflict was destructive of this common national community.

Thus, such AES analyses sought to pursue a national project not in the reactionary, right-wing form found in the West but akin to what they saw as the progressive anti-imperialist nationalisms of the 'global periphery'. In a 1977 *New Left Review* article, Tom Nairn observed that nationalism was 'always the joint product of external pressures and an internal balance of class forces', typically arising in societies disadvantaged or colonised due to world capitalism's law of uneven development, 'where conscious, middle-class élites have sought massive popular mobilization to right the balance'. Britain was unusual in this respect: it 'suffered far less from those external pressures and threats than any other [society], during a very long period'.[142] As a result, the 'great power' nationalism which developed in Britain was especially conservative, since it lacked 'the key, populist notion informing most real nationalism: the idea of the virtuous power of popular protest and action'.[143] Arguably, therefore, the AES's ideological construction of an oppressed Britain played a critical role in its attempts to viably advance this 'populist notion', a variant of British nationalism which sought to rally popular support to reverse Britain's economic decline and its increasingly wronged status in the global economy. By portraying Britain as oppressed, AES analyses could also attempt to portray their national focus as progressive.

## THE RIGHT-WING NATURE OF ANTI-PROTECTIONISM?

In response to charges of chauvinism from their left, AES proponents reproached their 'ultra-left' critics for capitulating to a free-trade philosophy shared by large sections of the right. The left-wing opponents of the AES were 'siding with the forces of the market' and '[burying] their heads in the sands of liberal free trade'.[144] The 'ultra-left' were 'couching their argument in revolutionary phrases about "international solidarity"' but ignoring 'the fact that free trade has more in common with 19th-century liberalism than Marxism'.[145] However, there were two main problems with this line of argument.

The first was that there was nothing inherently left-wing about opposition to liberal political economy; as pointed out above, protectionism had had a long history on the British right, including the antecedents of British fascism in the first half of the twentieth century. A post-war representative of that political tendency, the National Front leader John Tyndall, approached Britain's economic problems in terms not entirely dissimilar from those of the AES left. As he argued in a 1977 interview with the London *Times*, Britain was now 'reaping the harvest of having travelled for at least 100 years in a totally wrong direction. If you want me to encapsulate this in one word, it is liberalism'.[146] Tyndall defined this liberalism mainly in economic terms: weak government, laissez-faire instead of state control, bankers determining the nation's credit, and the relinquishing of authority to international institutions.[147] He attacked 'big business' and the City, called for a ban on all imports of manufactured goods, for Britain to grow at least 75% of its own food, and for its departure from the EEC.[148] The close parallels between the AES and the National Front did not, of course, extend to matters of militarism, foreign policy, race, immigration and the labour movement. Yet the National Front shared the AES's anxiety about a national economic decline, and both approaches called for state solutions which fortified the nation and distanced it from the world economy. If there was nothing left-wing about free trade, the case of the National Front indicated that there was nothing necessarily left-wing about a British 'planned trade' either.

The second problem was related to the fact that several proponents of the AES, while associating anti-protectionism with the right, upheld Marx as a key theoretical influence. This was true of the self-described Marxists in the CPGB and the CSE, but also Labour-left figures like Holland and Hodgson. However, Marx's own approach to free trade and protectionism radically contradicted that of the AES. Marx acknowledged that free trade and protection were both variants of capitalist policy, implemented at different stages of capitalism's historical and regional development, but he rejected socialist support for protectionism in the late 1840s and he endorsed free trade. Regarding protectionists in Germany—then a relatively weak industrial economy—he argued that their appeals to German workers were based on the 'very patriotic' idea that it was 'better to be exploited by one's fellow-countrymen than by foreigners'.[149] In reality, however, workers' interests did not lie with their nation's industrialists but with the collapse of the capitalist system; and free trade, by intensifying the contradictions within that system, had greater revolutionary implications than a policy for the artificial conservation of national capital by protective state measures:

> generally speaking, the Protective system in these days is conservative, while the Free Trade system works destructively. It breaks up old nationalities and carries antagonism of proletariat and bourgeoisie to the uttermost point. In

a word, the Free Trade system hastens the Social Revolution. In this revolutionary sense alone…I am in favor of Free Trade.[150]

As Engels put it forty years later, upholding Marx's position, the question of free trade or protectionism 'moves entirely within the bounds of the present system of capitalist production, and has, therefore, no direct interest for us socialists who want to do away with that system'.[151] Its indirect interest for socialists was the extent to which either policy created the conditions for the '[destruction of] the whole system'.[152] In other words, the object was to favour the policy that would accelerate capitalism's demise. The crucial difference between the approaches of Marx and the AES left was that the latter sought to devise policies by which the existing British economy could be stabilised and reinvigorated, at least as the immediate priority, since without this recovery of British industry Britain could neither trade on favourable terms with its international competitors, lower unemployment nor raise the wages of its workers. This approach bore less resemblance to Marx's position than to the tradition of patriotic protectionism Marx had identified and opposed more than a century prior.

That the AES left could not avoid aligning with this tradition was related, as discussed in Chapter 3, to its rejection of the viability of a revolutionary strategy. Its acceptance of reformism and the parliamentary road to socialism encouraged a nation-centred approach which saw the interests of the working class as tied to the prosperity of the nation. The first priority was thus to secure this prosperity, irrespective of the socialist or capitalist nature of British society: the 'first plank' of this strategy was '**an expansion of the economy**… [W]e want an economy of expansion starting *now*, not in the distant future'.[153] A political strategy which prioritised immediate economic regeneration (as the basic precondition for progressive reforms) over the capitalist system's destruction (*à la* Marx and Engels) could not but contain a strong preoccupation with Britain's position in the global economy. Thus, as shown above, the CPGB's official adoption of the reformist route in its 1951 party programme had accompanied an upsurge in nation-centred thinking among its leaders and intellectuals. As for the Labour left, whose party had never had a non-reformist past, it was heavily constrained by the nation-oriented politics that had characterised Labour's socialism since its formation.

## CONCLUSION

The AES's protectionist approach stood in a long line of responses since the late nineteenth century to the problem of Britain's economic decline, and put forward policies for economic growth through Britain's greater insulation from the global economy. Britain's membership of the EEC was called into question on the basis that its terms disadvantaged Britain with respect to its competitors, and the underlying concern was whether Britain could assert its own economic sovereignty through the EEC against interests inimical to the national economy. The AES policy of import controls was likewise premised on concerns about Britain's economic subjugation by forces abroad, which was seen to require the fortification of the British economy. However, as this chapter suggested, such AES opposition to global trade was not motivated primarily by an anti-free trade left-wing principle, but by practical considerations of economic exigency.

In their close dialogue with Marxist theory, AES proponents rejected charges of nationalism, and believed that their policies could form the basis for a progressive foreign policy and a socialist internationalism. Yet their depiction of Britain as an oppressed country indicated strongly their orientation towards a left-wing variant of a nationalist project for national regeneration and sovereignty. The AES left's emphasis on Britain's oppression by foreign interests, and its calls for a popular project for national economic reconstruction, raised the interesting question of how the AES would approach the matter of class conflict at home. According to one historian, behind the 'Bennite' left was 'the assumption that the class divisions in British society are less important than the forces which unite the nation against foreign capital'.[154] The following chapter will consider this idea further and examine the influence of the AES's national outlook on its approaches to the organised working class in Britain.

## NOTES

1. Hassan and Shaw, *The People's Flag and the Union Jack*, p. 256.
2. Benn et al., *A Ten Year Industrial Strategy for Britain*, p. 3.
3. Ibid.
4. See Budge, 'Relative Decline as a Political Issue', and Coates and Hillard, *The Economic Decline of Modern Britain*.
5. Gamble, *Britain in Decline*, p. xiv.
6. Hobsbawm, *The Age of Capital*, p. 29.
7. Ibid., p. 39.

8. Ibid., pp. 40–1.
9. Gamble, *Britain in Decline*, p. 53.
10. Ibid., p. 171.
11. Cited in Gamble, *Britain in Decline*, p. 173.
12. Snowden, 'Free Trade', p. 59.
13. Gamble, *Britain in Decline*, pp. 177–8.
14. Ibid., p. 178.
15. See Bradley, 'Master Plan for a Master Race'.
16. Gamble, *Britain in Decline*, pp. 177–8.
17. Thorpe, 'The Communist Party and the New Party', p. 485.
18. Pimlott, 'The Labour Left', p. 169.
19. Labour Party, *Labour's Call to Action*.
20. Hain, *The Democratic Alternative*, p. 57.
21. LCC, *There Is an Alternative*, p. 10.
22. Rowthorn, 'The Politics of the Alternative Economic Strategy', p. 4. For similar British Communist statements, see Aaronovitch, *The Road from Thatcherism*, pp. 5–6; Ramelson, *Bury the Social Contract*, p. 5; Hobsbawm, 'The Beginnings of Decline', p. 230.
23. Hodgson, 'Britain's Crisis and the Road to International Socialism'.
24. Barratt Brown, *From Labourism to Socialism*, p. 190. This was an argument Barratt Brown expanded on in his book *After Imperialism*.
25. CPGB, *The British Road to Socialism*, 1977.
26. Labour Party, *The New Hope for Britain*.
27. Warren and Prior, *Advanced Capitalism and Backward Socialism*, p. 4.
28. London CSE Group and the LCC, *The Alternative Economic Strategy*, p. 103.
29. Ibid., p. 88.
30. Ibid.
31. Ibid., p. 1.
32. Labour Party, *Labour's Programme 1976*, p. 30.
33. London CSE Group and the LCC, *The Alternative Economic Strategy*, p. 103.
34. Gaitskell, Speech against UK membership of the Common Market, 3 October 1962, p. 7. For a discussion, see George, *Britain and European Integration Since 1945*.
35. Labour Party, *Time for Decision*; Labour Party, *Now Britain's Strong*.
36. Labour Party, *Let Us Work Together*.
37. Ibid.
38. Labour Party, *Britain Will Win with Labour*.
39. Labour Party, *The Labour Way Is the Better Way*.
40. Callaghan, 'Rise and Fall of the Alternative Economic Strategy', p. 116.
41. Thompson, *Political Economy and the Labour Party*, p. 223. See also Harmon, *The British Labour Government and the 1976 IMF Crisis*, p. 2.

42. Labour Party, *The New Hope for Britain*.
43. Ibid.
44. Ibid.
45. Labour Party, *Labour's Programme 1976*, p. 109.
46. Ibid.
47. Kennet et al., *Sovereignty and Multinational Companies*, p. 27.
48. House of Commons Debate, *Hansard*, 8 May 1967, vol. 746, cc. 1061–184.
49. Kennet et al., *Sovereignty and Multinational Companies*, p. 27.
50. See Holland, *The Uncommon Market*, p. 26.
51. Ibid., p. 38.
52. Holland, 'Introduction', p. 6.
53. Holland, *The Socialist Challenge*, p. 337.
54. Ibid., p. 317.
55. Ibid., pp. 318, 322.
56. Ibid., p. 360.
57. Ibid., p. 322.
58. Ibid., pp. 322–3.
59. Holland, *Out of Crisis*, p. 101.
60. Holland, *Uncommon Market*, p. 132.
61. Holland, *The Socialist Challenge*, pp. 360–1.
62. Hodgson, *Labour at the Crossroads*, p. 220.
63. Ibid., pp. 220–1.
64. Hain, *The Democratic Alternative*, pp. 110–1.
65. Ibid., p. 111.
66. CPGB, *The British Road to Socialism*, 1977.
67. Ibid.
68. Ibid.
69. Callaghan, 'Rise and Fall of the Alternative Economic Strategy', p. 120.
70. Bob Rowthorn, 'The Alternative Economic Strategy'.
71. Cited in Callaghan, 'Rise and Fall of the Alternative Economic Strategy', p. 120.
72. Holland, 'Alternative European and Economic Strategies', p. 114, fn. 25.
73. Labour Party, *The New Hope for Britain*.
74. Michael Barratt Brown, *From Labourism to Socialism*, p. 203.
75. Wickham-Jones, *Economic Strategy and the Labour Party*, pp. 74–5.
76. Labour Party, *Labour's Programme 1976*, p. 14.
77. Ibid., p. 12.
78. Ibid., p. 13.
79. Ibid.
80. Cripps and Godley, 'A Formal Analysis of the Cambridge Economic Policy Group Model', p. 335.

81. Cripps and Godley, 'Control of Imports as a Means to Full Employment and the Expansion of World Trade', p. 328.
82. Ibid., pp. 329–9.
83. Rowthorn, 'The Politics of the Alternative Economic Strategy', p. 4.
84. Bearman, 'Anatomy of the Bennite Left'.
85. Rowthorn, 'The Alternative Economic Strategy'.
86. Rowthorn, 'The Politics of the Alternative Economic Strategy', p. 4.
87. Cripps and Godley, 'Control of Imports as a Means to Full Employment and the Expansion of World Trade', p. 333.
88. Labour Co-ordinating Committee, *There Is an Alternative*, p. 19.
89. Hodgson, *Socialist Economic Strategy*, p. 40. His italics.
90. Glyn, *Capitalist Crisis*, pp. 36–7.
91. Hodgson, *'Militant' and the Alternative Economic Strategy*, p. 5.
92. Meacher, *Socialism with a Human Face*, pp. 172–3.
93. Foote, 'Interview with Tony Benn', p. 29.
94. Ibid.
95. Hain, *The Democratic Alternative*, p. 69.
96. Meacher, *Socialism with a Human Face*, p. 172.
97. Labour Party, *The New Hope for Britain*. Its emphases.
98. Rowthorn, 'The Alternative Economic Strategy'.
99. Hain, *The Democratic Alternative*, p. 69.
100. Ibid.
101. Hodgson, *Socialist Economic Strategy*, p. 41.
102. Ibid., pp. 40–1.
103. Labour Party, *Labour's Programme 1976*, pp. 124–42.
104. Rowthorn, 'The Alternative Economic Strategy'.
105. Barratt Brown, *From Labourism to Socialism*, pp. 203–4.
106. Meacher, *Socialist with a Human Face*, p. 184.
107. See Nowzad, 'The Resurgence of Protectionism', pp. 14–19; Strange, 'The Management of Surplus Capacity', pp. 303–34; Kahler, 'European Protectionism in Theory and Practice', pp. 475–502.
108. Hodgson, *Socialist Economic Strategy*, p. 41.
109. Meacher, *Socialist with a Human Face*, p. 183.
110. Hodgson, *Socialist Economic Strategy*, p. 41
111. Hodgson, *Labour at the Crossroads*, pp. 211–12. His italics.
112. Holland, 'Planning Disagreements', p. 142. See also Barratt Brown and Holland, *Public Ownership and Democracy*, p. 4.
113. Holland, 'Planning Disagreements', p. 142.
114. Ibid.
115. Ibid.
116. Holland, 'Alternative European and Economic Strategies', p. 108.
117. Deutscher, 'On Internationals and Internationalism'.
118. Lenin, 'The Discussion on Self-Determination Summed Up'.

119. Lenin, 'The Right of Nations to Self-Determination'.
120. See Lenin, 'The Socialist Revolution and the Right of Nations to Self-Determination'. For a critique, see Nairn, 'The Modern Janus'.
121. Ramelson, *Bury the Social Contract*, p. 28.
122. CPGB, *Draft Programme of the C.P.G.B. to the Comintern*.
123. CPGB, *The British Road to Socialism*, 1951.
124. Ibid.
125. Ibid.
126. Aaronovitch et al., *The American Threat to British Culture*, pp. 3, 6.
127. Ibid., p. 6.
128. Montagu Slater, 'Literature', p. 37. 'Dashniell Hamnett' is a misspelling of Dashiell Hammett, the American author of popular detective novels who was, incidentally, imprisoned during McCarthyism for contempt of court while being tried for Communist activity.
129. Aaronovitch, *The American Threat to British Culture*, p. 15.
130. Ibid., pp. 17, 19.
131. CPGB, *The British Road to Socialism*, 1977.
132. Cronin, *New Labour's Pasts*, pp. 43–4.
133. Holland, *The Socialist Challenge*, pp. 346–7.
134. Meacher, *Socialism with a Human Face*, p. 192.
135. Benn, *The Case for a Constitutional Civil Service*, p. 14.
136. Foote, 'Interview with Tony Benn', p. 20.
137. Ibid., p. 21.
138. Ibid.
139. Benn, *The Speaker, the Commons and Democracy*, p. 1.
140. Benn, *Parliament, People and Power*, p. 40.
141. Ibid., pp. 99–100.
142. Nairn, 'The Twilight of the British State'.
143. Ibid.
144. Hodgson, *Socialist Economic Strategy*, pp. 40–1.
145. Ramelson, *Bury the Social Contract*, p. 27.
146. Bradley, 'Master Plan for a Master Race', p. 10.
147. Ibid.
148. Ibid.
149. Marx, 'The Protectionists, the Free Traders and the Working Class', p. 280.
150. Marx, 'Speech on the Question of Free Trade', p. 465.
151. Engels, 'On the Question of Free Trade'.
152. Ibid.
153. Ramelson, *Bury the Social Contract*, p. 22. His emphases.
154. Foote, *The Labour Party's Political Thought*, p. 334.

# CHAPTER 6

# Class Conflict and Class Collaboration: The AES and the Working Class

## INTRODUCTION

AES debates on the working class and industrial democracy occurred in a period of working-class militancy and large-scale instability in industrial relations. Industrial democracy was a policy response to a concrete problem, an active domestic threat to the stability of British capitalism. As the next chapter will argue, this era was ended in Britain by the decisive defeats suffered by organised labour by the mid-1980s and the accompanying collapse of socialist politics. Thereafter workers came to be discussed by their left-wing sympathisers increasingly in terms of their hardship and helplessness, and left-wing opposition to government policies against workers (whether welfare cuts or anti-union policies) began to be framed by emphases on workers' vulnerability as opposed to their collective power.[1]

In the 1970s and early 1980s, however, a starkly different view of Britain's workers existed, both on the left and the right. The organised working class was seen as a social force whose ideas and actions could change the course of economic and political history. The very existence of industrial democracy as a prominent topic of political discussion presupposed British workers as a collective force to be reckoned with. Both left and right figures in British public life discussed industrial democracy in terms of its ability to address what was considered a central concern in the sphere of domestic policy-making—industrial unrest arising from the inability of British industry to meet workers' demands in the workplace,

© The Author(s) 2020

B. Tufekci, *The Socialist Ideas of the British Left's Alternative Economic Strategy*,
https://doi.org/10.1007/978-3-030-34998-1_6

a seemingly irreconcilable struggle between the forces of labour and capital. The extent of working-class strength in this period was demonstrated by the broad recognition that the future of Britain's economic prosperity depended on the policies and attitude of organised labour.

Along with the right, AES analyses regarded union strength and militancy as important obstacles to Britain's economic recovery.[2] Of course, the recognition of organised labour as a barrier to capitalist recovery and restructuring did not in itself imply a certain position on the labour movement; depending on the political interpretation of the problem, it could suggest fundamentally different political programmes. For the right, the solution may involve legislation against trade-union freedoms to weaken workplace organisation and thereby reduce workers' ability to defend their jobs and wages, thus increasing their susceptibility to market discipline and the will of management. At the other end of the political spectrum, the solution may be the replacement of an economic system seen as unable, particularly under conditions of strong workplace organisation, to emerge from economic crisis and secure growth but by reducing the material position of the working class and its rights to industrial organisation.

AES positions were distinct from both these approaches. Although their critiques varied, in general AES proponents rejected the right-wing emphasis on increased state repression as a solution to the industrial-relations problem. In addition, however, they opposed what they called the 'insurrectionist' strategies of the left, and their analyses suggested that a growth of the existing economy could occur without sacrificing, and indeed by raising, the living standards of workers. In between the left-right approaches pointed to above, AES proponents called for (what they believed would be) an empowerment of the working class in the workplace as a solution to a British economy torn by class conflict and low productivity. Whether labelled 'workers participation', 'industrial democracy' or, in its most radical form, 'workers' control', an underlying justification for 'empowering' the labour force was that the present situation in industrial relations was unsustainable and destructive of the kind of social and economic progress AES proponents sought to realise.

Such ideas were devised in the political context of a cross-party interest in workers' participatory schemes to improve industrial relations.[3] Although more closely identified with the left in the AES period, interest in such schemes cut across the left-right divide in mainstream British politics. It was a sign of the times that organisations from the Conservative Party and the British Institute of Management (BIM), to the Labour Party, the

TUC and the Institute for Workers' Control (IWC), devoted considerable attention to a policy realm that would by the 1990s become virtually absent from mainstream political discourse. As Labour MP Giles Radice put it in 1974,

> 'Industrial democracy' is now on the political agenda for the first time since the 1930s...All three major political parties will be putting to the electorate proposals to increase 'participation'. Journalists, management consultants, enlightened managements spend much time discussing the issue. Even the CBI [Confederation of British Industry] has agreed that some changes are needed.[4]

In the one-nation, pro-consensus wing of Conservative opinion, workers' participation was acknowledged as a possible means to industrial co-operation. The Conservative government published a White Paper in 1973 which upheld employee participation, and the Queen's Speech of October 1973 pledged a Green Paper 'containing proposals for promoting a greater degree of employee participation in industry'.[5] Despite their criticism of participation initiatives based on trade-union leadership, Conservative politicians expressed support for workers' participation in principle. As one Conservative MP put it in a parliamentary debate on industrial democracy, the Tories shared 'a commitment to extend the opportunities for people to participate in and influence the decisions of their own companies and the places where they work, so long as this involves all employees and not just the members of trade unions'.[6]

Within British Liberalism, meanwhile, endorsement of workers' participation in industry had had a long history. In 1928, under the leadership of Lloyd George, the Liberal Party published *Britain's Industrial Future*, a document contributed to by Keynes which called for workers' participation on the basis that 'the evoking of a team spirit' was key to successful management.[7] Throughout the post-war period, Liberal general-election manifestos advocated greater labour participation in workplace decision-making (along with profit-sharing and bonus schemes to 'encourage the worker to do his best') as a means to industrial peace and economic productivity (workers' participation could '[induce] agreement and co-operation').[8] In an attempt to establish an electoral existence in between the parties of capital and labour dominating post-war British politics, Liberal politics sought to combine a criticism of big-business tycoons and union barons with overtures to 'ordinary people' and the ordinary employee.[9]

In contrast to the Conservatives and the Liberals, Labour was, of course, alone in upholding industrial democracy in socialist terms. Where Labour's parliamentary opponents saw a measure of workers' participation as compatible with the capitalist economy, the Labour left in the AES period posed industrial democracy as perhaps the most essential element of its socialist strategy. This signalled a recognition by AES proponents that the other planks of their strategy (public ownership, import controls, etc.) were in themselves devoid of any necessary socialist content. What would provide those core aspects of the strategy with socialist substance was the additional policy for an empowered working class. As Tony Benn put it:

> what is it that differentiates a Socialist approach to intervention and public ownership from these corporatist ideas that are widely accepted by our opponents? The answer lies in the whole area of industrial democracy or workers' control.[10]

Stuart Holland made a similar point in *The Socialist Challenge*: without workers' control initiatives, 'new public enterprise and strategic planning could as easily promote state capitalism and a corporatist state as socialism'.[11] The Conference of Socialist Economists (CSE) also argued that the AES 'could not claim to be a socialist strategy' without 'moves towards real...democracy in industry'.[12]

However, AES proponents accepted a premise not entirely distinct from that of Labour's parliamentary opponents: the immediate need for an economic recovery. This was accompanied by a focus on the low productivity of labour in British industry; as Thompson points out, the AES left shared the Conservative New Right's belief that 'Britain's economic difficulties were largely a consequence of supply-side failures...a function of the deficient quality and commitment of labour'.[13] The aim of this chapter is to discuss how AES proponents dealt with this possible dilemma. If the immediate goal of the AES was to reverse Britain's economic decline and raise the productivity of labour in industry, to what extent were these aims compatible with a policy for workers' empowerment in the workplace?

## THE BACKGROUND: MANAGEMENT, UNIONS AND UNRULY WORKERS

The rise of interest in industrial democracy in the 1970s was connected to the failure of existing tripartite methods of managing workplace unrest. The apparent inability of trade-union control to provide a lasting solution to the unofficial strikes of the 1960s gave way to calls for an alternative strategy for the workplace. In the late 1960s, the Donovan inquiry had acknowledged the 'importance of the question of workers' participation in management for industrial relations', but had seen it as 'subsidiary to reforms in collective bargaining'.[14] Its main concern was to solve the problem of unofficial industrial action, the discord between the 'formal' and 'informal' systems of industrial relations, where the ability of trade unions to regulate workplace collective bargaining and earnings had been undermined by the rise of 'unofficial and unconstitutional' action by workers.[15] The rise of wages beyond the levels agreed at TUC and government level meant that real incomes were rising faster than productivity. The TUC, for its part, agreed that this was a problem, but saw that the solution should involve a 'voluntary but also collective effort, both sides of industry working with Government, so that in the longer run, and indeed in the not very long run, incomes policy would find justification in a faster increase in real incomes than would otherwise have been achieved'.[16]

It was within the context of the post-Donovan persistence of labour unrest and bargaining at the 'informal' level that industrial democracy was increasingly discussed, including by British management. In a 1968 report on industrial democracy, the British Institute of Management criticised the Donovan inquiry's 1968 report as overly focused on 'modernising the system of collective bargaining' while leaving in the air 'the question of industrial democracy' and giving little encouragement to the 'idea of workers directors'.[17] The BIM's enthusiasm for industrial democracy was led by its concern for the acquisition of working-class consent to company decisions at a time when British industry needed to 'rationalise and modernise at an increasing rate', when 'mergers and regroupings must go on' and workers must be 'retrained and moved to new centres of employment'.[18] The existing 'safety valves' in industry were not functioning: the current situation in industrial relations was creating unrest and tension and 'radical relief' was 'required to avoid an explosion', the danger of which, the BIM argued, was visible not far abroad.[19]

The need for workers' collaboration with company management occurred within the context of, and was compounded by, the rise of productivity bargaining between firms and trade unions in the 1960s. In response to the failure of incomes policy to restrain wage rises, employers sought to secure productivity deals in return for these wage rises. Covering areas such as the deployment of labour, working tempo and the length of break times, productivity deals, as a CBI leader put it, aimed to 'genuinely trade a new way of work (and life) for a new wage structure'.[20] This broadening of the parameters of workplace negotiation, requiring greater consultation of workers by management as to workplace rules and practices, coincided with new management ideas for a new participatory regime in industry.[21]

However, the industrial democracy debate also reflected older concerns with the failure of nationalisation and joint consultation to foster contentment within the British workforce. Labour's official post-war definition of industrial democracy had understood it as 'a flourishing partnership between Government, management and workers' in the interests of productivity, and complained that too many managers 'still pay lip-service to joint consultation and then do little to make it effective'.[22] There was indeed a widespread concern among the left that nationalisation had failed to solve 'the problem of the place of the worker in industry', as a 1949 Fabian Society pamphlet put it, as workers in nationalised industries continued to experience the class hierarchies and inequalities that defined the private sector.[23] A virtue of increased workers' participation was therefore its potential to 'neutralise' this 'adversed feeling'—to satisfy workers 'that there was a genuine change in the attitude of the management' and make them recognise 'in themselves a power which they did not have before'.[24] From the left, Tony Topham and Frederick Singleton argued in similar terms: had nationalisation contained a greater degree of industrial democracy, 'there would have been much stronger popular resistance to the anti-nationalisation propaganda which was so successful in the years preceding the 1959 election'.[25]

## The Bullock Inquiry

Labour's 1974 manifesto had pledged to introduce an Industrial Democracy Act 'to increase the control of industry by the people',[26] and in December 1975 Labour prime minister Harold Wilson launched an inquiry, chaired by Lord Bullock, whose terms of reference accepted 'the need for a radical extension of industrial democracy in the control of companies by means of representation on boards of directors' and (controversially with business) 'the essential role of trade union organisation in this process'.[27] The Bullock inquiry on industrial democracy published its report in 1977, almost a decade after the Donovan report, and in the context of the post-Donovan failure of the trade-union machinery to adequately contain militancy (notwithstanding TUC claims that it had made 'solid advances' in this regard).[28] The trade-union movement had effectively brought down the Conservative government of Edward Heath in 1974, and, as mentioned, there was wide-ranging interest in new policies for industrial harmony.

Thus the Bullock report emphasised the increased assertiveness of British workers since the Second World War and their decreasingly deferential attitude to managerial hierarchy. Workers had

> become less prepared to accept unquestioningly unilateral decisions by management...Traditional management prerogatives have therefore come under attack, and the modern manager has had to develop a style of participative management, which has recognised the necessity and the benefits of involving employees in decision-making, rather than imposing decisions upon them without consultation.[29]

The Bullock report repeated what was a common belief in the 1970s: workers' deference to hierarchy had been eroded, what the political theorist Ralph Miliband called the 'state of de-subordination' that had taken hold at the point of production with the weakening of the post-war consensus between labour and capital.[30] As the Industrial Participation Association (IPA) put it, the 'present generation...makes demands and has expectations that no previous generation would have contemplated'.[31] A key 'pressure for participation' was that the 'modern tendency to challenge authority in every sphere inevitably spills over into industry'.[32] If the 'industrial system' was to survive, the BIM argued, it needed to accommodate the aspirations to which it had given rise.[33] A special supplement by Industrial Relations Services (IRS) made a similar point, arguing that 'the Bullock majority answers the question of how do we ensure that capitalism survives with the solution of changing its face so as to make it acceptable to employees'.[34]

In the end, the Bullock inquiry neither produced industrial democracy nor calmed industrial tensions—industrial disorder peaked in the winter of 1978–1979, and the subsequent election of Margaret Thatcher marked a decisive turn away from state policies for industrial consensus and collaboration. As Williamson has argued, there was unlikely to be agreement between the representatives of labour and capital that the latter should cede greater power to the former.[35] However moderate it may have been, the Bullock and TUC proposal of the '2 × plus y' formula—company boards to be composed of an equal number of employee and shareholder representatives in addition to a third group of co-opted directors—challenged the decision-making prerogatives of existing management. Any compulsory system requiring company managers to submit to interference by ordinary employees in board-level decisions—particularly via trade unions—was unlikely to receive keen endorsement from those who saw organised labour as a leading cause of low productivity.

Despite the disagreements it exposed, however, the Bullock inquiry also showed the extent to which the organisations of labour and capital agreed upon the need for greater collaboration. Even the CBI, though strongly rejecting any 'rigid formula for Board level representation by trade union nominees', expressed support for employee participation as a means to 'greater efficiency and better industrial relations'.[36] While it opposed a change in the 'manager's role as decision maker', it endorsed 'employee involvement' and 'open management' as means to help the manager 'achieve the consent which he needs to put his decisions into action'.[37] In its evidence to the Bullock inquiry, the City Company Law Committee (CCLC) made a similar point: 'Employee participation is to be welcomed if…it contributes to the efficiency and profitability of the private sector.'[38]

Indeed, it was the fact that the Bullock majority report had based its case for workers' participation so strongly on its capacity to deliver improved economic efficiency and better industrial relations which allowed it to be convincingly challenged also primarily on those terms. The CCLC argued that workers' participation should be judged according to its contribution to efficiency and profitability, and it opposed the Bullock recommendations on the basis that they likely would not contribute much.[39] Likewise, an Institute of Economic Affairs (IEA) booklet on industrial democracy challenged Bullock according to the latter's own criteria: its recommendations would 'radically derange the structure of firms in British industry', while improving neither efficiency nor 'employer-employee relations'.[40] It was the BIM that perhaps best identified the inconsistency in left-wing calls for industrial democracy. Few advocates of industrial democracy were 'clear what they want and how it is to be achieved without weakening the economic and industrial organisation of the country on which the welfare society, the motor car owning democracy and the affluent consumer society is perilously based'.[41] The BIM was categorical as to the purpose of workers' participation:

> If industrial relations in Britain were fully satisfactory, there would be less need to examine participation. Since this is not the case, it is right that we should consider ways of improving relationships by working more constructively with trade unions and by giving employees greater scope to take part in decisions. If by doing so we can gain the commitment of *all* employees to the achievement of common objectives, without at the same time restricting management initiative, there is a real chance that the productive efficiency of this country will improve.[42]

The BIM was right to suggest that, in a capitalist economy, economic growth and prosperity, as well as the long-term provision of social services, ultimately depended upon the profitability of capitalist industry. It was also true that the success of capitalist industry required the general compliance of the working class in the interests of that industry. If it was accepted that this success was the premise upon which all else depended, the only legitimate function of industrial democracy could be to facilitate it. In other words, industrial democracy could be worthwhile not for its own sake, but insofar as it improved the conditions for capitalist profitability. The rest of this chapter will consider how the left-wing proponents of the AES addressed this question.

## THE OPTIONS: (I) COLLABORATION

Of the two broad left-wing approaches to the problem of the working class—conflict and collaboration—the collaborationist approach was the more dominant and mainstream. This approach directly upheld the view, shared by management organisations and sections of Conservative opinion, that better collaboration between labour and capital was part of the solution to Britain's economic and social problems, and that this collaboration could not be delivered without the institution of greater working-class input at the level of workplace decision-making. This was the basic understanding that underpinned the support for industrial democracy by what came to be called the 'Bennite' left.

One of this left's more radical members in the early 1980s, Peter Hain, advanced this viewpoint with some clarity in his 1983 book *The Democratic*

*Alternative.* For Hain, low productivity was the most serious symptom of Britain's economic decline, and greater investment alone would not 'guarantee a comparable increase in output'.[43] The root of the problem was political rather than economic, the 'class-ridden and elitist structure of society in Britain', which had led to 'industrial and managerial backwardness'.[44] Hain defined industrial democracy as giving 'a real say to workers under both public and private ownership and positively [involving] them in the process of economic decision-making'.[45] Again, the goal was economic reconstruction, and the effective collaboration of British workers was seen as central to it. Industrial democracy was not 'simply a democratic bonus for the workforce, but an indispensable cog in the machinery of recovery'.[46]

Michael Meacher likewise regarded workers' satisfaction via industrial democracy as key to Britain's economic recovery. Industrial democracy was vital because it offered the best hope for ending the class conflict that Meacher saw as a cause of Britain's industrial weakness. Labour's planning agreements and the National Enterprise Board offered 'a direct means to promote desperately needed investment in manufacturing', but the condition for their viability was 'trade union and worker co-operation'.[47] These agreements would therefore

> represent both a highly significant extension of industrial franchise and also perhaps the best means of breaking out of the institutionalised trench warfare that has sapped the strength of British industry for decades.[48]

Running British industry 'like the British army' was no longer acceptable to workers, nor did it 'make for high productivity or efficiency'.[49]

A detailed elucidation of a version of this idea was provided in Geoffrey Hodgson's 1984 book *The Democratic Economy*, which criticised official Labour and trade-union positions on industrial democracy for their 'scant recognition' of its economic necessity, and their treatment of it as a moral ideal or 'merely as a short logical extension to trade union collective bargaining'.[50] Endorsing E. F. Schumacher's view that economic development did not start with goods but with the 'education, organization and discipline' of people, Hodgson contrasted the productive potential of workers' participation to the more conventional, top-down management techniques of Taylorism.[51] While the latter had become mostly ineffective as means to raise productivity, there was 'overwhelming evidence that increased worker participation reduces work alienation and raises productivity'.[52]

To illustrate this, Hodgson gave the example of female workers in an American toy factory, employed to undertake the repetitive task of painting wooden toys at high speed and in overheated conditions. Despite a wage bonus system, absenteeism and staff turnover were high, and labour morale and productivity were low. With the intervention of management, a consultant was introduced to confer with the workers and advise the foreman. After a number of meetings, a ventilation system was installed and the workers were allowed to introduce a schedule of slow, medium or fast pace of work depending on their mood. The innovation was a success. The women became more interested and involved in how their work was organised, morale reached a record high, and there was evidence of satisfaction with working conditions. Despite the women controlling their own work pace, the average speed of work also increased, and productivity rose between 30 and 50%. As Hodgson put it:

> The first moral of this story is clear: increased productivity and reduced alienation are both possible through an increase in worker participation, and without repression, authoritarianism, increased exploitation, or a further subdivision of labour.[53]

In other words, management could raise workers' contentment by means other than wage increases or even improvements in working conditions *per se*. Workers' participation was a way to raise workers' morale and their identification with the productivity goals of their workplace, and thereby extract more labour from the worker without changes to the wage rate. By reducing workers' 'alienation', workers' participation could succeed where monetary inducements had failed. The toy-factory example showed that there was 'scope for the extension of real worker participation, and the survival and multiplication of workers' co-operatives under capitalism'— and that 'big gains in productivity are possible even within capitalism'.[54]

Hodgson did seek to address the criticism that such participation entailed class collaboration, that participation was 'a means of securing the compliance of labour to capital'.[55] He argued that, if this were true, it could also be said to apply to trade-unionism, where 'compromise rather than confrontation prevails', and argued that trade unions had been 'instrumental in securing compliance to government policies on incomes and economic austerity'.[56] In reality, both trade-unionism and worker participation contained contradictions and opposing tendencies, and each could produce either compromise or confrontation depending 'on the balance of class forces, the nature of the leadership, and the political and institutional context'.[57]

Yet the bulk of Hodgson's case for workers' participation was that better co-operation between workers and management was the key to raising the productivity of British industry. Furthermore, he saw workers as an 'interest group', a sectional interest among several other legitimate interest groups. As a result, the workers' participation he endorsed was limited even on its own terms: 'Worker participation does not necessarily mean majority representation on company boards in all cases; there may be arguments for the representation of other interest groups as well.'[58] The basic problem here was that Hodgson advanced workers' participation both as a spur to workers' combativity and class consciousness against management and capitalism, and as a system of personnel management to induce workers' co-operation with what would remain, at least for now, a capitalist economy. It was the latter of these two irreconcilable positions that dominated Hodgson's case for workers' participation.

### Tony Benn's Constitutional Settlement Between Labour and Capital

Among Benn's key concerns had long been the misfortune of British industry's wasteful and destructive relationship with its workers. In *The Regeneration of Britain*, published in 1965, he had argued that a fuller utilisation of Britain's workforce was crucial to Britain's economic revival, which could 'only be achieved by releasing energy now bottled up by outmoded traditions and methods and the maintenance of obsolete privileges'.[59] *The Regeneration of Britain* was published prior to Benn's frequently noted leftward shift in the 1970s. However, it revealed an enduring feature of Benn's approach to industrial democracy—the belief that, by improving industrial co-operation, industrial democracy could be a foundation for social harmony and unleash the productive potential of British labour.

With the rise in trade-union militancy from the late 1960s, Benn's warnings took on a greater sense of urgency. In 1970, he argued that the pressure for industrial democracy had reached 'such a point that a major change is now inevitable'.[60] Workers would not be 'fobbed off' with a few shares in their companies or satisfied with 'having a statutory worker on the Board or by a carbon copy of the German system of co-determination'.[61] The demand for workers' control may have sounded revolutionary and conjured up 'Trotskyite bogeys', but it was vital that Labour took it seriously.[62]

Indeed, Benn presented workers' control as a protection against revolution-ary upheaval. It was true, Benn argued, that some proponents of workers' control believed in a revolutionary overthrow, but then so had some pro-ponents of working-class suffrage. Yet it was the 'genius of the British'—a blend of 'realism, laziness, decency and humanity' that had 'given us 300 years free of violent revolution'—that 'the powers that be, in the end, granted the demands in full'.[63] There was no reason why these powers could not also grant in the workplace the kind of democratisation that their predecessors had granted the masses in the House of Commons.

Benn also upheld workers' control as a boon to the British economy. At present, British workers possessed an 'enormous negative power to dislo-cate the system', and workers' control could convert that negative power into 'positive and constructive power', engendering 'common interest with local managers struggling to make a success of the business', bridging the gap between management and workers and leading to a 'natural conver-gence of two streams of thinking'.[64] A major advantage of workers' con-trol was its capacity to instil, in the interests of the 'community', a sense of responsibility into relations between workers and employers in industry:

> One of the real potential beneficiaries will be the community, since an effective workers' control system probably stands the only real chance of creating the sort of responsibility in industrial affairs that is now lacking and that the legislative proposals for dealing with prices and incomes or industrial relations seemed or seem unlikely to achieve.[65]

This understanding of industrial democracy shaped Benn's views as he became a prominent spokesman for the IWC. At an IWC meeting in November 1974, as the Secretary of State for Industry, and with the Labour government recently re-elected to office on an AES platform for a 'social contract' for economic growth and class harmony, Benn argued that indus-trial democracy was 'one of the key components' in this social contract agenda to bring 'Britain through the present crisis'.[66] The trade-union movement was still exercised largely by its 'veto power', which was 'so strong in many firms and industries as to be a bar to the full develop-ment of Britain's industrial potential'.[67] Industrial democracy was also a way of battling inflation because it would shift workers' focus away from constant wage demands: it could increase production and 'supply more goods at a lower unit cost', and 'if workers' demands were to focus more precisely on the transfer of power these demands would not of themselves be inflationary, and would be more likely to achieve consent'.[68] The overall suggestion was that increased workers' empowerment in the workplace was the necessary foundation for a better-functioning tripartite system engendering greater consent and productivity—a new 'constitutional settlement' between labour, capital and the government. As he put it in the early 1980s:

> until there is a new constitutional settlement between capital and labour and the electorate, what will happen is that capital when it's strong will be deadlocked by labour and the economy will fail.[69]

### Holland's Theory for Ending the '"Them Versus Us" Syndrome'

Stuart Holland shared these concerns with the failure of existing tripartite engagements to foster an effective social consensus and regarded greater 'economic democracy' as a means to it. *Out of Crisis*, the 1983 book Holland authored with his European colleagues, 'stress[ed] the potential of economic democracy' to '[make] explicit issues which otherwise may explode in social confrontation'.[70] The improved negotiating system that economic democracy would facilitate could enable 'commitment to the agreed resolution of the problem by more of those involved'—such as trade unions—and bring 'higher returns both to the groups involved and to society as a whole'.[71] Social change needed to be a product of 'social negotiation', since no 'elite group' could 'of itself deliver a blueprint for change commanding real consensus from a variety of interested social groups and classes'.[72] Economic progress could only result from this kind of cross-class democratisation, a 'powerful coalition' across classes to mobilise 'real progress in our economies'.[73]

*The Socialist Challenge* contained three chapters on the role to be played by the working class in the AES regime. In one, 'Social and Industrial Democracy', Holland called for a workers' democracy that would encompass not only the enterprise and shop-floor level but also national and regional decision-making.[74] In a chapter titled 'Democracy of the Proletariat', Holland's rhetoric was radical, demanding a 'genuine "democracy of the proletariat" in the context of a reinforced national democracy'. Workers' self-initiative was also recommended: the tactics for industrial democracy would to a large extent be left 'to workers themselves within the enterprise'.[75]

Radical rhetoric aside, however, a key objective here was improved class harmony, the ability of tripartite industrial democratisation to end 'the trench warfare between management and workers in companies of strategic importance to the economy'.[76] As an economist, Holland accepted, for example, that decisions for the closure of certain firms were an inevitable part of a dynamic, evolving market economy. But with the better incorporation of workers' representatives in the making of these decisions, the scope for industrial confrontation could be reduced, since 'one of the main potential gains from the establishment of a wide-ranging National Enterprise Board is the increased capacity which this will bring to the government in organizing the provision of new jobs in areas of high unemployment or redundancies'.[77]

Holland sought to promote this new tripartism as advantageous not only to unions but also management. Upon accepting a workplace closure as justified, the government could 'seek advance information from the unions on the proportion of the existing labour force which would freely accept severance and redundancy pay'.[78] In the case of involuntary redundancies, the government could intervene to 'assure the provision of alternative jobs at comparable levels of pay'.[79] The closer links forged between the government, management and the unions would increase the likelihood of a smoother, less conflictual process of redundancy and workplace closure. As he argued in *Strategy for Socialism*, if bargaining negotiations were 'too distant from the shopfloor or office to involve working people directly', they would not 'overcome the present psychology of the "them versus us" syndrome'.[80]

As with Hodgson's approach, therefore, for Holland the working-class was only one element in a society made up of other essential elements; as shown in Chapter 4, Holland envisioned entrepreneurs and state representatives as constituting vital components in a well-functioning modern economy. Furthermore, workers' participation at times appeared more as an optional rather than integral element in his socialist model, which seemed primarily concerned to provide workers with opportunities to participate alongside management and the government, rather than envisaging workers at the core of the new corporate decision-making process:

The main aim of this new dimension to democratic planning should be to open the door to workers to take part if they so choose in the negotiation with government and management of the main features of their companies' programmes over the medium term.[81]

Indeed, for Holland, it was entirely possible and legitimate that the wider 'public interest' may conflict with the interests of workers—a view at odds with Marxism's theoretical subordination of other class interests to those of the working class, or its universalising of workers' fundamental interests as the human interest.[82] *The Socialist Challenge* sought to address the 'conflict between the public interest and the workers' interest' in cases where economic efficiency required plant closures, and asked how it could 'possibly result in greater readiness of the workers to accept such closures in favour of the build-up of a smaller number of rationalized plants'.[83] Holland's answer was that the 'revolutionary reforms' of the AES would create the 'worker-management relations' necessary for working-class acceptance of industrial 'modernisation' and 'rationalisations'.[84] Since Holland accepted market competition and the indispensable role of the entrepreneur, his approach needed to seek out ways of securing working-class collaboration with the tasks of economic restructuring as and when such restructuring was deemed necessary by the new tripartite system of decision-making.

A means to this collaboration was increased transparency on the part of industry, the AES demand to 'open the books', i.e. to expand the communication of corporate information. This would also reduce what Holland saw as a primary barrier to working-class co-operation: organised labour's suspicion of the employer. Many British companies were 'frustrated in undertaking the expansion of which they are technically capable through being called—unsuccessfully—to serve three masters: the government, the unions and the shareholders.'[85] The union suspicion inherent in union-employer negotiations could be reduced if unions were privy to greater information regarding the true levels of profitability of the companies concerned, which could enable the employer to convince the union of the necessity to proceed with a particular course of action. By opening the books, management could show that 'it deserved the confidence and support of the unions in a socially responsible use of its corporate power'.[86]

## *The Social Contract and Incomes Policy*

This labour-capital alliance for economic revitalisation envisaged by Holland was at the crux of the theoretical tension within the 'Bennite' left's workers' control policy. It was difficult to see how a reformed arrangement in the balance of power between labour and capital was enough to prevent the ultimate subordination of workers' interests to those of capital. The approaches of Holland, Benn, Hodgson, Meacher and Hain were each underpinned by the idea that Labour's socialist strategy was in the interests not only of British workers but also of British capital. As Hain put it, Labour's strategy was 'dependent on winning the support of significant sections of capital'; while severe opposition could be expected from finance capital, there was less reason to expect hostility from manufacturers presently hit by Conservative deflation, or small businesses and progressive sections of management.[87] Yet this idea of a cross-class alliance for economic progress further called into question the possibility of asserting the primacy of workers' interests in an AES economy whose success would depend on the success of British capital in the competitive global market economy.

It was perhaps AES positions on incomes policy which best demonstrated the contradiction inherent in a strategy that sought to uphold the interests of workers and capital simultaneously. Although nominally opposed to statutory incomes policy as a first-resort measure against economic crisis, the Labour left acknowledged the inevitable necessity of wage controls in an AES economy en route to socialism. Labour-left proponents of the AES endorsed a *just* incomes policy, one that would presuppose the existence of sufficient employment, price controls and social services. Until then, Holland argued, no Labour government could legitimately demand 'long-term voluntary wage restraint from unions'[88]; Labour's social contract could legitimately secure voluntary wage restraint from workers only if it fulfilled its promise of 'trans-socialist formation on the lines of Labour's Programme 1973 and the two 1974 manifestoes'.[89] Likewise, Hodgson called for a 'conditional incomes policy', the conditions being price controls, redistributive measures and democratic planning. Once these conditions were met, incomes policy could legitimately operate, and could continue to do so insofar as workers' living standards were raised or at least maintained.[90] For Hain, a socialist incomes policy would need to be accompanied by 'a firm commitment to achieve full employment, a programme to extend public ownership, to make corporation tax bite and to implement the rest of the alternative economic strategy'.[91] With these commitments made by the Labour government, the trade unions would be more likely to turn their focus away from wage demands and towards 'higher priorities ', since 'to gobble up all the extra resources released by [economic] expansion in a wages scramble would leave nothing for job creation and improvement in public services'.[92]

Brian Sedgemore insisted strongly that the AES would be unworkable without industrial democracy precisely because it was a means to moderate wage demands and increase the saleability of incomes policy to organised labour.[93] As he grappled with the arithmetic of incomes policy, it was clear that his main concern was the acquiescence of trade unions:

> I would hesitate to quantify the figures but a 15% overall increase in wages and salaries on a percentage-plus-differential basis with additions for real productivity increases might be saleable if its introduction were accompanied by a 4-month price freeze, followed by a genuine price and profit control as an earnest of real intent by Government to control inflation and back substantial further tax cuts and/or increases in public expenditure. A medium term strategy with growth of 5% per annum might go a long way to secure union backing for such a policy.[94]

Sedgemore believed that his strong advocacy of incomes policy was controversial among his Labour-left colleagues.[95] Yet the idea that it was legitimate to request wage sacrifices from workers if social services, price controls, etc., were delivered by a Labour government underlay Labour's official pitch to the organised working class in the AES period, and was openly endorsed by leading Labour-left figures. As outlined in Chapter 2, the willingness of union leaders to co-operate with this 'social contract' helped facilitate a major downturn in workers' living standards during the life of the 1974–1979 Labour governments. After 1979, sections of the Labour left were vocal in condemning the reality of the social contract, the fact that sacrifices were demanded from workers while little was delivered to them in return.[96] Yet the theoretical groundwork for such demands had been laid, at least partly, by the Labour left itself. In accepting the legitimacy of incomes policy on principle, AES proponents were perhaps in a weak position to reject any responsibility for the practical reality of the Labour government's wage policies.

All in all, the collaborationist approach to class did not represent a significant divergence from the nation-oriented approach that had characterised Labour's brand of socialist politics since its foundation. This approach was well theorised by Leo Panitch, who argued that Labour's 'predominant ideological orientation' was nation-centred rather than class-centred.[97] Performing an 'integrative' role, Labour sought to obtain compromise between classes in the professed interests of the nation as a whole, seeing itself as a national party not in the sense of leading a hegemonic nation-wide class movement (*à la* Gramsci) but 'in the conventional idealist sense of defining a "national interest" above classes'.[98] Incomes policy was central here, as 'an integrative function without peer', necessitating collective co-operation from workers.[99] While other forms of economic policy requiring working-class co-operation, such as fiscal policy, saw workers consenting largely as single individuals—taxes were collected individually and 'the individual worker [faced] the state atomistically'—the success of incomes policy depended on the compliance of workers as a class, their acceptance that there was 'a community of interests within existing society, that the harmony between classes posited by a national integrative political party does in fact exist'.[100]

The AES of figures like Benn, Holland, Meacher, Hain and Hodgson did not fall outside the national orientation that Panitch had attributed to Labour's brand of socialism. They each pointed to the need for better class collaboration, albeit on terms they believed to be favourable to the working class. They perceived the working class as just one component, in a complex social formation, requiring its legitimate demands to be met just as the legitimate demands of management and business needed to be met. The legitimacy of those demands was to be determined by the needs of society as whole, a society whose economy would continue to be based on capital, market competition and the sale and purchase of labour power. Hence the endorsement of a more 'progressive' incomes policy, for those inevitable moments when the wage demands of labour would conflict with the Labour government's strategy to produce growth by facilitating increased industrial productivity in the interests the nation's prosperity. This is not to state that the main political sympathies of the 'Bennite' left did not lie with the working class, or even that it saw the interests of capital and labour as equal in importance; on the contrary, it believed that capital could be made to better serve labour, as well as the wider 'community'. But its theory did not look beyond the capital–labour relationship, and, as a result, it saw improved collaboration between capital and labour as the only way forward that was both progressive and realistic.

## The Options: (II) Conflict

Not all AES approaches to the problem of the working class emphasised collaboration, however. The analyses of leading theorists from the IWC, the CSE, along with some trade unionists and figures from the CPGB, at times implied a diametrically opposed approach, one which suggested that the strategic aim of workers' control was to intensify the conflict between capital and labour rather than foster greater harmony in British industry. As discussed in Chapter 3, CPGB figures such as Bob Rowthorn described the AES as a strategy to heighten the class struggle, and the policy for working-class representation on company boards was justified as a means to further expose the contradictions inherent in the capitalist system. As the CSE put it in its joint pamphlet with the Labour Co-ordinating Committee, a resolution of the current crisis needed to be achieved 'in a manner which leaves the working class in a stronger position and exposes further contradictions in our system of political economy'.[101] The CPGB's 1977 *British Road to Socialism* also called for industrial democracy in the nationalised industries as part of its self-described revolutionary strategy and opposed workers' participation in the management of private companies as a form of 'disguised class collaboration'.[102]

However, the most prolific and well-known exponents of this understanding of workers' control in the AES period were those in the IWC, and this section will therefore focus on their analyses and arguments. Formed in 1968 after a series of conferences on workers' control beginning in 1964, the IWC was conceived as a forum for left-wing discussion and did not, therefore, advance a single set of positions. Since it is well beyond the scope of this chapter to provide a detailed discussion of the various positions held by what was a diverse and heterogenous organisation, this section will aim to determine the extent to which prominent figures within the IWC diverged from the collaborationist viewpoint discussed above. As Hyman pointed out in a lengthy analysis of the IWC, its most dominant component was a group whose main spokesman was Ken Coates, and which also included Tony Topham and Michael Barratt Brown.[103] This section of the chapter will, therefore, focus on the positions of these three figures, not only because of their prominence within the IWC, but also because their analyses represented perhaps the most determined AES attempt to break with the collaborationist, tripartist approach dominant on the Labour left.

In a 1976 *New Left Review* article, one left-wing critic called the IWC's stance 'a sort of Fabianism of the factory', which merely upheld a theory of 'encroaching control' whereby 'the abuses encountered by the workers in their employment are annihilated one by one'.[104] Indeed, Coates et al.

themselves defined 'workers' control' as distinct from 'workers' management', the latter only feasible in a future socialist society where 'full industrial democracy' had become a realistic possibility.[105] Workers' control was far more modest in relation. It was simply the establishment of a measure of 'control' by workers 'over the hitherto unfettered decisions of the ruling party in industry, namely the employers and their managers'.[106] Moreover, aspects of workers' control already existed in British industry, for example via trade-union preventions of arbitrary dismissals, or shop stewards' informal regulation of the speed of work. In this sense, workers' control was not 'something which is either established or not'—it varied in degree and scope depending on time and place, and industry and occupation.[107] The aim was to increase the influence over company decisions that the trade-union movement to an extent already practiced. Workers' control would be 'a valuable school for self-management', but in itself it represented simply 'the aggressive encroachment of Trade Unions on management powers in a capitalist framework'.[108]

IWC literature nevertheless endorsed workers' control in highly radical terms. Coates et al. upheld the line of the radical socialist Tom Mann, who in the 1920s had demanded the application of "'workers' control until we get complete control".[109] Measures for industrial democracy today, however limited, would be transitory, existing as preparatory steps towards the eventual hegemony of workers in industry. The movement for workers' control would create a situation of 'dual power' in society, in which the agenda of labour would stand as a competing force in a power struggle within industry. This idea was central to the IWC's justification of workers' control in revolutionary terms:

> All concessions won by Labour from capital from the Ten Hour Bill to the latest Health and Safety Bill can be seen as 'making capitalism work'; but, if they increase the knowledge and power of the workers and reduce the arbitrary power of capital, then increasingly capitalism is 'working' on the workers' terms. Such a situation of 'dual power' is we believe inherently unstable and after whatever length of time and fierceness of struggle would have to be resolved in the hegemony of the workers.[110]

The attempt to install a revolutionary justification into industrial democracy was also evident in the IWC's policy to 'open the books'. According to Barratt Brown, to open the books was not 'just a matter of reading hitherto concealed facts and figures', but a starting point for evaluating and interpreting a complex industrial situation in order to determine and fight for 'a policy of advance towards democratic control of industry'.[111] As Coates and Topham put it, the demand for company information was 'a demand for power and democracy'.[112] In his critique of the IWC, Hyman argued that its 'open the books' policy tended to suggest an acceptance of the management's criteria for production. If management could demonstrate, for instance, that a certain ceiling for wages was necessary at the existing level of the firm's productivity, was the wage militancy of that firm's workforce no longer appropriate or legitimate? Perhaps the goal of socialist policy was not to 'open the books but to transcend them', as Hyman put it.[113] While this ambiguity did exist in their accounts, Coates and Topham justified 'opening the books' as a means to expose the class relations which underlay the subjugation of the worker, to unmask the 'essentially *social* nature of production and economy'.[114] Thereby the 'possibility of genuinely communal, democratic planning' would also become revealed; and this planning, by confronting the 'arbitrary powers of the giant companies', would '[intensify] the struggle for workers' control'.[115]

### IWC and Trade-Unionism

The 'new unionism' demanded by Coates et al. also challenged the self-restricted parameters of British trade-unionism and, in particular, its traditional aversion to industrial democracy. The old union leaders had by and large accepted the restriction of union functions to the regulation of wages and working conditions, and the 'managerial prerogative' over 'the process of production, location of industry, investment, expansion, contraction, distribution of product, safety, health, welfare, education, technology, etc.'[116] By adhering to the narrow path of collective bargaining over wages and conditions, the old unionism had helped distort a key aim of the labour movement: the assertion of democratic principles in industry.[117]

In this vein, the IWC theorists warmly welcomed the turn to industrial democracy that sections of British trade-unionism had witnessed since the late 1960s. For Coates et al., the rise of union leaders like Jack Jones and Hugh Scanlon was reason for great optimism. Scanlon authored the first in the long series of IWC pamphlets, in which he called for increased workers' control as part of a strategy for a socialised and democratic economy that would better utilise what was 'probably the most industrially experienced work-force in the world'.[118] Jones, who served as an IWC vice president, saw workers' control as a means for union representatives to limit the 'unilateral authority of management' and involve 'workers through their unions in the decisions which affect their working lives'.[119]

Coates et al. held Jones and Scanlon in high regard; as Hyman argued, their criticism of Jones and Scanlon, when it did occur, was limited in its extent and muted in its tone.[120] Barratt Brown celebrated the fact that industrial democracy was 'central' to the policies of Jones and Scanlon, while Coates and Topham argued that these policies were key to the increased 'democratization of their unions'.[121] When, for example, Coates and Topham criticised Jack Jones's collaborative approach to industrial democracy—such as his view that the reforms 'agreed between the unions and company in the case of the ICI Works Councils' represented an 'entirely positive step'—it was merely with the suggestion that such negotiations would be more fruitful if accompanied by the 'language of "control"' rather than that of 'participation'.[122] Hyman suggested that a reason for the subdued nature of these criticisms was the IWC's core objective of cultivating prominent left-wing leaders like Jones, Scanlon and Tony Benn as central figures within the IWC.[123] However, perhaps a more important reason, as discussed below, was the lack of fundamental *political* divergence between the approaches of Coates et al. and that of the Labour-leftism of Jones, Scanlon and Benn.

### Strategic Ambiguity: Crisis or Stability?

A characteristic feature of Coates et al., and perhaps the main source of their political ambiguity, was their attempt to combine into a single strategy two fundamentally different and conflicting left-wing approaches. In their response to Hyman's criticisms, they argued that:

> Extensions of workers' control from wages and conditions to employment and investment policies are all aspects of that changing balance [of class power]; and while they raise consciousness, they do also have a certain viability before they are sufficiently widespread to provoke a crisis of dual power. The encroachment of workers' control is not regarded by ourselves as a gradualist recipe which can avoid violent resistance at some stage; but this is just because each new encroachment is seen as moving towards a real abrogation of the power of capital.[124]

There were two main ideas being expressed here, which, when combined, represented the theoretical tension in the approach of Coates et al. The first idea was that workers' control would represent a further 'encroachment' into the power of capital, shift the balance of class power, and create a situation of dual power in society, i.e. the condition for a revolutionary crisis. The second idea, meanwhile, was that policies for workers' control could have 'a certain viability' within the existing system, i.e. that they were, at least to an extent, immediately workable policies for industry as it currently stood. Together they formed the view that the establishment of a viable system of workers' control in the capitalist economy could be the foundation from which a revolutionary transition to a socialist economy of workers' self-management could occur.

These were contradictory ideas because they represented conflicting socialist traditions and strategic positions. Whereas the second idea was reformist in character, the first idea took its inspiration from the Marxist notion of transitional demands, associated, in the period of the AES, in particular with Trotskyism. According to Trotsky in the late 1930s, a transitional programme would bridge the gap between the presently non-revolutionary political consciousness of workers and the socialists' demand for the seizure of working-class power—a minimum programme of demands relating to workers' day-to-day concerns (regarding employment, wages, housing, etc.), but one constructed in such a way that the process of workers fighting for it would raise their consciousness of the necessity of the maximum demand for socialism. Crucially, this would occur because the minimum demands would not be able to be met by the capitalist system. In general, there could not be any 'discussion of systematic social reforms and the raising of the masses' living standards', since 'every serious demand of the proletariat and even every serious demand of the petty bourgeoisie inevitably reaches beyond the limits of capitalist property relations and of the bourgeois state'.[125]

As an example of these demands, Trotsky identified the call for a sliding scale of wages, whereby the workers' movement would demand the institution of automatic wage increases to match price increases. Since capital, in a period of economic crisis, would not be in a position to provide such wage increases, it would become increasingly clear that capitalism could not sustain workers' living standards and that socialism stood as the only alternative to workers' further impoverishment. In this sense, therefore, it was precisely the 'unviability' of such demands under capitalism which gave them a revolutionary implication:

Property owners and their lawyers will prove the 'unrealizability' of these demands. Smaller, especially ruined capitalists, in addition will refer to their account ledgers. The workers categorically denounce such conclusions and references... If capitalism is incapable of satisfying the demands inevitably arising from the calamities generated by itself, then let it perish. 'Realizability' or 'unrealizability' is in the given instance a question of the relationship of forces, which can be decided only by the struggle. By means of this struggle, no matter what immediate practical successes may be, the workers will best come to understand the necessity of liquidating capitalist slavery.[126]

The strength of Trotsky's approach was that it appeared to provide a way out of the pitfalls both of reformism and sectarianism, a strategy distinct from the moderate left-wing programme for gradual changes to the existing system, but also from the platforms of the small, 'sterile', self-proclaimed revolutionary groups on the left satisfied with 'a repetition of the same meagre abstractions' while refusing to struggle for 'the elementary interests and needs of the working masses, as they are today'.[127] As a result, aspects of this strategy proved attractive to Coates et al. Coates, who had previously been a leading figure within the section of the British Trotskyist movement associated with the Fourth International,[128] praised Trotsky's understanding 'that the conventional social-democratic and communist view of a disjunction between "maximum" and "minimum" programmes is acutely disruptive of socialist consciousness'.[129] According to Coates, 'Trotsky saw the need for a programme of immediate demands which led out of one social order into another, and about this need he was certainly profoundly right.'[130] At the same time, however, Trotsky's actual programmatic proposals belonged in his own era, and 'Dedication to revolutionary models established during the first five years of the Comintern does not produce the kind of mentality which can meet the challenges of working-class democracy in late capitalist society'.[131]

In essence, Coates's position was that, in the present period, the 'transitional stage' in Trotsky's formulation would need to be extended if the approach of the transitional programme was to be able to provide a strategic basis from which to advance to a revolutionary situation at a point in the future, but also provide a means by which British socialists could address and immerse themselves in the working-class movement as it currently stood. Coates endorsed the American Trotskyist Felix Morrow's argument in the 1940s that capitalism would experience a prolonged period of stability within which socialists would need to focus on pursuing 'maximally democratic demands, effectively extending the notion of "transitional" politics over a relatively longer period, instead of siting them within a convulsive immediate trauma'.[132] This was broadly in line with the strategy put forward in the 1960s by the Belgian Trotskyist Ernest Mandel, a leading theorist of the Fourth International in the post-war period and an acknowledged influence on Coates and his close co-thinkers in the IWC. Mandel believed in the unlikelihood of a capitalist crisis in the 1970s of a similar gravity to that of 1929–1933, and thus called for a strategy of 'structural reforms' that would seek to link workers' day-to-day struggles to a wider, anti-capitalist and socialist platform. In an essay published as an IWC pamphlet, *A Socialist Strategy for Western Europe*, he included demands for workers' control of production and 'opening the books' as key components of this strategy—as 'the only way to avoid giving the strategy of structural reforms a technocratic character and giving it a life in the factories, on the shopfloor and in offices', as well as to '[make] the duality of power a real threat to the survival of capitalism'.[133]

In Coates's case, this idea of an extended period of capitalist stability was an important influence on his own enthusiasm for workers' control, but also his endorsement of Labour-leftism, socialist campaigns within parliament, the initiatives of left-wing trade-union leaders, and, as discussed below, a Labour government social contract. It was this aspect of the IWC position which provided a bridge between the radical pronouncements of the IWC and the reformist and collaborationist politics of Labour-left figures such as Tony Benn. The interpretation of the existing political and economic juncture as unfavourable to 'insurrectionist' politics created theoretical justification for a political strategy for improvements to the existing economic system.

### *Yugoslavia*

Coates and his colleagues' critical endorsement of the Yugoslav model was also relevant here. The industrial system instituted in Yugoslavia after its expulsion from the Cominform in 1948 was regarded favourably by a number of AES proponents of industrial democracy,[134] as strict state-centralisation of the economy had given way (according to its Yugoslav advocates) to a model of commodity production combined with 'self-managing economic organisations' that was believed to offer not only an alternative to the autocratic command systems of the Soviet bloc but also a means towards workers' management and even the 'withering away of the state' itself.[135] The appeal of the Yugoslav model to AES proponents was its apparent demonstration that workers' control could co-exist with the incentives to production provided by a market subjected to social control. As Topham put it in 1963, Yugoslav Communists had 'sought a form of economic organisation which will give them the advantages of both capitalism and socialism'.[136] The Yugoslav system had

> harnessed the acquisitive spirit of the individual worker to the social goal of increased industrial efficiency and has provided a structure which involves the worker in a high degree of democratic control over the decisions which affect the achievement of that efficiency. The Yugoslav worker knows that if he and his fellow workers produce more, they will receive direct material benefit from the increased output of their factory.[137]

The Yugoslav model had seemed to have combined market incentives with workers' control and the social good, and to an extent therefore it could suit those AES socialists who also defined socialism as a socially directed market economy. Coates and Topham did lay the blame for the limitations of Yugoslav socialism directly on the growing influence of its market forces.[138] They also posed the 'power of the market' as something that the socialist society of the future would ultimately need to overcome.[139] Yet they were also aware of the benefits—however short term—that market forces had brought not only to the Tito regime, but also, it seemed, to the Yugoslav working class. The introduction of market relations had 'stimulated both individual and collective effort to raise productivity—the overriding need of the stricken and isolated economy'.[140] The market system had also fostered a measure of social harmony with the peasant farming sector, a collision with which could have resulted from any introduction of 'the drastic methods of a siege economy'.[141] Coates and Topham upheld a vision of a future society without the constraint of the market on the human potential; but their location of the Yugoslav model as a real-life example of workers' self-management seemed to suggest that, in the immediate term at least, the interests of the British working class and those of a British market economy could correspond.

### *The Labour Party and Its Social Contract*

The attempts of Coates et al. to figure out an independent working-class solution to the economic crisis were also confronted by their commitment to the Labour Party and to the prospect of its socialist transformation. Coates rejected Miliband's pessimism about Labour's socialist potential and argued that British socialists lacked a viable alternative to the Labour Party.[142] Barratt Brown made a similar argument in his *From Labourism to Socialism*, which argued that the socialist potential of Labour could not be determined solely by its 'past performance' but mainly by its 'potential for the future'.[143] According to Barratt Brown, Labour's Clause 4 already committed it to socialism formally, and therefore the party's democratisation would enable it to realise its already existing capacity to become a socialist party.[144] Coates et al. were prepared to criticise Labour's past record in the strongest terms. However, as with others on the Labour left, they were not prepared to look beyond Labour, and they believed that revolutionary socialist politics should be devised in a way that was, as Coates put it, 'intelligible and acceptable to Labour Party members'.[145]

In the early 1970s, Coates et al. believed that the Labour Party, with its new left-wing programme and the apparent radicalisation of Labour politicians like Tony Benn, could form a genuinely socialist government in alliance with the workers' movement. This optimistic belief underlay their faith in the legitimacy of working-class co-operation with such a government. This was perhaps most evident in the fact that they, along with others on the Labour left, accepted in principle the legitimacy of a Labour government social contract. As described in Chapter 2, IWC figures such as Jack Jones and Hugh Scanlon were the leading advocates of the social contract within the trade-union movement. As Jones stated in his 1986 autobiography:

> I never doubted the value of the Social Contract, which I saw a major step towards economic equality and better conditions for working people, and used every democratic means to gain the co-operation of fellow trade unionists.[146]

Although Coates et al., as with others on the AES left, upheld price controls as preferable to wage restraint, they did not reject the Labour left's justification of incomes policy—that it could be legitimate, and indeed unavoidable, as long as the required preconditions (price controls, investment, redistribution, etc.) were met by a socialist Labour government. A reason for this was the aforementioned optimism with which they approached the prospect of an incoming Labour government in the early 1970s, as well as the trade unions' role within that government. In 1972, Barratt Brown had argued that the left-wing trade unions

> will not be prepared to accept any form of incomes policy involving restraint on money wage increases, at least until they have seen the evidence of economic growth *and* price control from a government that proposes such a policy.[147]

Barratt Brown's misjudgement here was not simply the product of a naivety regarding the left union leaders, but also an expression of the high level of optimism that existed in the early 1970s about the kinds of political shifts and transformations that could be possible in the years ahead. While 'insurrectionist' strategies were dismissed as unrealistic, it was believed that Labour could defy its origins, traditions and seventy-year-long practices to become, with the help of a left-wing union bureaucracy, a force for revolutionary change in British society. While the reality, as later admitted by Coates,[148] proved very different, the misplaced optimism of those years tended to obscure the serious pitfalls of working-class co-operation with Labour. In *What Went Wrong*, a 1979 multi-author charge sheet against the Wilson-Callaghan government edited by Coates, much blame was placed on the Labour right. Coates also criticised Scanlon's receipt of a life peerage (and state patronage in general), and in another chapter he outlined some of the failures of the Bullock inquiry.[149] In the same book, Barratt Brown discussed the 'unprecedentedly low rate of economic growth' over which the Wilson-Callaghan government had presided,[150] and laid the blame for low incomes on the Labour government's failure to challenge 'capitalist institutions'.[151] The shortcomings of the IWC's own approach—in particular its inability to break decisively from the class-collaborationist politics of Labour-leftism—were not evaluated.

## THE LIMITATIONS OF LABOUR-LEFT CRITICISMS OF WORKERS' CONTROL

The class-collaborationism of industrial democracy did not go wholly uncriticised on the Labour left. An outspoken opponent of the workers' control policy was Arthur Scargill, the left-wing miners' union leader in Yorkshire, and later the leader of the National Union of Miners during the 1984–1985 miners' strike. In line with others on the British left, Scargill envisioned socialism as the nationalisation of the 'commanding heights' of the economy by a Labour government, bolstered by trade-union strength and free collective bargaining. His opposition to workers' control was shaped by these two principles: workers' control would represent a diversion from public ownership, undermine trade-union rights and independence, and thereby 'retard progress towards the ultimate goal of a socialist Britain'.[152]

Scargill criticised workers' control in very strong terms. Workers' control would mean effectively 'the castration of the trade union movement', represent 'a total collaboration as far as the working class is concerned', and 'result in compromise with society as it exists'.[153] Scargill argued that, with the economic and industrial instability and unrest of the 1960s and 1970s, 'industrial democracy appeared as the best method to enlist workers in co-operating with managerial decisions at local level'.[154] The leaders of large companies were 'frequently faced with important decisions about investment in new technology, capital re-equipment and transfer of production', and they sensed that 'if they did involve employees in such decisions, strong trade unions were likely to resist changes that threatened workers' livelihoods and security'.[155] However, although the left-wing supporters of workers' control saw it as a means to build socialist consciousness and wrest power from the capitalist employer, the capital–labour conflict meant that workers' control under capitalism was a contradiction in terms:

> There is a fundamental incompatibility between the employers' need to control the workforce and maximise profits and the workers' desire to secure the highest wages, best conditions, and resist control...[156]

This fundamental incompatibility between the interests of labour and capital, along with the greater relative power of capital over labour in capitalist society, meant that labour-capital co-operation would only advantage the employer. In capitalist society, 'workers on boards of directors inevitably become part of the institutions of the boardroom, in much the same way that labour politicians often become "constitutionalised" in capitalist parliamentary institutions'.[157]

Scargill also pointed to the limitations of the workers' control policy to 'open the books'. He argued that, had miners in 1972 been part of the management of the National Coal Board, they 'would have had before them the statistical data then available and, undoubtedly, the decision would have been taken not to concede a wage increase because the finances were not available...What was required in 1972, and what was eventually decided, was a political decision and not simply an economic decision.'[158] If the account books of the employer were accepted as a legitimate basis for determining the validity of strike action and militant confrontation in general, it was entirely possible for these books to encourage retreat and conformity. In other words, the focus on company accounts risked accepting the terms of the capitalist employer, and, according to Scargill, thereby helped shift focus away from the need for anti-capitalist politics.

### The UCS Work-In

Indeed, this lack of political challenge to the logic of capitalist production was arguably present even in the boldest displays of workers' militancy in this period. The Upper Clyde Shipbuilders' (UCS) work-in in 1971—in which the workers continued production in the face of a Conservative threat to scale down the industry—was a defiant rejection of government policy. In terms of its own alternative, however, the work-in also showed the limitations of a political campaign which could only tie workers' objectives to the interests of the industry in which they worked. In their defence of the UCS workers, IWC figures emphasised the economic viability of the Upper Clyde yards as well as their mismanagement by the employers and the government. According to Coates, there was no basis for the industry's description as a 'lame duck', since its productivity 'had been rising with extraordinary force' until its mismanagement via misguided policies.[159] Tony Benn also stressed the industry's viability: cuts to the industry were 'not an economic decision' and there was 'no shred of economic justification for imperilling 20,000 jobs in a yard which is within months of viability'.[160] The IWC did make an additional case for the Upper Clyde yards, calling for a 'social audit' of the industry as a means to shift its priorities towards 'human' concerns and away from those based on narrow commercial profitability.[161] However, such arguments coexisted with a defence of jobs on the basis of their value to the existing economy.

In the end, the harsh logic of capitalist production prevailed, and British shipbuilding, along with its workforce, continued to decline. An Independent Labour Party (ILP) pamphlet argued that the achievement of the UCS lied 'not in its results but in the utilisation of tactics. The UCS struggle demonstrated for the first time that the workers should, and could, exercise control over the right to work', and therefore provided the impetus that led to later workplace occupations.[162] In reality, however, due to the politics with which it was guided, the success of the UCS work-in depended ultimately on the success of the British shipbuilding industry. The UCS leadership believed that the shipbuilders had a business plan superior to that of Heath's Conservative government, one that would not be based on strike action but on an increased effort by the workforce to ensure the industry's wellbeing. In his famous 'no hooliganism, no vandalism, no bevvying' speech to the UCS workers, the leader of the work-in, the CPGB official Jimmy Reid, sought to reassure the government and the media that workers' discipline would be maintained in the interests of the industry. As Reid's daughter put it after his death in 2011, the significance of the work-in was that it sought to create 'an ethos where workers, management, police and public can work together'[163]—precisely the kind of co-operation Scargill warned against.

### *The Lucas Plan*

The aim to advance an alternative business case for a capitalist enterprise also underpinned the well-known plan put forward by shop stewards at Lucas Aerospace in 1976. In response to the threat of company restructuring and large-scale redundancy, a group of staff at Lucas Aerospace, led by Mike Cooley, a designer at the firm, called for a shift in the firm's production to 'socially useful' goods such as medical equipment and civilian vehicles. The plan argued that redundancies could be avoided if the enterprise employed the skills of the workforce in society's interests. Since about half of the output of Lucas Aerospace supplied military contracts which depended on public funding, as did many of their civilian contracts, the business case of the alternative plan was that 'state support would be better put to developing products that society needed, rather than the state supporting workers through paying redundancy money when they were put out of work'.[164] In an attempt to convince management and the government of its viability, the plan sought to advance a superior financial and managerial model for the future prosperity of Lucas Aerospace. As one academic has outlined:

> The Plan included market analyses and economic argument; proposed employee training that enhanced and broadened skills; and suggested re-organising work into less hierarchical teams that bridged divisions between tacit knowledge on the shop floor and theoretical engineering knowledge in design shops.[165]

In a speech at an IWC conference, Mike Cooley expressed his support for the plan using the radical language of Marxism and 'dual power'. He accepted that some interpretations of workers' control 'could represent a compromise with the system which oppresses us'. In reality, no ruling class 'acquiesces in its own destruction', and therefore 'there is a need ultimately for a Party and for an organisation of the working class which can face up to that power'.[166] The problem, however, was that the necessary level of class consciousness did not currently exist in Britain, hence the value of experiences like that at Lucas Aerospace:

> insofar as workers' control can begin to move towards a dual power situation in industry, the workers begin to flex their own muscles, begin to be conscious of their own great intellect...If through workers' control, they have the opportunity of sensing [their] power, the opportunity of using it in practice, and thereby understanding how parasitic and how irrelevant those are who control our society, to that extent do I believe that workers' control can be important.[167]

The idea was that, by displaying to themselves that they had the capacity to shape the practices and objectives of their workplace, workers could come to understand the irreconcilability of their interests with those of the capitalist economy. Yet it was unclear how this would occur—how a successful restructuring along the lines of the Lucas plan would enhance the independence of labour and intensify the combativity of the workforce, if it was shown that closer co-operation between labour, capital and the state could, however temporarily, prevent redundancy and better serve the apparent interests of society. In addition, the Lucas plan's approach to co-operative production was distinct from that of Marx's, who had endorsed co-operatives within capitalism insofar as they did not seek state aid and were 'the independent creations of the workers and not protégés either of the governments or of the bourgeois'.[168] In contrast, the Lucas plan sought the help of the British Labour government as well as the approval of management.[169] It was therefore difficult not to accept Scargill's judgement that participation along such lines would undermine workers' independence and their consciousness of the incompatibility of interests between capital and labour.

## The 1984–1985 Miners' Strike

Scargill had valid ground, therefore, to criticise workers' control for tying workers' interests to those of British capitalism. However, his adopted strategy for the British coal industry also suffered from this political weakness, and showed the limitations of the principle of free collective bargaining for socialist politics. From the perspective of a socialist strategy for working-class combativity in industry, it was difficult to disagree that free collective bargaining was superior to an industrial democracy which encouraged class collaboration. In itself, however, free collective bargaining was neither a novel nor a specifically left-wing policy, having historically had the right-wing of the trade-union movement as among its keenest proponents.[170] As Minkin has pointed out, the principle of free collective bargaining was 'virtually a closed area of Labour Party policymaking' in the interwar period, so deeply rooted was it as 'a fundamental principle to the majority of affiliated trade unions'.[171] This had changed with the increased state incorporation of the trade-unions during and after the Second World War, which had certainly undermined trade-union independence. However, there was little that was necessarily radical about the principle of free collective bargaining if it did not exist within an overall strategy for socialist transformation.

Throughout the 1984–1985 miners' strike Scargill upheld *Plan for Coal*, the policy statement adopted by the National Coal Board, the NUM and the British government in 1974, promising expansion of the British coal industry in the aftermath of the 1972 miners' strike. Scargill commended the fact that this 'tripartite agreement' had turned Britain's coal industry into 'the most efficient and technologically advanced in the world', and he lamented its abandonment by Thatcher in the early 1980s.[172] Centred around arguments for the coal industry's importance and viability for the British economy, *Plan for Coal*, like the Lucas Plan and the UCS work-in, had presented a business case for output and productivity. This proved to be the dominant NUM position against pit closures. NUM literature against the Thatcher government emphasised the economical nature of British coal. As one NUM document put it, 'few pits are really "uneconomic"' if account was taken of the fact that the Conservatives had 'artificially depressed the market and the price that can be obtained for coal', or the '[huge] cost of dependence on foreign sources, or nuclear power'.[173] Militant trade-unionist demands against pit closures, or for concessions such as a four-day working week and early retirement, co-existed with what was in essence an alternative, NUM case for the viability of miners' continued employment within the existing economic system. Scargill's opposition to what he saw as the class collaboration intrinsic to industrial democracy did not prevent him from calling for a form of class collaboration in defence of the mining industry. The idea that the coal industry should be defended on the basis of good 'economic sense'—i.e. as central to the prosperity of the country—adhered to the nation-oriented logic underlying the AES concept of industrial democracy. In tying the interests of workers to those of the capitalist economy, it legitimised the counter-argument that employment in the mining industry must be based on the requirements of that economy.

A defence of miners' interests centred around arguments about economic viability was unlikely to provide the ideological weaponry required to sustain a movement to defend jobs in an industry experiencing long-term decline in the British capitalist economy.[174] Yet this was precisely the line of argument favoured by the remnants of the AES left during the 1984–1985 strike. According to the CPGB, the miners' victory would 'safeguard a precious resource, Britain's independent energy supply, which will be essential in an expanding industrial future'; coal was a 'precious national asset', and the closures proposed by the NCB's Ian MacGregor would 'spell nothing but economic disaster'.[175] For the Labour Research Department, the 1974 *Plan for Coal* had 'recognised that coal production should be planned for the benefit of the national economy'; coal could produce electricity at only two-thirds of the price of oil, it was 'cheaper and less hazardous than nuclear power stations', and the use of British coal reduced the need to import energy from abroad.[176] Even for Andrew Glyn, the Trotskyist critic of the AES, pit closures could be opposed on the basis of insufficient business justification: 'under present circumstances *there is no economic case whatsoever for pit closure before exhaustion of mineable reserves.*'[177] Through an examination of NCB accounts and a calculation of the likely effect of pit closures on the national economy, Glyn sought to establish the viability of the mining industry for the British economy.

### The Miners' Next Step

This approach to the agency of the working class stood in sharp contrast to that of an earlier tradition within the British labour movement, one which some AES proponents of workers' control sought to claim as an influence on their own approaches: the radical syndicalist current in the early twentieth-century British labour movement. A classic text of that tradition,

*The Miners' Next Step* (*MNS*), a pamphlet published in 1912 by socialist miners and submitted to the executive of what was then the South Wales Miners' Federation, provided inspiration to the workers' control movement re-emerging in the late 1960s. The pamphlet was reprinted in 1964, and a number of left-wing publications in the AES period were named in its honour.[178]

However, the fact that the *MNS* represented a politics fundamentally different from that which dominated the AES was evident throughout its pages. In contrast to the AES's prioritisation of economic viability and productivity, the *MNS* expressed no interest in maintaining the profitability of capital, whether in the short or the long term. Indeed, the employer was 'vulnerable only in one place, his profits!', and effective pressure on the employer thus meant 'methods which tend to reduce profits'.[179] Where AES proponents called for state ownership in industries in crisis, the *MNS* saw nationalisation as an attempt to salvage the profitability of capital, and it defined industrial democracy as the total removal of the employer and the imposition of independent working-class objectives. In addition, where IWC figures like Barratt Brown, Ken Coates and Tony Topham sought to convince trade-union leaders of the virtues of workers' control, the *MNS* was hostile to trade-union bureaucracy and sought to depend on radicalising grassroots action. It described the labour leader as 'compelled to become an autocrat and a foe to democracy', who must 'keep the men in order' to maintain the respect of 'the employers and the "public"', and who 'prevents solidarity' by undermining workers' unity and their loyalty 'not to an individual, or the policy of an individual, but to an interest and a policy which is understood and worked for by all'.[180]

Perhaps the most distinctive, however, was the *MNS*'s categorical rejection of collaboration with the employer. It called for a fighting organisation and emphasised class confrontation as its priority. Top on its list of proposals 'to remedy the present evils' was a call for:

> I. A united industrial organisation, which, recognising the war of interest between workers and employers, is constructed on fighting lines, allowing for a rapid and simultaneous stoppage of wheels throughout the mining industry.[181]

Elsewhere in the pamphlet, opposition to class collaboration was again emphasised first in its list of policies:

I. The old policy of identity of interest between employers and ourselves be abolished, and a policy of open hostility installed.[182]

The successful adoption of the 'irritation strike' depended 'on the men holding clearly the point of view' that their interests and those of the employer 'are necessarily hostile'.[183] Conciliation boards and wages agreements only led workers 'into a morass'; workers' needed an organisation 'constructed to fight rather than negotiate', one 'based on the principle that we can only get what we are strong enough to win and retain'.[184] It was this 'militant aggressive policy'[185] demanded by the *MNS* which set it apart from the official leadership of the 1984–1985 miners' strike, as well as the ideas of the AES proponents of industrial democracy and workers' control.

## CONCLUSION

A product of the turbulent years surrounding the First World War—a period which saw workers' uprisings across Europe, and in which the Labourist, nation-oriented ideas of class co-operation had a weaker influence among the militant layers of the British working class—*The Miners' Next Step* was a trade-unionist manifesto for class war. Whatever its syndicalist limitations, its foremost emphasis was on the irreconcilability of the interests of labour and capital; it envisaged a social organisation of economic production on the terms of the working class; and it regarded the intensification of workers' collective hostility to the employer as the only means by which this future society could be fought for and won.

Products of yet another period of capitalist instability and intensifying class conflict, AES approaches to the working class were led by very different ideas. In comparison to the revolutionary ambition of their predecessors, AES theories for industrial democracy, even at their most radical, granted a limited agency to British workers. AES ideas were marked by the orientation to class co-operation that had, as argued in the previous chapter, dominated British leftism since the Second World War. Unlike the earlier syndicalist radicals in British trade-unionism, the AES socialists' radicalism regarding the role of the working class was tempered, to one extent or another, by their accompanying—and often overriding—commitment to the immediate regeneration of the British economy. The strength of this commitment undermined any express determination to foster an independent and revolutionary strategy for working-class emancipation, created theoretical inconsistencies, and tied the interests of the working class, at least in the immediate term, to those of British capitalism.

However, as pointed out in the introduction to this chapter, the very fact that the working class was discussed in these terms by AES figures itself signalled a political environment in many ways unrecognisable from that which came to supersede it from the late 1980s to the present period. The working class was a central factor in each political consideration of the AES, whether state planning of the economy, import controls or, of course, industrial democracy. In a sense, the AES occurred at a turning point in British political history, representing the final attempt of British left-wingers to rest their theories and policies upon a conception of the working class as an organised collective force in society and politics. The real-life retreat and disorganisation of this collective force gave way to its demise as a political phenomenon, and a very different politics of the left emerged by the twenty-first century. The next chapter will discuss some of these politics, and explore their relationship with the AES and its defeat and decline.

## NOTES

1. For a discussion of some of the trends related to this development, see Furedi, *Politics of Fear*, pp. 142–58. 'Vulnerable' appears to be key among Labour leader Jeremy Corbyn's preferred adjectives for working-class people. As he told the TUC after his election as Labour leader in 2015: 'The [Conservative] Welfare Reform Bill is…all about building on the cuts they have already made, making the lives of the most vulnerable and poorest people in our society even worse…I simply ask the question: what kind of a society are we living in where we deliberately put regulations through knowing what the effects are going to be on very poor and very vulnerable people who end up committing suicide?' (Corbyn, 'Speech to the TUC').
2. See, for example, Barratt Brown, *Labour and Sterling*, p. 8; Warren and Prior, *Advanced Capitalism and Backward Socialism*, p. 7.
3. Williamson, 'The Bullock Report on Industrial Democracy'.
4. Radice, *Working Power*, p. 1.
5. Cited in Williamson, 'The Bullock Report on Industrial Democracy', p. 124.
6. John Nott, House of Commons Debate, *Hansard*, 26 January 1977, vol. 924, cc. 1492–512. For a similar view, see Conservative Trade Unionists, *Participation—A New Way Ahead*, pp. 3, 8.
7. Dostaler, *Keynes and His Battles*, p. 114; Liberal Industrial Inquiry, *Britain's Industrial Future*, p. 227.

8. Liberal Party, *The Nation's Task*; Liberal Party Research and Information Department, 'Employee Participation', p. 20.
9. See, for example, *What a Life!* the Liberal Party's 1970 general-election manifesto.
10. Benn, 'The Industrial Context', p. 72.
11. Holland, *The Socialist Challenge*, p. 255.
12. London CSE Group and the LCC, *The Alternative Economic Strategy*, p. 62.
13. Thompson, *The Left in the Wilderness*, p. 51.
14. Report of the Royal Commission on Trade Unions and Employers' Associations 1965–1968 ('Donovan Report'), p. 275.
15. Ibid., p. 261.
16. TUC evidence to the Royal Commission on Trade Unions and Employers' Associations, p. 79.
17. British Institute of Management, *Industrial Democracy*, pp. 6, 9.
18. Ibid., pp. 7–8.
19. Ibid.
20. Sir Peter Runge cited in Cliff, *The Employers' Offensive*.
21. Amalgamated Engineering and Foundry Workers' Union, 'Industrial Democracy in Great Britain', p. 5.
22. Labour Party, *Let Us Win Through Together*. Influenced by the industrial relations academic Hugh Clegg, Labour revisionists like Crosland and Douglas Jay also 'avoided what they saw as the trap of workers' control by redefining the meaning of "industrial democracy" in such a way as to allow for the continuation of the respective traditional functions of trade unions and management' (Ellison, *Egalitarian Thought and Labour Politics*, p. 100).
23. White, *Workers' Control?* pp. 25–6.
24. Ibid. See also, Boyd, *Is Industrial Democracy Compatible with Efficiency?* p. 3.
25. Singleton and Topham, *Workers' Control in Yugoslavia*, p. 27.
26. Labour Party, *Let Us Work Together*.
27. Report of the Committee of Inquiry on Industrial Democracy ('Bullock Report'), p. v.
28. TUC, *Industrial Democracy*, p. 7.
29. Report of the Committee of Inquiry on Industrial Democracy ('Bullock Report'), p. 23.
30. Miliband, 'A State of De-subordination', p. 402.
31. Industrial Participation Association, *Works Councils, Employee Directors, Supervisory Boards*, p. 4.
32. Ibid.
33. British Institute of Management, *Employee Participation*, pp. 9–10.
34. Industrial Relations Services, *Special Supplement: The Bullock Report*, p. 13.

35. Williamson, 'The Bullock Report on Industrial Democracy'.
36. Confederation of British Industry, *In Place of Bullock*, p. 29.
37. Confederation of British Industry, *Guidelines for Action on Employee Involvement*, pp. 3–4.
38. City Company Law Committee, *A Reply to Bullock*, p. 23.
39. Ibid., p. 23.
40. Chiplin et al., *Can Workers Manage?* p. 8.
41. British Institute of Management, *Industrial Democracy*, p. 7.
42. Ibid., p. 9. Its italics.
43. Hain, *The Democratic Alternative*, p. 60.
44. Ibid.
45. Ibid., p. 61.
46. Ibid., p. 67.
47. Meacher, *Socialism with a Human Face*, pp. 179–80.
48. Ibid., p. 189.
49. Ibid., p. 201.
50. Hodgson, *The Democratic Economy*, p. 130.
51. Ibid., p. 129.
52. Ibid., p. 135.
53. Ibid.
54. Ibid., pp. 144, 138.
55. Ibid., p. 144.
56. Ibid., p. 145.
57. Ibid.
58. Ibid., p. 151.
59. Cited in Warde, *Consensus and Beyond*, p. 74.
60. Benn, *The New Politics*, p. 16.
61. Ibid., pp. 16–17.
62. Ibid., p. 17.
63. Ibid.
64. Ibid.
65. Ibid., p. 18.
66. Benn, *Industrial Democracy*, p. 1.
67. Ibid.
68. Ibid., p. 8.
69. Cited in Foote, *The Labour Party's Political Thought*, p. 329.
70. *Out of Crisis*, p. 136.
71. Ibid.
72. Ibid.
73. Ibid.
74. Holland, *The Socialist Challenge*, p. 255.
75. Ibid., p. 294.
76. Ibid., p. 274.

77. Ibid.
78. Ibid., p. 275.
79. Ibid.
80. Holland, *Strategy for Socialism*, p. 72.
81. Holland, *The Socialist Challenge*, p. 271.
82. Llorente, 'Marx's Concept of "Universal Class"'.
83. Holland, *The Socialist Challenge*, pp. 284–5.
84. Ibid., p. 285.
85. Ibid., p. 276.
86. Ibid.
87. Hain, *The Democratic Alternative*, p. 73.
88. Holland, *The Socialist Challenge*, p. 173.
89. Holland, *Strategy for Socialism*, pp. 80–1.
90. Hodgson, *Labour at the Crossroads*, p. 213.
91. Hain, *The Democratic Alternative*, p. 71.
92. Ibid.
93. Sedgemore, *The How and Why of Socialism*, pp. 26–7.
94. Ibid., pp. 39–40.
95. Ibid., p. 31.
96. See Coates, 'What Went Wrong?'.
97. Panitch, *Working-Class Politics in Crisis*, p. 14. See also Tufekci, '"Politics of Containment"'.
98. Panitch, *Working-Class Politics in Crisis*, p. 14.
99. Panitch, *Social Democracy and Industrial Militancy*, p. 3.
100. Ibid.
101. London CSE Group and the LCC, *The Alternative Economic Strategy*, p. 77.
102. Communist Party of Great Britain, *The British Road to Socialism*, 1977. See also Ramelson, *Bury the Social Contract*, p. 32.
103. Hyman, 'Workers' Control and Revolutionary Theory', p. 242.
104. Monds, 'Workers Control and the Historians', pp. 83–4.
105. Coates and Topham, *The New Unionism*, p. 55. See also Coates, 'Democracy and Workers' Control', p. 293.
106. Coates and Topham, *The New Unionism*, p. 55.
107. Ibid.
108. Coates, 'Democracy and Workers' Control', p. 293.
109. See Barratt Brown, *From Labourism to Socialism*, p. 186.
110. Barratt Brown et al., 'Workers' Control Versus "Revolutionary" Theory', p. 303. See also Coates and Topham, 'Participation or Control?'.
111. Barratt Brown, *Opening the Books*, p. 2.
112. Coates and Topham, *The New Unionism*, p. 108.
113. Hyman, 'Workers' Control and Revolutionary Theory', p. 247.
114. Coates and Topham, *The New Unionism*, p. 108.

115. Ibid.
116. Ibid., p. 44.
117. Ibid., p. 45.
118. Scanlon, *The Way Forward for Workers' Control*.
119. Cited in Barratt Brown, *From Labourism to Socialism*, p. 180.
120. Hyman, 'Workers' Control and Revolutionary Theory', p. 264.
121. Barratt Brown, *From Labourism to Socialism*, p. 183; Coates and Topham, *The New Unionism*, p. 202.
122. Coates and Topham, *The New Unionism*, p. 202.
123. Hyman, 'Workers' Control and Revolutionary Theory', p. 265.
124. Barratt Brown et al., 'Workers' Control Versus "Revolutionary" Theory", p. 304.
125. Trotsky, *The Death Agony of Capitalism*.
126. Ibid.
127. Ibid.
128. Palmer, 'Ken Coates Obituary'.
129. Coates, 'Socialists and the Labour Party', pp. 161–2.
130. Ibid., p. 162.
131. Ibid., p. 163.
132. Ibid., p. 162. See also Morrow, *The First Phase of the Coming European Revolution*.
133. Mandel, *A Socialist Strategy for Western Europe*, pp. 9–10.
134. Including Stuart Holland. See his *The Socialist Challenge*, pp. 264–6, for a critical yet partly positive appraisal.
135. See Pasic et al., *Workers' Management in Yugoslavia*. Tito, the Yugoslav leader, had announced as early as 1950 that his policies for the 'decentralisation of the state administration, especially in the economy' would begin the process of the withering away of the Yugoslav state (Tito, *Workers Manage Factories in Yugoslavia*, pp. 23–4).
136. Singleton and Topham, *Workers' Control in Yugoslavia*, p. 26.
137. Ibid., p. 25.
138. Coates and Topham, *The New Unionism*, pp. 226–7.
139. Ibid., p. 234.
140. Ibid., p. 225.
141. Ibid.
142. Coates, 'Socialists and the Labour Party'.
143. Barratt Brown, *From Labourism to Socialism*, p. 239.
144. Ibid.
145. Coates, 'Socialists and the Labour Party', p. 175.
146. Cited in Medhurst, *That Option No Longer Exists*, p. 57.
147. Barratt Brown, *From Labourism to Socialism*, p. 206.
148. See Coates, 'Whatever Happened to Industrial Democracy?', pp. 124–36.
149. Coates, 'What Went Wrong?' and 'Whatever Happened to Industrial Democracy?'.

150. Barratt Brown, 'The Growth and Distribution of Income and Wealth', p. 34.
151. Ibid., p. 73.
152. Scargill, *A Debate on Workers Control*, p. 4.
153. Ibid.
154. Scargill and Kahn, *The Myth of Workers' Control*, p. 3.
155. Ibid.
156. Ibid., pp. 20–1.
157. Ibid., p. 21.
158. Scargill, in *The Harrogate Debate*, p. 11.
159. Eaton et al., *UCS: Workers' Control*, p. 4.
160. Cited in Eaton et al., *UCS: Workers' Control*, p. 12.
161. See Barratt Brown, *UCS: The Social Audit*; Coates and Topham, *The New Unionism*, pp. 6–7.
162. Graham, *The Workers' Next Step*, p. 6.
163. Smith, 'The Truth Behind That Speech'.
164. Salisbury, 'Story of the Lucas Plan'.
165. Smith, 'The Lucas Plan'.
166. Cooley, *A Debate on Workers Control*, p. 3.
167. Ibid.
168. Marx, *Critique of the Gotha Programme*.
169. Salisbury, 'Story of the Lucas Plan'.
170. Minkin, *The Contentious Alliance*, p. 13.
171. Ibid., pp. 12–13.
172. Scargill, 'In His Own Words', p. 16.
173. SERTUC and Kent NUM, *Winning the Argument: Speaker's Notes*.
174. See Richards, *The Miners' Next Step*, for a polemical treatment of this argument.
175. Communist Party of Great Britain, *Solidarity with the Miners*, pp. 1–2.
176. Labour Research Department, *The Miners' Case*, London: LRD Publications Ltd., p. 2.
177. Glyn, *The Economic Case Against Pit Closures*, Yorkshire: NUM, p. 1. His italics.
178. Graham, *The Workers' Next Step*; A Group of Sheffield Steel Workers, *Steel Workers Next Step*; Hull and London Port Workers' Control Groups, *The Dockers' Next Step*.
179. Unofficial Reform Committee, *The Miners' Next Step*, p. 27.
180. Ibid., p. 14.
181. Ibid., p. 17.
182. Ibid., p. 24.
183. Ibid., p. 27.
184. Ibid., pp. 19–20.
185. Ibid., p. 26.

# CHAPTER 7

# Conclusion: The AES, New Times and the Death of British Socialism

## Introduction

As discussed in Chapter 1, the academic literature has tended to emphasise the radicalism of the Alternative Economic Strategy (AES). This has
involved depicting the AES period as one in which left-wing ideas flour-
ished in Labour's ranks, leading the party to adopt radical programmes
and manifestos between 1973 and 1983. The suggestion has been that, in
between 1950s revisionism and the 'modernisations' of Kinnock and Blair,
the AES stands out as a markedly radical strategy in Labour's post-Second
World War history.

This chapter will discuss the AES in the context of the left-wing politics
that succeeded it and consider the extent to which the AES differed from
but also represented a bridge towards the shift that took place in British
left-wing politics in the 1980s onwards. The first part of the chapter will
attempt to place the decline of the AES within the context of change in the
late 1970s and early 1980s. The second part will discuss some of the left-
wing challenges to the AES in the 1980s. The chapter then will consider the
relationship between the AES and the 'New Times' ideas that influenced the
rise of New Labour in the 1990s, particularly with respect to the questions
of economic strategy, the nation state and the working class.

© The Author(s) 2020                                                    175
B. Tufekci, *The Socialist Ideas of the British
Left's Alternative Economic Strategy*,
https://doi.org/10.1007/978-3-030-34998-1_7

## A NEW POLITICAL CLIMATE

By the end of the 1970s, state policy confronted pressures against tripartist solutions to industrial conflict. With the rise of monetarism, Keynesian policy also appeared to stand rejected: as Thompson states, by the mid-1970s Keynesianism had fallen victim to 'the combined pressures of a sterling crisis, the International Monetary Fund (IMF) and the US Federal Reserve and was jettisoned by many of its erstwhile supporters within the Labour Party'.[1] The apparent discrediting of Keynesianism occurred within the lifetime of a Labour government closely identified with a variant of Keynesian strategy promising closer co-operation with the unions to secure wage restraint for economic growth and inflation control. As Panitch and Leys point out, in 1974 Labour

> had once again come to office with the belief that its main contribution to managing the economy lay in being better able *to secure the moderation of the unions through incomes policy*. The monetarists' message was clear – this whole perspective was passé; at best irrelevant, at worst counterproductive, to the real challenge of public policy, which was *to win the confidence of the financial markets through monetary policy*.[2]

This shift from tripartist Keynesianism was problematic especially for Labour because, as David Coates argues, the entire basis of its post-war strategy had been 'its mobilisation of a coalition of interests between organised labour and private capital behind a common commitment to growth and employment'.[3] That strategy had now come unstuck; and the Conservatives, with a far less entrenched attachment to the post-war consensus, readily took advantage, replacing Heath with a Thatcher leadership standing for a radical break with tripartism. Callaghan's 'that option no longer exists' speech at the 1976 Labour conference, in which he decried the inflationary consequences of state spending, marked a retreat from Keynesian state policy. However, the Labour government in the late 1970s continued to resort to the corporatist components of that policy:

> Submerged in the daily pressures of government, and with their own credibility at stake, Labour ministers could only appeal again and again to the trade unions for restraint; and were unable to see beyond trade union power to the more basic shifts in the capitalist world order which were rendering their political project anachronistic.[4]

A crucial turning point, as mentioned in Chapter 2, was the 'winter of discontent' of 1978–1979, which appeared to demonstrate beyond much doubt that Labour's approach could neither foster industrial peace, solve the economic crisis nor raise workers' living standards. The strikes of that winter helped bring into power a right-wing government that was, in the eyes of the left, seeking to destroy the very foundations of post-war social democracy: as Hay argues, 'Thatcherism as a state project, though conceived long before, was born in the context of crisis during the winter of discontent'.[5] For many on the left, a powerful and new type of right-wing ideology had emerged, fundamentally reconfiguring politics and necessitating a fundamentally adjusted type of progressive, left-wing initiative. More and more left-wing figures began to see in the AES precisely the kind of left-wing approach that was now discredited and from which Labour urgently needed to advance beyond.

The AES differed from the left-wing politics that succeeded it by its emphasis on the working class, its attempt to 're-class' Labour, at a time when, as argued in chapter two, it had become imperative that Labour strengthen its links with organised labour after the Wilson government of the 1960s. By the late 1970s, however, and in particular after 1983, there was a very different mood among sections of the left, and a different response to the problem of Labour's declining working-class base: the momentum was now with those who sought to 'de-class' Labour, to again decrease its proximity to class politics. The backdrop to this was the growing weakness of organised labour, along with the profound change that had taken place in state policy towards the labour movement. In the early 1970s, the Heath government's attempts to reverse the growing self-confidence of organised labour via policies of confrontation had led to its defeat by union power and to Labour's election on a platform pledging control of industrial unrest via union-government co-operation. These political conditions encouraged the growth of pro-worker ideas within the left in and around Labour, creating political space for positions with emphases on the working class and, at times, even class struggle.

However, a version of the Labour strategy which had brought the party into government in 1974, was decisively rejected at the 1983 general election. Indeed, in the early 1980s the Labour left was already in the midst of its long-term decline. The brief post-1979 advance of the Labour left ended in 1981: Benn was defeated in the deputy-leadership election, the left's majority in the National Executive Committee (NEC) was reversed, and the left lost its treasurership of the party.[6] But it was Labour's electoral devastation in 1983—which saw significant losses of support from the working class, particularly skilled and semi-skilled workers[7]—which appeared to signal the final end of Labour's ability to sell tripartist policies to the electorate. Labour's 1983 manifesto continued to stress partnership with the unions 'to rebuild our country', without which 'all else will fail'.[8] But state policy had moved on from corporatist solutions to class conflict. Whatever the disunity and mismanagement that appeared to plague Labour's 1983 election campaign, it was the conclusion of that prior era that reduced the political purchase of the corporatist solutions to which Labour had still clung. Labour's stark failure to fulfil its pledge to solve industrial conflict in favour of workers via closer union-government co-operation—among its core pledges to the electorate throughout the AES period—dented its credibility and produced a large exodus of support from the party.

A key feature of this transformation was the changed role of organised labour. As Chapter 2 discussed, in post-war Britain the unions had acquired a degree of importance as respectable institutions not only for workplace representation but also for the stable government of British society. By the 1980s, that respectability and importance had been heavily eroded, which fundamentally altered the political value of Labour's union alliance. Whereas, in 1974, Labour could still plausibly base its legitimacy on its ability to 'work with the unions', in May 1979 it faced a very different situation. As Thorpe puts it, 'the years 1964 and 1979 seem poles apart...[The] link with the trade unions, which had served Labour well at various points in the past...now appeared to be a millstone around the party's neck.'[9]

This helped to further discredit the Labour left, whose politics were closely associated with Labour's union alliance in the 1970s. By the 1980s, with a Labour government brought down by its own social base in 1979, and with Labour's evident failure to implement the AES, left-wing disquiet with the Labour-left policies and tendencies of the 1970s intensified, as the optimism of the early 1970s left gave way to calls for an admission of failure and a political 'modernisation'. Central to this change would be Labour's break from what became called 'class politics'.

## THE 'NEW REVISIONISM' VERSUS 'CLASS POLITICS'

Labour's policy changes under Neil Kinnock are well-known.[10] Kinnock's first general-election manifesto in 1987 removed the AES's signature commitment to a fundamental shift in the balance of power and wealth in favour of the working class. After the party's third successive general-election defeat that year, Kinnock oversaw a 'policy review' which removed key planks of the 1987 manifesto that had still tied Labour to its former left-wing positions: reversal of Conservative privatisation, repeal of Thatcher's anti-union laws, and unilateral nuclear disarmament.[11] A commitment to co-operation with the European Community (EC)—already present in the 1987 manifesto but mentioned only once—was emphasised numerously in the 1992 manifesto, regarding a range of issues from cutting unemployment and protecting consumers, to racial equality, environmental security and peace in the Middle East.[12] Along with this policy 'modernisation', there was a 'modernisation' of Labour's party organisation, as it became a 'more centralised and disciplined party, with power firmly located within its inner parliamentary circle'.[13] In addition, this period saw the growth of Labour's preoccupation with media relations and 'spin doctoring',[14] as the party's newly prominent media strategists treated the media 'as the arbiters of what it was sensible for the party to advocate, in a way that even the National Executive members were not'.[15] These changes gained added force under Blair's leadership after 1994, as Labour distanced itself yet further from its past as a mass organisation, and, as discussed below, from its former association with nationalisation, the nation state and the trade unions.

In important ways, dominant centre-left ideas in the 1990s had their intellectual roots in the left-wing debates of the 1980s, in the reappraisals of the old Labour-left politics to which the AES was seen as tied. This section will summarise some of these early debates, focusing particularly on figures associated with the Communist Party of Great Britain (CPGB) magazine *Marxism Today*, which, once a proponent of the AES, was a key intellectual arena for left criticism of 'old left' politics in the 1980s. In the early 1980s it had published articles advancing the pro-AES positions of the CPGB as informed by its party programme *The British Road to Socialism*.[16] However, individuals associated with the magazine voiced implicit criticisms of the AES as early as the late 1970s. In a 1986 edition of *Marxism Today*, Sam Aaronovitch, a former proponent of the strategy, put forward what were by now common objections to the AES left: its attachment to state control of the economy; its desire to '[escape] from the pressures of the world capitalist economy'; and its confinement within 'the traditions of a male dominated [labour] movement'.[17] In their place was a call for a modernised approach with new 'moral and human values', without 'the "grandeur" and ambition of the AES in its proposals for economic planning and large-scale extensions of public ownership', and with 'a positive project for international economic relations', particularly within the European Economic Community (EEC).[18] These notions became central to the left's new approach by the 1990s.

Thatcher's dominance of the 1980s undoubtedly gave added impetus to the left-wing reappraisals, which gradually led Labour to its 'modernisation' under Kinnock, the extent of which, according to Bob Rowthorn in 1989, would not have been possible 'without the trauma of Thatcherism'.[19] However, the debates launched by the seminal articles of Eric Hobsbawm and Stuart Hall—respectively 'The Forward March of Labour Halted?' and 'The Great Moving Right Show'—began before Thatcher's election, at a time of growing left-wing concern not with a Conservative government but with the failures of Labour. Sections of the left responded to these failures by continuing to uphold the AES and demanding Labour's greater democratisation so that, the next time, the strategy's implementation would not be thwarted by a right-wing party leadership. Hobsbawm and Hall led a different response within the British left. Its underlying message, particularly after the 1979 Conservative victory, was that the left urgently needed a change of direction to be able to viably challenge what, by 1987, Hobsbawm was calling 'by far the most dangerous and disastrous [government] in twentieth-century British history'.[20] For this left-wing section, the problem was not so much the Labour government's reluctance to implement Labour-left policies, but those policies themselves. A specific focus for this section was what it saw as the Labour left's outdated attachment to a certain interpretation of 'class politics'.

In 1985, Ralph Miliband called this vein of left-wing reappraisal the 'new revisionism', succeeding that of Gaitskell and Crosland in the 1950s.[21] For Ellen Meiksins Wood, another left-wing critic, it represented a 'New "True" Socialism', based on Marx and Engels' label for a left-wing idealism that saw socialism as expressing not 'the needs of a particular class and a particular time' but as 'a question of the "most reasonable" social order'.[22] For the authors of *Class Politics*, meanwhile, a pro-AES pamphlet by figures in the CPGB opposed to its Eurocommunist faction around *Marxism Today*, this 'newer left' was a modern type of Fabianism, with 'remarkable similarities' to that current of anti-Marxist socialism that had emerged at the turn of the twentieth century, with its hostility to the labour movement and its 'unprincipled search for alliances'.[23]

These critiques each laid special emphasis on what they saw as a growing left-wing abandonment of class. As Miliband put it,

> 'Class politics' has become the shorthand for much which the new revisionism most strongly repudiates: above all, it has come to stand for the insistence on the 'primacy' of organized labour in the challenge to capitalist power and the task of creating a radically different social order.[24]

For the authors of *Class Politics*, the newer left's shift from class was at the root of its flawed perspectives; each of its propositions was thus 'partial and one-sided', and its abandonment of class politics rendered the 'terrain of debate' itself unacceptable to Marxists.[25] Similarly, Wood argued that class was central to the coherence of the socialist project, and key to its being grounded in the material world of historical development.[26] As a result, no revised socialism could 'have the same force without a similarly coherent and organic conception of ends, means, social processes, and historical possibilities'.[27]

Class was indeed central to this 'new revisionism'. Two key texts in this broad current—Hobsbawm's aforementioned article and André Gorz's book *Farewell to the Working Class*—each placed, as their titles suggested, a decline of the working class at the core of their analyses. For Gorz, workers were being replaced by a 'post-industrial neo-proletariat' distinct from the proletariat of Marxism. Resembling twenty-first century notions of a growing 'precariat'—and arguably with a somewhat romantic view of past labour stability[28]—he argued that the neo-proletariat lacked 'job security or definite class identity': the only certainty it felt was that it did not belong to a class, and certainly not to the working class, since its labour was not a basis for a collective workplace identity.[29] Unlike the proletariat of Marxism, the neo-proletariat was not a 'social subject': it had 'no transcendent unity or mission, and hence no overall conception of history and society'.[30]

Gorz was optimistic about this fragmentation of workforce identity and the neo-proletariat's non-subjectivity. Combining ideas of diversity, individual autonomy and a green promotion of small-scale production, he saw neo-proletarians as 'constantly changing individuals' aiming for individual self-empowerment by 'disengaging from the market rationality of productivism'.[31] The old proletariat was now a declining and conservative force:

its work was the source of its self-definition and self-realisation, and so it could have no interest in abolishing work in favour of automation. This was the neo-proletarians' objective, to abolish what could 'never be a source of personal fulfilment or the centre of their lives'.[32] Thus Gorz called for a 'dual' society upholding both the general interest and diversity and individual autonomy, the latter via apparently non-market 'autonomous activities', and the former through 'heteronomous, wage-based social labour'.[33] His proposals were partly motivated, therefore, by his opposition to an oppressive 'compulsion to seek a social identity',[34] his aversion to the old left-wing objective to establish a collective social subject for its politics. As discussed below, this opposition to old-left emphases on class commonality was, by the 1990s, integral to the left's view that the growth of 'diversity' in lifestyle and identity had rendered class politics largely obsolete.

Gorz's claim that the working class had become a conservative minority was perhaps at the extreme end of the 'new revisionism'. However, his position belonged to a wider left-wing trend to demote the political significance of the working class and thereby redefine socialist strategy. A key text in this regard, Laclau and Mouffe's 'post-Marxist' *Hegemony and Socialist Strategy*, directed its argument against the notion of a class-based subjectivity. Left-wing politics could exist as a 'discourse of radical democracy' but 'no longer [as] the discourse of the universal', i.e. the 'classic discourse of socialism'.[35] Class-based socialist politics, along with the notion of objectively determined class interests or 'discourses', had been eradicated and 'replaced by a polyphony of voices' constructing their own 'irreducible discursive [identities]'.[36] As they wrote in *Marxism Today*, there were now 'new political subjects – women, national, racial and sexual minorities, anti-nuclear and anti-institutional movements etc'.[37] This final 'etc', as Heartfield points out in his discussion of the 'new social movements', was a common habit of their intellectual proponents. Rather than simply a matter of grammatical convenience, it expressed a certain ambiguity as to precisely who would constitute the new radical agency, appearing as 'the endless sequence that can always be expanded by the addition of another forgotten or excluded social movement'.[38]

Laclau and Mouffe presented Marxism as flawed from the beginning: from Marx to Gramsci, it contained elements of class reductionism which prevented its realisation as a 'radical democratic' project. This differed somewhat from Hobsbawm, who, as Pimlott argues, adopted the rhetoric of 'realistic Marxism' against class politics.[39] For Hobsbawm, the British working-class had undergone sociological, political and cultural changes that had undermined its class consciousness, increased its sectionalism and reduced its political cohesion. The latter was key to Hobsbawm's analysis, which, as Callinicos pointed out, identified 'the fate of the [British] working class with the electoral fortunes' of Labour.[40] For Hobsbawm, 'the political expression of class consciousness' was 'in practice, support for the Labour Party', and the decline of this consciousness necessitated a new direction for the party of British workers.[41] Although his article did not mention the AES, it heralded his later endorsement of Labour's 'modernisation' away from that strategy's class emphases. Famously called Kinnock's 'favourite Marxist',[42] Hobsbawm supported Kinnock against the 'hard left' in Labour's 1983 leadership election, and 'naturally welcomed [his victory] with enthusiasm'.[43] Claims that he was 'Kinnock's guru' were 'baseless', Hobsbawm argued in 1989, since Kinnock did not need have 'read Hobsbawm in order to talk common sense about the Labour Party'.[44]

However, as with Kinnock, Hobsbawm's political focus in the 1980s was on the politics needed for Labour's modernisation. Although his arguments often appeared, as Wood suggests, to stand 'in the tradition of the old Communist Popular Front strategies'[45]—the call for cross-class alliance to defeat the reactionary enemy, upon which the Communists' position would be strengthened—Hobsbawm's main preoccupation was not with the future of the CPGB but of Labour. In addition, though he refused to explicitly deny the centrality of workers for socialist strategy,[46] he envisaged a future in which Labour had decreased its identification with the labour movement. Labour's future depended on 'men and women, blue collar, white collar, no collar, ranging from zero CSE to PhD', and people who remember the date the Beatles disbanded but 'not the date of the Saltley pickets'.[47] Labour's politics needed to make sense to these broad strata—'in their own terms'.[48]

As an example of this model for cross-class appeal, Hobsbawm pointed to the Italian Communist Party (PCI), the pioneer of the Eurocommunist centrism to which he and *Marxism Today* were seen to belong. The PCI had known not only how to maintain its working-class base but also to 'extend its support to new social strata and groups, in new conditions'.[49] Under PCI administration, the party's stronghold of central Italy had become 'probably the spearhead of Italy's economic development'—the kind of area which, had it been non-Communist, Thatcher's Conservatives would point to as a model of 'a go-ahead economy'.[50] The PCI had increased its support by showing that 'the left can have a policy for this kind of development':

> In Bologna and Florence even businessmen would be worried if the Christian
> Democrats took over: for one thing, because they would be strikingly more
> inefficient and corrupt.[51]

The implication was that Labour had failed to convince the public that it could be a similar force for economic modernisation, thus giving credibility to Thatcher's right-wing politics of modernisation. This idea was central to the reappraisals of the left-wing milieu Hobsbawm represented.

Perhaps the most insightful of this milieu's analyses was provided by Stuart Hall, whose ideas on 'Thatcherism' were integral to *Marxism Today*'s approach in the 1980s. For Hall, the rise of 'Thatcherism' was related principally to contradictions in the relationship between British workers and British social democracy. To win elections in the 1960s and 1970s, Hall argued, Labour had to emphasise its role as the unions' political representative in its claim to be 'the natural party of the crisis'. In government, however, Labour had to win support from capital, since its solutions to crisis were framed within the limits of British capitalism. To do so, Labour had to employ its links with workers 'not to advance but to *discipline* the class' and its unions.[52] But it could only do this by forming an 'alternative articulation', one which emphasised 'the people' or 'the national interest'. The latter was 'the principal ideological form in which a succession of defeats [had] been imposed on the working class' by Labour in power, as it stood '"on the side of the nation" *against* "sectional interests", "irresponsible trade union power", etc., i.e. against the class'.[53]

It was this contradiction in Labour's politics that 'Thatcherism' had homed in on, 'deploying the discourses of "nation" and "people" against "class" and "unions"'.[54] The political terrain on which Thatcher could attack working-class politics was prepared by Labour. Yet whereas Labour in the 1970s could only oppose particular instances of industrial action rather than trade-unionism in general, Thatcher could construct an assault on 'the very foundation of organized labour'.[55] Hence the success of her 'authoritarian populism'—'authoritarian' because its implementation required increased state power, but 'populist' because it drew on popular disillusion with the social-democratic state.[56] An hegemonic project in the Gramscian sense, it sought to 'construct a social authority throughout all levels of social activity',[57] and posed as a *radical* alternative to a status-quo politics that was, by the mid-1970s, suffering a crisis of hegemony.[58] As Hall put it in 1985, the new right's novelty was that it had established '*itself* as the radical political force, the political force that was going to change things'.[59]

Hall's analysis of the Social Democratic Party (SDP) breakaway in 1981 demonstrated his acute awareness that the value of Labour's 'class connection' had been fundamentally altered in the Thatcher period. In the past, Hall argued, the loyalty of Labour's right-wingers to the party was assured insofar as the right gained from Labour's association with unions. The Labour right had not had a dispute with the unions as such but with the left in the labour movement, and indeed it had depended on the right wing of the unions for its political base.[60] What was different in the early 1980s was that the SDP regarded the union link as 'a constraint rather than a lifeline'.[61] It was not so much the SDP's 'reformism' that distanced it from Labour—as Hall pointed out, many in the Labour Party shared this reformism—but its belief that 'class politics' was no longer pertinent:

> the unions, though not necessarily standing for anything but a reformist type of politics, nevertheless constitute a link with class questions and relationships. And the [SDP] reformists reject this, they think politics is no longer about this.[62]

As discussed below, this SDP belief also informed Hall and his co-thinkers as they sought to formulate a progressive Labour politics that did not feature 'class questions' as its central focus. Hall thus presented it as progress that individuals from what he called the 'hard left' were being won to the side of Kinnock and the Labour Co-ordinating Committee (which had, by the mid-1980s, transmuted from Bennite faction to 'soft left' moderniser).[63] He berated the hard left for not accepting contemporary realities, and for its attachment to a definition and model of socialism 'which in no way adequately reflects the actual social composition of the class forces and social movements necessary to produce it'.[64] The hard left represented 'a blockage to a long, difficult but necessary process' towards 'the renewal of the socialist project and the generation of new strategic perspectives for the Left'.[65] But precisely what would this renewal entail? What kind of strategy did the left now need? By 1990, Hall and his colleagues were ready to provide some clarifications.

## New Times/New Labour

The parallels between New Labour and post-war revisionism have been much debated.[66] Yet it is worth underlining that New Labour drew its ideas and personnel not primarily from old revisionists like Roy Hattersley, but from those formerly in and around Labour's left.[67] Numerous figures previously associated with the left became leading figures in the New Labour project,[68] and the LCC, which had backed Benn for deputy leader in 1981, and had included Tony Blair among its ranks in the early 1980s,[69] had by the 1990s become a leading proponent of Labour's 'modernisation'. When deemed appropriate, New Labour continued to pay verbal homage to Labour's past traditions, whether those of Crosland and Wilson or Hardie and Bevan.[70] However, by the 1990s, calls for Labour's 'modernisation' were framed by a view that the world had entered an epoch fundamentally different from the past, which demanded a progressive politics quite different from those based on social and political conflicts that no longer really mattered, at least not centrally.

*Manifesto for New Times*, published by the CPGB a year before the party's dissolution in 1991, was a representative statement of this 'modernising' left-wing approach, a culmination of its reappraisals since the late 1970s. As a codification of *Marxism Today*'s outlook, *New Times* contained several of the core themes that had risen among the left in the 1980s and that would dominate British 'centre-left' thinking in the 1990s. The influence of *Marxism Today* debates on New Labour's Third Way is well known.[71] Blair contributed to the magazine in 1991,[72] and Gordon Brown endorsed the *New Times* project in its pages in 1989.[73] *Marxism Today* editor Martin Jacques founded Demos in 1993, an influential think-tank linked to New Labour. Geoff Mulgan, a leading writer for *Marxism Today* in its final years, was the think-tank's first director, and later became head of the policy unit at 10 Downing Street under Blair,[74] to whom Charles Leadbeater, another regular contributor to the magazine, was also a leading adviser.[75] In 1994, Stuart Hall referred to Blair as the '*Marxism Today* candidate'[76]; as Bob Rowthorn recalls, New Labour was 'in a certain sense a Communist project almost. Communists made a big input into it'.[77]

Geoff Andrews underplays this link with New Labour, which, he argues, was distinct from the transformative agenda of *New Times*.[78] In the last, one-off edition of *Marxism Today* published in 1998, Hall and Martin Jacques themselves criticised New Labour for its continuities with 'Thatcherism', for upholding the modernising agenda of *New Times* but without a commitment to its left-wing aspirations.[79] As a product of discussions in and around the CPGB, *New Times* did contain proposals that did not feature in New Labour's politics. It called for abolishing the House of Lords and, in 'the long run', the monarchy, both of which were arguably given a new lease of life under Blair—the former as a parliamentary centre of scrutiny and expertise, the latter as an institution 'in touch with public opinion', particularly after the death of Diana Spencer in 1997.[80] *New Times* also expressed a commitment to 'sustaining and renewing critical, democratic Marxism',[81] and certainly to what it saw as a type of socialism, a word which did not feature in any general-election Labour manifesto under Blair or Brown (or indeed under Ed Miliband or—at the time of writing—Jeremy Corbyn, having last been used in 1987).

However, *New Times* represented a worldview in keeping with dominant left ideas in the 1990s. It also, as mentioned, posed as a radical and even Marxist document, and therefore arguably represented a more self-avowedly left-wing reappraisal than did the more self-consciously centrist pronouncements of New Labour. It is therefore a useful document to gauge the extent of the discontinuity between the ideas of the AES and those of the British left that *New Times* represented.

### Economic Policy

*New Times* expressed a qualified commitment to the market and a thorough renunciation of centralised state planning. This prefigured Blair's 'Clause 4 moment' in 1995, which discarded Labour's constitutional commitment to nationalisation and called for partnership between 'a thriving public sector' and 'the enterprise of the market and the rigour of competition'.[82] *New Times* called for a strategy that would 'use both planning and market mechanisms to achieve its objectives'.[83] However, the market was presented as the source of 'incentives and discipline', as well as 'innovation, flexibility and diversity'.[84] There were 'some goods such as education and health [that] should not be provided through the market's ability to pay', and, overall, public intervention was needed to direct the market in the public interest.[85] Yet this intervention would be distinct from the state involvements of the old labour movement, which had a 'conservative approach to the state'.[86] Instead, *New Times* looked to 'development agencies, financial institutions and local regulatory bodies to promote new businesses and local economic regeneration', as well as to guide the market in the public interest (giving the example of a 'green bank' to 'fund businesses specialising in recycling or developing environmentally safe products').[87] The old left was identified with state control of the economy, and the 'new right' with an uncontrolled market. Progressive politics needed to differ from both, as Blair also emphasised in Labour's 1997 manifesto.[88]

A noteworthy feature of this post-left/right economics was its emphasis on environmentalism and 'sustainable development'. These gained significant traction under New Labour, which set up the Sustainable Development Commission in 2000, affirming the severity of the 'environmental impacts of our consumption and production patterns'.[89] For *New Times*, environmental damage had profoundly challenged existing ideas about economic development, consumption and socialism. Society's 'criteria for progress' now required a 'different ethic of consumption and lifestyle'.[90] Britain already produced enough wealth to meet its needs 'without further economic growth'.[91] This disquiet about economic growth, previously a feature of relatively marginal neo-Malthusian figures and organisations like Paul Ehrlich and the Club of Rome in the 1960s and 1970s, became increasingly central to left-wing politics from the 1990s, as fears about the environment led to an intense disquiet about the pro-growth ideas that had once been central to left-wing campaigns.[92]

### The Nation-State

The *New Times* embraced international organisations and simultaneously promoted state decentralisation and 'localism'. This was also a key feature of New Labour, which accepted 'the global economy as a reality and [rejected] the isolationism and "go-it-alone" policies of the extremes of right or left'.[93] In this vein, it called for Britain's greater involvement in an enlarged EU, and for Britain to play a greater role in the 'international community' to promote the progressive politics of global development, environmental security, peace and human rights.[94] In addition, however, it supported state decentralisation at home, against the over-centralisation that had been 'a problem in governments of both left and right'.[95] The nation-state was 'too small a stage for resolving the big issues and too big a stage for resolving the small ones', as Gordon Brown had put it in the late 1980s.[96]

For *New Times*, the rise of transnational corporations meant that progressive development was impossible without their regulation 'by both national and international bodies'.[97] Globalisation had altered the 'character and sovereignty of the nation state' and created the impetus for a 'realignment' *within* nation states.[98] Power was 'tending to move downwards as well as upwards', giving new meaning to 'identities', as in the rise of Scottish and Welsh nationalism and the demands for regional power in England.[99] Cold War bipolarity was also breaking up, creating the basis for greater international integration. The left had to embrace this development as a basis for a new internationalism, and discard its attachment to the 'political demarcation lines of the old world'.[100] A socialist Britain would press 'the United Nations to expand its influence' and urge the creation of 'new international institutions to regulate the economy'.[101]

New Times thus represented an early statement of the ardent pro-European outlook that came to dominate the British centre-left from the 1990s till the present period.[102] It saw Britain's 'progressive role' in Europe as key to the left's 'new international outlook'; Britain's membership of the EC 'must define the way we conceive of our future', it stated.[103] New Times was aware that a strengthened EC would redefine state sovereignty and 'mean more power is transferred to Brussels'.[104] It also saw that 'Europeanisation' was 'leading to widespread industrial restructuring, job losses and the further concentration of economic power'.[105] However, this merely reinforced the need for progressives to engage with Europeanisation. The nation-state foundation of the old right/left politics had been uprooted.

### The Working Class

New Times upheld 'universal human values', which had 'primacy over class divisions'.[106] Work under 'post-Fordism'—a shift away from the old mass-production methods of industry—was 'taking on more flexible, diverse, fragmentary forms'.[107] In addition, the service industry was now the main source of new jobs, and new workforce divisions were weakening the old strongholds of union power and creating 'ever greater social fragmentation, diversity and polarisation'.[108] As Leadbeater argued, the old left's 'mass' aims were based on mass interests formed by the old types of production and work.[109] There were now new identities based around '[choice] in consumption, lifestyle, sexuality'.[110] Echoing Gorz, he argued that the 'traditional sources of solidarity and common identity forged through work' had decayed, giving way to 'the growth in the importance of individual choice in consumption, the revolt against centralising sameness, the pursuit of diversity'.[111]

Like Gorz, New Times saw the fragmentation of identity as an opportunity for a new progressive politics, albeit one very different from the past socialist politics emphasising class unity and commonality. There would now be movements representing different 'moods, currents and forces in society' which, though lacking any 'automatic cause to unite', were in a position to 'offer an alternative vision of modernisation'.[112] There needed to be a 'modernisation of class politics', and Britain had become a 'more unequal, more exploitative society'.[113] However, class traditions no longer provided 'such a strong point of common identity, commitment and purpose', and we now wore

> different identities which we take up and discard with amazing rapidity and ease: teachers in one capacity, we are parents in another; producers in one situation, we are consumers in the next; members of a family, part of a workforce; hillwalkers today, motorised polluters of the countryside tomorrow and so on.[114]

A viewpoint which ranked class alongside identities formed around pastimes and consumption choices, and in which these identities were politically significant and simultaneously ephemeral, underlay a belief that class in general, and trade-unionism in particular, were not to feature centrally in the progressive politics for the new times, at least not necessarily. Unions were just one among a number of diverse interests: left-wing strategy would represent 'the plurality of social groups and concerns—for instance, independent trade unions, collective organisations for black people, women, lesbians and gay men, consumers, writers and artists'.[115] As Wood argued, it seemed as if class could be reduced 'to just another personal "identity"'.[116] Indeed, for Anthony Giddens, among New Labour's key intellectual influences, the individual now faced the class system 'not just as a producer but as a consumer'; as such, 'Lifestyle and taste…become as evident markers of social differentiation as position in the productive order'.[117]

The transformation of Labour's image under Blair involved its categorical rejection of union militancy, promising unions 'no favours from a Labour government'.[118] Unions would now facilitate workplace training and skills-raising,[119] acting in partnership with business, and not as a 'trade-union movement' as such but as a body promoting 'basic minimum rights for the individual at the workplace'.[120] Class was less a source of collective agency than a hindrance on the individual's economic advancement. For Giddens, the link between class and collective social engagement had sharply weakened, and, for the most part, class was 'no longer experienced as class', i.e. as a 'collective fate', but as a source of an individual's personal constraints and opportunities.[121]

*New Times* also envisioned the unions as partners in the progressive economy. On the one hand, unions should become 'a bridge between the social movements, the voluntary sector, pressure groups and the Labour Party', and the union-Labour link should not be broken but recast.[122] After ten years of Conservative anti-union legislation, 'a positive legal framework for organised labour' was also required.[123] However, *New Times* did not emphasise unions as organisations upholding their members' interests, or even the interests of workers as a whole (as in the old Marxist critiques of union sectionalism). Instead, unions had to prove their value to society by winning 'the public over to a modernised view of them as organisations capable of making a real contribution to the quality of life'.[124] They should champion the cause of consumers, for example, articulating their 'concerns about quality of services, price rises and the protection of the countryside'.[125] The significance of this approach was not in its call for unions to broaden their political horizons—that call had long accompanied radical-left critiques of trade-unionism—but its demotion of workers' organisation at the level of production, its presentation of the political value of trade-unionism as akin to that of consumer campaigns. There was a marked shift away from the view of unions as industrial combat organisations for upholding workers' interests against the employer, which did not receive any emphasis in *New Times*.

## THE AES VERSUS THE NEW-TIMES LEFT

*New Times* saw the AES as part of a failed left-wing politics: although it had represented the left's ability to develop 'new ideas', it did not belong to a 'popular, modernising perspective able to coalesce disenchantment with the post-war settlement'.[126] Wickham-Jones's book on the AES also points to its fundamental difference from New Labour: Blair 'presented an image of the party as being transformed almost beyond recognition', and the AES's economic proposals 'seem far removed from those put forward by the party he leads'.[127] Yet, in some ways, *New Times* and New Labour can be seen as having developed upon some of the key ideas of AES analyses. While, as discussed below, *New Times* did represent an outlook distinct from the social-democratic tradition to which the AES belonged, its ideological 'realignment' did not emerge in a vacuum but, to an extent, out of the ideological shifts already established by its left-wing predecessor.

This was perhaps most clear in the parallels in their approaches to economic strategy. As discussed in Chapter 4, Stuart Holland's theory had already represented a significant break with approaches to the state and the market that had previously dominated Labour-left thinking. While the post-war Labour left had tended to equate socialism with nationalisation, Holland's AES called for a 'public control' of the economy without an emphasis on state ownership, and, like *New Times*, he believed that a market economy could be compatible with socialism. Furthermore, like *New Times*, AES economists like Holland and Geoffrey Hodgson saw lack of markets as a cause of bureaucratisation and authoritarian government. As Holland later recalled, his AES 'was not "Old Labour" looking back but already a "New" Labour case', one which sought a new type of Labour politics 'recognising trends in globalisation'.[128] Along with other prominent AES proponents, he shared the *New Times* view that the market would remain in the future economy as the primary engine of economic productivity and efficiency.

Environmentalist critique of economic growth, although perhaps more common among sections of the Labour right in this period,[129] was also given some space within the AES. Labour's manifestos during the AES period made commitments to environmental improvement, and the party published a Green Paper in September 1973 which called the provision of funds to overseas family-planning programmes.[130] In the late 1970s, Holland and his European colleagues criticised mass consumption, a primary focus of mainstream environmentalism in the 1990s: 'Spurred on by advertising, consumption in our society tends towards a model which includes a large measure of frivolous, ostentatious or, at the very least, non-essential consumption.'[131] Michael Meacher's version of the AES, meanwhile, contained an open hostility to economic growth, arguing that Britain should reduce its dependence not only on the global economy but on its own economy, too—via measures including a greater focus on non-industrial growth and a 'containment strategy' to reduce the material consumption of the British population.[132]

In terms of Britain's international role, Chapter 5 noted that, while protectionism was prominent in AES analyses, this was not due mainly to an anti-free-trade principle or any ideological commitment to autarky. AES approaches were nation-focused but their opposition to free trade tended to be pragmatic and not envisaged as a long-term policy for the British economy; indeed, it was argued that import controls could ultimately *increase* international trade. This principally practical concern suggested that AES socialists could, under different practical circumstances, perhaps be open to rather different policy options regarding Britain's role in the world market economy.

Indeed, while it is true that opposition to the EEC was a major rallying point for the AES left, and that the 1983 Labour manifesto called for Britain's withdrawal from the EEC, by the 1980s there were significant elements of self-criticism *within* the AES left regarding Europe. The failure of the Mitterrand government's left-wing policies in France in the early 1980s 'began to appear in socialist discussion as evidence of the problems a purely national reflationary strategy would encounter'.[133] There was increasing doubt that national solutions could be effective against international crises, or that left-wing reforms were implementable in a single country.[134] Hostility to the EEC remained strong among some sections of the Labour left during the 1980s, including Benn, who opposed the EU till his death in 2014. However, the arguments of Jacques Delors, the French left-wing politician and president of the European Commission from 1985 to 1995, were finding favour among key AES advocates, including Stuart Holland, Bob Rowthorn and Ken Coates (who became a Member of the European Parliament in 1989), as well as in the Trades Union Congress (TUC).[135] According to one account, Delors was instrumental in convincing British left-wingers and trade union that the EEC need not be 'constructed along free market, anti-union lines', presenting it as a possible means to redress Thatcher's attacks on workers' rights and social protection.[136]

Finally, there were also parallels on the question of class. As discussed, the new-times left marginalised the working-class as a politically relevant social 'identity', presenting it as in competition now with identities based around nation, ethnicity, consumption, etc., to which a modern left would need to relate. Yet AES approaches to the working class had also contained a view of workers as merely one important element in a broader social picture containing a number of other legitimate elements or 'interest groups'. As discussed in the previous chapter, the AES Labour left sought a new tripartite arrangement between government, management and the unions which could form the basis for improving the social position of the working class, but also for raising its productivity. As argued below, this approach had important differences from the 'identity politics' of the new-times left. However, the AES had already contained a limited view of workers' socialist agency. Although some of its radical proponents presented it as a 'transitional strategy' to intensify class conflict en route to socialism, in the main the AES sought improved class co-operation and social cohesion, albeit on improved terms for the working class.

Along with these similarities, however, the AES also contained important differences from *New Times*. Whereas the new-times left established its prominence in a period in which Britain appeared to be coming to terms with its industrial decline and its role as a service economy,[137] the AES emerged in a context of deep political anxiety about Britain's industrial decline. As discussed in the chapters above, Britain's industrial regeneration was preeminent among AES demands. The AES saw the growth of Britain's industrial base as the fundamental prerequisite for the country's future prosperity, as well as for progressive social changes. The *New Times* position was very different in this regard: it argued that Britain already produced enough, and incorporated an environmentalism troubled by the prospect of future industrial growth. While the ideas associated with this environmentalism did exist in the AES, they did so relatively marginally, along the borders of a far more dominant case for an immediate industrial revival.

The AES also contained a far greater emphasis on the economic role of the state. As discussed above, *New Times* saw the old left's view of the state as outdated and conservative, called for state decentralisation and looked to other types of local and international organisations to fulfil the economic tasks that the left had traditionally assigned to the state. Despite Holland's distancing from state ownership, his ideas were still framed by the tripartist outlook of post-war politics. This saw the state as the primary agent of economic restructuring, and the main arbiter in disputes between labour and capital in the interests of industrial productivity. With the increased irrelevance of state-procured class co-operation for capitalist stability by the end of the 1980s, however, the type of tripartist politics to which the AES belonged was rendered largely obsolete, leading to rather different left-wing ideas about the state's purpose.

There were also significant dissimilarities on the question of Britain's role abroad. Whereas the new-times left upheld the transfer of aspects of state authority to international organisations, national sovereignty was a fundamental demand in AES approaches. These tended to pose Britain as a country oppressed by outside forces—America, NATO, the EEC, the IMF, multinational corporations—and thus called for a reassertion of Britain's sovereignty as the basis for reviving and democratising the British economy. State sovereignty was regarded as the precondition for the implementation of the AES. Although, for example, Holland's *Socialist Challenge* was not closed to co-operation within Europe via the EEC, this was on the condition that such co-operation occurred between sovereign nation-states rather than on the basis of a transnationalism undermining the authority of national governments. Others on the AES left, including those, like Peter

Hain, who would later play a central part in New Labour's pro-European project, saw the EEC as a self-evident block on national governments' implementation of socialist policies.[138] While many former AES proponents later came to endorse the European project, they did so as they distanced themselves from the politics of the AES in general.[139] The AES view of national sovereignty as a matter of practical necessity, differed significantly from the diminished regard for national sovereignty that would gain prominence on the British left by the twenty-first century, as support for EU integration was posed as an essential attribute of progressive politics.

The rise in left-wing support for the European project coincided with the left's distancing from the working class, its old social constituency.[140] While the new-times left spoke of the erosion of that constituency and promoted diversity of identity and 'new social movements', the AES, though it failed to break with the politics of tripartism, *presupposed* class and class conflict. Indeed, its strong tripartist inclinations were themselves products of the reality that class conflict was a central feature of the historical period in which the AES emerged, products because the basis for tripartist arrangements was the volatility of class relations in industry. That AES approaches devoted so much attention to industrial democracy, posing it as a vital bulwark against the strategy's degeneration into an authoritarian corporatism, represented what was at the heart of the strategy's preoccupations: to discover suitable means to incorporate the working class into the arrangements of an AES-led Labour government, a solution that would satisfy working-class concerns and thereby unite the nation for a future of stable economic prosperity and progressive social changes.

The situation by the 1990s was very different in this regard. The self-confidence and strength of organised labour in the early 1970s was replaced by its growing weakness and despondency by the mid-1980s. The defeat of the year-long miners' strike of 1984–1985 was a crucial turning point, effectively eliminating what had long been considered by the British left the vanguard of British trade-unionism, with the ability to lead general strikes (as in 1926) and bring down Tory governments (as in February 1974). Unlike in the early 1970s, the miners received limited support from other unions in 1984–1985, and, as Benn argued, 'virtually no support' from the Labour leadership.[141] As for Thatcher, the miners were 'the enemy within', and the Battle of Orgreave demonstrated her readiness to employ extraordinary measures for its defeat.[142] Kinnock has attributed his lack of support for the strike to its lack of backing by a national ballot,[143] the absence of which had indeed left the strike vulnerable to the charge of an 'undemocratic' attack on elected government. However, the disengaged nature of Kinnock's response in 1984–1985 perhaps also reflected the fact that the strike went against the grain of an ongoing 'modernisation' project increasingly dissociated with trade-unionism. As Wood argued at the time, the strike represented a 'significant test' for this left-wing current, and a lesson which (according to Wood) it failed to learn, choosing instead to interpret the miners' defeat as having 'sounded the death knell of class politics'.[144]

Yet, with the power of hindsight, it is difficult to disagree that the defeat of the miners marked the end of an era, dealing a major blow not only against trade-unionism but also its political significance. Strike activity, which had already dipped in the early 1980s, decreased dramatically from the second half of that decade,[145] a progressive decline which has continued into the present period. Fig. 7.1 illustrates that an exceptional period of industrial calm was in the process of emerging in Britain by end of the 1980s, in stark contrast to the large-scale militancy of the 1970s, while Fig. 7.2 shows the steep decline of unions as mass organisations since the rise and peak of union membership in the 1970s. If Stuart Hall was right to argue that Labour's prior role was to 'discipline' the unions to master capitalist crises, by the 1990s, it seemed, there was little left of the unions to discipline. Their political and economic significance had greatly diminished, thus further underlining the redundancy of Labour's 'class politics'.

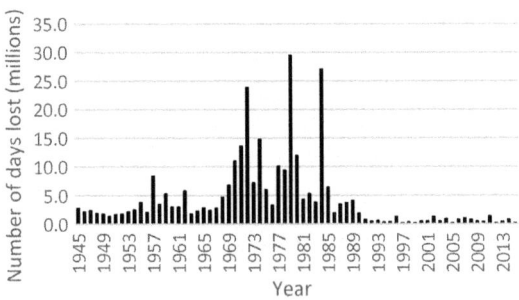

**Fig. 7.1** Total number of working days lost to strikes in the UK, 1945–2015 (*Source* Office for National Statistics)

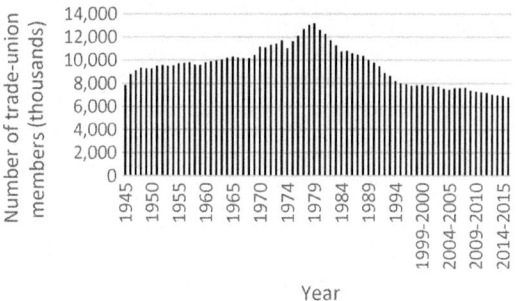

**Fig. 7.2** Number of trade-union members in Great Britain, 1945–2015/2016 (*Source* Department for Business, Energy and Industrial Strategy)

## Conclusion: The AES and the Death of British Socialism

With the increased irrelevance of class conflict to party politics, the terms of the old debates around socialist strategy could also become extraneous. The AES, as discussed in Chapter 3, was marked by its engagement with wide-ranging debates around socialist strategy, often attempting to reconcile its reformist approach with what it saw as its revolutionary objective. Revolution and reform, class and party, class conflict and class collaboration, Marxism and social democracy—these were all within the ambit of AES discussion, often discussed not as academic questions pertaining to a prior era but as germane to the formulation of a radical Labour-left strategy for the present.

However, the perceived pertinence of each of these debates rested greatly on the political significance that they ascribed to class and class conflict, as forces pivotal to how socialist strategy should be conceived. Once class was rid of any major political significance, however, the strategic questions formed around it could also be largely dispensed with. As Hyman noted of Gorz's theory of the near extinction of the working class, he neither engaged with nor contested a 'century of debate on socialist political strategy' on the role of the party, parliamentary participation and reform versus revolution.[146] For Gorz, society had entered a period that had shaken if not dissolved the old certainties of class-based socialism. 'The crisis of socialism is above all a reflection of the crisis of the proletariat', as Gorz put it, locating the 'degeneration of socialist theory and practice' in the large disappearance of 'proletarianised social producers'.[147] Similarly for Laclau and Mouffe, what were previously defined as the means to socialism—'the essentialism of the traditional Left, which proceeded with absolute categories of the type "*the* Party", "*the* Class", or "*the* Revolution"'[148]—could have little relevance for a left-wing strategy in the present. As Laclau argued in 1989, 'The political productivity of the two conceptions of socialism which have dominated the last 70 years—social-democracy and communism—is exhausted', and the defeat of 'Thatcherism' required 'a complete transformation of the political and intellectual horizon of the Left'.[149]

Arguably, therefore, it was primarily in this respect that the AES was distinct from the left-wing politics that emerged dominant in the 1990s: the theories, traditions, language and frames of reference of the old socialist politics were now seen as anachronistic preoccupations.[150] Indeed the label 'left-wing' itself was called into question as a representation of the new progressive politics, since left and right belonged to an era of class politics now past. As Blair put it, many of the old left-right struggles had 'no relevance whatsoever to the modern world—public versus private, bosses versus workers, middle class versus working class'.[151] For Giddens, to be 'beyond left and right' meant recognising that the old left politics had become moribund and backward-looking, harking back to old traditions and forms of government, seeking 'mainly to conserve'; while conservatism had itself 'become largely dissolved', as the right had set in play 'radical processes of change, stimulated by the incessant expansion of markets'.[152] The Third Way was therefore a *product* of the demise of political categories that had acquired meaning through class divisions that, while not gone away, were no longer a driving force of politics.[153]

Hence the seeming effortlessness with which the Third Way could reconcile in its politics the old left-right differences to which the AES had given a far greater significance. As Fairclough notes, the phrase 'not only... but also' pervaded New Labour's discourse as it sought to bring together the old markers of left and right politics (social justice and economic dynamism; fairness and enterprise; opposing the 'destructive excesses of the market and the intrusive hand of state intervention'), making compatible, according to Fairclough, 'two previously incompatible terms'.[154] Yet, as Heartfield suggests, the prior incompatibility of left-right distinctions was not merely a matter of logic but based on confrontation between opposing social forces: 'The ease with which Tony Blair maps out a Third Way...arises out of the real-world minimisation of the social conflicts around left and right.'[155]

The rise of 'compassionate conservatism' in David Cameron's Conservative Party, which toned down or discarded a number of its former right-wing emphases,[156] perhaps validated the expectation that Conservatism would fall alongside socialism, the politics against which it had formerly been compelled to define itself. Yet it is difficult to avoid the conclusion that the main political casualty of the new-times era—which took capitalist production as read and generally accepted Thatcher's mantra that no alternative to it existed—were not the politics of capitalism but the politics for socialist change. As Perry Anderson wrote at the turn of the present century:

> For the first time since the Reformation, there are no longer any significant oppositions—that is, systematic rival outlooks—within the thought-world of the West...Virtually the entire horizon of reference in which the generation of the sixties grew up has been wiped away—the landmarks of reformist and revolutionary socialism in equal measure.[157]

The AES, then, was the last project in mainstream British left-wing politics to have engaged seriously with these past left-wing traditions. Despite its attempts to reconcile Labour's reformist heritage with radical ideas from the Marxist left, the AES failed to break from the boundaries of a Labour socialism tied to gradualism and class co-operation in the 'national interest'. Yet it was also a type of left-wing politics fundamentally different from New Labour, in the sense that, in many ways, the latter sought to overturn and replace *all* past traditions of socialism, Marxist *and* reformist.

## NOTES

1. Thompson, *Left in the Wilderness*, p. 191.
2. Panitch and Leys, *The End of Parliamentary Socialism*, p. 108. Their italics.
3. Coates, *Crisis of Labour*, p. 77.
4. Ibid., p. 78.
5. Hay, 'Narrating the Crisis', p. 254.
6. Thorpe, *A History of the British Labour Party*, p. 216.
7. Thompson, *Left in the Wilderness*, p. 4.
8. Labour Party, *The New Hope for Britain*.
9. Thorpe, 'The Labour Party and the Trade Unions', p. 133.
10. The party's policy and organisational changes in this period have been detailed in Eric Shaw, *The Labour Party Since 1979*. A discussion of the changes in Labour's political economy can be found in Noel Thompson,

*Left in the Wilderness*. For a critical account, see Panitch and Leys, *The End of Parliamentary Socialism*.

11. Panitch and Leys, *The End of Parliamentary Socialism*, p. 222.
12. Labour Party, *Britain Will Win with Labour*.
13. Shaw, *The Labour Party Since 1979*, p. 108.
14. Ibid., pp. 126–7.
15. Panitch and Leys, *The End of Parliamentary Socialism*, p. 221.
16. Rowthorn, 'The Politics of the Alternative Economic Strategy'. This was followed by a number of *Marxism Today* articles with the same title: Adam Sharples, April 1981, pp. 25–7; John Harrison, May 1981, pp. 27–8; and Brian Nichols, June 1981, pp. 27–8—as well as Jean Gardiner and Sheila Smith, 'Feminism and the Alternative Economic Strategy', October 1981, pp. 24–30.
17. Aaronovitch, 'The Alternative Economic Strategy', p. 22.
18. Ibid.
19. Rowthorn, 'No Such Miracle', p. 3.
20. Hobsbawm, 'Snatching Victory from Defeat', p. 181.
21. Ralph Miliband, 'The New Revisionism in Britain'.
22. Wood, *The Retreat from Class*. The quotations are from Marx and Engels (*The German Ideology*), as cited in Wood, p. 1.
23. Fine et al., *Class Politics*, p. 8.
24. Miliband, 'The New Revisionism in Britain', p. 8.
25. Ben Fine et al., *Class Politics*, p. 7.
26. Wood, *The Retreat from Class*, p. 90.
27. Ibid., pp. 90–1.
28. As Richard Hyman wrote in a lengthy critique of Gorz's book: 'The dynamics of capitalist production relations, with their complex patterns of division of labour and hierarchies of control, have always involved elaborate trajectories of skill, de-skilling, and at times re-skilling. Ever since the early nineteenth century, socialists and capitalists alike have repeatedly discerned the final abolition of skill and associated job controls' (Hyman, 'Andre Gorz and His Disappearing Proletariat', p. 286.)
29. Gorz, *Farewell to the Working Class*, p. 69.
30. Ibid., p. 11.
31. Ibid., p. 75.
32. Ibid., p. 7
33. Ibid., p. 97.
34. Ibid., p. 97.
35. Laclau and Mouffe, *Hegemony and Socialist Strategy*, pp. 191–2.
36. Ibid., p. 191.
37. Laclau and Mouffe, 'Socialist Strategy: Where Next?', p. 17.
38. Heartfield, *The 'Death of the Subject' Explained*, p. 147.
39. Pimlott, 'From "Old Left" to "New Labour"?', p. 178.

40. Callinicos, 'The Politics of *Marxism Today*'.
41. Hobsbawm, 'The Forward March of Labour Halted?', p. 20.
42. Kinnock reportedly called Hobsbawm 'The Most Sagacious Living Marx-ist'. See Davies, *Challenging Governance Theory*, p. 45.
43. Hobsbawm, 'Preface', p. 3, fn.
44. Ibid.
45. Wood, *The Retreat from Class*, pp. 2–3, fn. 3.
46. Hobsbawm, 'The Retreat into Extremism', p. 88.
47. Hobsbawm, 'The Debate on "The Forward March of Labour Halted?"', p. 40.
48. Ibid.
49. Hobsbawm, 'Labour's Lost Millions', p. 74.
50. Ibid., p. 74.
51. Ibid.
52. Hall, 'The Great Moving Right Show', p. 26. His italics. (The article was first published in the January 1979 edition of *Marxism Today*, and then republished in partly rewritten form in 1983 as a chapter in *The Politics of Thatcherism*, which Hall edited with *Marxism Today* editor Martin Jacques. All references here are to the book version.)
53. Ibid. His italics.
54. Ibid.
55. Ibid.
56. Gamble, *The Free Economy*, p. 182.
57. Hall cited in Gamble, *The Free Economy*, pp. 178–9.
58. Gamble, *The Free Economy*, pp. 174–8.
59. Hall, 'Faith, Hope or Clarity', pp. 16–7. His italics. For Benn's criticisms, see Benn, 'Who Dares Wins', pp. 12–5.
60. Hall, 'Redrawing the Political Map', p. 16.
61. Ibid.
62. Ibid., pp. 16–7.
63. Hall, 'Realignment—For What?', p. 12.
64. Ibid., p. 14.
65. Ibid.
66. See Diamond, *The Crosland Legacy*; See also Meredith, 'Mr Crosland's Nightmare?'.
67. Hattersley rejected that New Labour had any close association social democracy. (See Hattersley, 'It's No Longer My Party'.)
68. Other than the *Marxism Today* figures pointed to below, these included former the Labour-leftists Peter Hain, Chris Mullin, David Blunkett, Patricia Hewitt, Alan Johnson and Michael Meacher.
69. *Telegraph*, 'The Full Text of Tony Blair's Letter to Michael Foot'.

70. According to John Prescott, Blair's deputy prime minister, 'The Values That Motivated Keir Hardie Are the Same Ones That Motivate Tony Blair'—a claim Hattersley mocked as less plausible than to claim that Kinnock had won 'At Wimbledon or Invented the Hovercraft' (Hattersley, 'Trustee of Keir Hardie's Cloth Cap').

71. See Andrews, *Endgames and New Times*, pp. 237–43; Pimlott, 'From "Old Left" to "New Labour"?', p. 196. For a lengthy journalistic account, see Harris, 'Marxism Today'.

72. Blair, 'Forging a New Agenda', p. 32.

73. Napolitano et al., 'Debate: Smaller Worlds', pp. 37–9.

74. Wintour and White, 'Blair Pins Hopes on Sweeping Changes to Reinvigorate Policy Thinking'.

75. Andrews, *Endgames and New Times*, p. 224.

76. Pimlott, 'From "Old Left" to "New Labour"?', p. 196.

77. Author's interview with Bob Rowthorn, *Cambridge*, 10 June 2015.

78. See Andrews, *Endgames and New Times*, pp. 237–43.

79. Hall, 'The Great Moving Nowhere Show', and Jacques, 'Good to Be Back'.

80. ITV News, 'The Queen at 90'.

81. CPGB, *Manifesto for New Times*, p. 7.

82. The New Labour Clause 4 can be read in full here: http://www.labourcounts.com/oldclausefour.htm (accessed January 2018).

83. CPGB, *Manifesto for New Times*, p. 82.

84. Ibid.

85. Ibid.

86. Ibid., p. 49.

87. Ibid., p. 79.

88. 'The old left would have sought state control of industry. The Conservative right is content to leave all to the market. We reject both approaches. Government and industry must work together…' (Labour Party, *New Labour Because Britain Deserves Better*).

89. UK Government, *Securing the Future*, p. 7.

90. CPGB, *Manifesto for New Times*, pp. 62–3.

91. Ibid., p. 62.

92. Ben-Ami, *Ferraris for All*. For another polemical treatment from a left-wing perspective, see Heartfield, *Green Capitalism*. In 2007, the prominent environmentalist George Monbiot supported a recession on the basis it could save the earth, partly by restraining working-class consumption (Monbiot, 'In this age of diamond saucepans, only a recession makes sense').

93. New Labour, *New Labour Because Britain Deserves Better*.

94. Ibid.

95. Ibid. See also Ellison and Ellison, 'Creating "Opportunity for All"?'

96. Napolitano et al., 'Debate: Smaller Worlds', pp. 37–9.

97. CPGB, *Manifesto for New Times*, p. 78.

98. Ibid., pp. 66–7.
99. Ibid., p. 67.
100. Ibid., p. 69.
101. Ibid., p. 17.
102. In June 2016 this outlook stood somewhat shaken—though by no means overturned—via its rejection by 52% of British voters, including many within Labour's old working-class heartlands (See Harris, 'If You've Got Money, You Vote In').
103. CPGB, *Manifesto for New Times*, p. 69.
104. Ibid., p. 70
105. Ibid., p. 71.
106. Ibid., p. 17.
107. Ibid., p. 24.
108. Ibid.
109. Leadbeater, 'Power to the Person', p. 15.
110. Ibid.
111. Ibid., p. 16.
112. CPGB, *Manifesto for New Times*, pp. 25–6.
113. Ibid., p. 47.
114. Ibid.
115. Ibid., p. 15.
116. Wood, 'Debate on the Manifesto for New Times', p. 31.
117. Giddens, *Beyond Left and Right*, p. 143.
118. Labour Party, *New Labour Because Britain Deserves Better*.
119. Labour Party, *Ambitions for Britain*.
120. Labour Party, *New Labour Because Britain Deserves Better*.
121. Giddens, *Beyond Left and Right*, p. 143.
122. CPGB, *Manifesto for New Times*, pp. 52–3.
123. Ibid., p. 76.
124. Ibid.
125. Ibid., p. 53.
126. Ibid., p. 23.
127. Wickham-Jones, *Economic Strategy and the Labour Party*, p. 223.
128. Holland, 'Demythologising "Old Labour"', p. 27.
129. As Foote argues, an emphasis on environment took root among figures from the old revisionist right with the evident failure of Keynesian policies for economic growth in the 1970s. By way of coming to terms with the failure of their economic model, these figures shifted their focuses away from the more radical aims of revisionism that had presupposed continued economic growth (such as equality and welfare), and towards ecology and smaller-scale production (Foote, *The Labour Party's Political Thought*, pp. 260–1).
130. See Tinker, 'The Environment: No Parsnips from Labour', p. 667.

131. Archibugi et al., 'The International Crisis', p. 176.
132. Meacher, *Socialism with a Human Face*, pp. 188–9.
133. Callaghan, 'Rise and Fall of the Alternative Economic Strategy', p. 120. As Sam Aaronovitch argued in 1986: 'The experience of the Mitterrand government since 1982 seemed to confirm the view that no second rank state could go it alone in implementing such a strategy [as the AES]; or, if it did, major sacrifices would be required from working people. And the result could well be politically destabilising' (Aaronovitch, 'The Alternative Economic Strategy', p. 22).
134. Callaghan, 'Rise and fall of the Alternative Economic Strategy', p. 125.
135. Ibid. In the early 1990s Holland served as adviser to Delors, with whom he had already collaborated intellectually since the 1970s (See Holland, 'Eurobonds'). Delors contributed to Holland's edited volume *Beyond Capitalist Planning*. See also Stuart Holland, *The European Imperative: Economic and Social Cohesion in the 1990s* (Nottingham: Spokesman, 1993).
136. Roberts, 'How One Man Changed How British Politicians Felt About Europe'; Hassan and Shaw, *The People's Flag and the Union Jack*, p. 160; and Thompson, *Left in the Wilderness*, pp. 256–80.
137. This was once again brought into question after the 2008 global financial crisis. See Christensen et al., 'The Finance Curse'.
138. Hain, *The Democratic Alternative*, pp. 110–1.
139. It is worth noting that Stuart Holland, while not opposed to European integration, has continued to emphasise the need for greater national sovereignty and democracy, calling for 'a process of decentralised europeanisation, to be juxtaposed against an authoritarian federation that has not been put to European electorates, is unlikely to be endorsed by them, and, critically, offers them no assurance of higher levels of employment and welfare' (Varoufakis et al., *A Modest Proposal*; see also Holland, 'Interview: Hope Amidst Despair?', where Holland calls the EU 'an anti-democratic disaster' ideologically dominated by 'neoliberal austerity').
140. See Heartfield, *The European Union*.
141. Cited in Jones, 'Class War'.
142. The Battle of Orgreave featured thousands of police officers equipped with riot gear and 'utilising dogs, horses and snatch squads before any aggressive behaviour... was undertaken by the pickets'. East et al., 'The Death of Mass Picketing', pp. 309–10.
143. *Wales Online*, 'I Felt Helpless During Miners' Strike'.
144. Wood, *The Retreat from Class*, p. 180.
145. See Wrigley, *British Trade Unions Since 1933*.
146. Hyman, 'Andre Gorz and his Disappearing Proletariat', p. 292.
147. Gorz, *Farewell to the Working Class*, p. 66.
148. Laclau and Mouffe, *Hegemony and Socialist Strategy*, p. 190.
149. Laclau, 'Debate: Roads from Socialism', p. 41.

150. As Hall had identified the problem in the mid-1980s: 'it is the "hard Left" as a peculiar and distinctive political style, a set of habits, a political-cultural tradition, stretching right across the actual organisational sub-divisions of the Left, which is at issue. It is the "hard Left" as keeper of left consciences, as political guarantor, as the litmus paper of orthodoxy, which is the problem' (Hall, 'Realignment—For What?', pp. 13–4).
151. Labour Party, *New Labour Because Britain Deserves Better*.
152. Giddens, *Beyond Left and Right*, pp. 8–9.
153. This point in made well in Heartfield, *The 'Death of the Subject' Explained*. See also Furedi, *The Politics of Fear*.
154. Fairclough, *New Labour, New Language*, pp. 10–1.
155. Heartfield, *The 'Death of the Subject' Explained*, p. 178.
156. Norman and Ganesh, *Compassionate Conservatism*.
157. Anderson, 'Renewals', pp. 13–4.

# Correction to: The Socialist Ideas of the British Left's Alternative Economic Strategy

**Correction to:**
**B. Tufekci,** *The Socialist Ideas of the British Left's Alternative Economic Strategy,*
https://doi.org/10.1007/978-3-030-34998-1

The original version of the book was inadvertently published with an incorrect affiliation of the book author "Baris Tufekci". The corrections to this affiliation have been updated.

The updated version of the book can be found at
https://doi.org/10.1007/978-3-030-34998-1

C1
B. Tufekci, *The Socialist Ideas of the British Left's Alternative Economic Strategy,*
https://doi.org/10.1007/978-3-030-34998-1_8

# Afterword: Corbyn—A Socialist Rebirth?

At the time of writing, Labour is led by Jeremy Corbyn, a Labour-left figure who did not join Blair, unexpectedly elected as leader in 2015 in a leadership contest otherwise comprising 'Blairites' and former New Labour Ministers, i.e. figures associated with the 'post-left' project discussed in the chapter above. Encouraged by Labour's strong (albeit second-place) performance in the 2017 general election, numerous figures on the left have interpreted 'Corbynism' as representing something of a socialist revival in British politics, as a break with a previously dominant New Labour 'neoliberalism', a re-emergence of class politics and Labour as a mass party, and evidence of the broad popularity of 'traditional' Labour-left policies for public ownership, wealth redistribution and workers' participation in economic ownership and workplace decision-making.[1] To what extent, therefore, does the emergence of 'Corbynism' challenge this book's assertion of a 'death of British socialism' upon the demise of the AES in the 1980s? Is Corbyn's rise evidence that socialist politics is again a major force in British politics?

## AES Parallels

Insofar as Corbyn, often called Tony Benn's protégé, has looked to the policy repertoire of Labour-left tradition, his attempts to forge a political platform credibly distinct from New Labour have to an extent involved a

B. Tufekci, *The Socialist Ideas of the British Left's Alternative Economic Strategy*,
https://doi.org/10.1007/978-3-030-34998-1

reiteration of some of the old AES themes. Echoes of these can be found in *For the Many, Not the Few*, Labour's manifesto for the 2017 general election, which has pointed to the decline of Britain's manufacturing base, the weak growth of British productivity and underinvestment in infrastructure.[2] *Alternative Models of Ownership*, a Labour-commissioned report also published in 2017, has repeated these concerns and identified the 'predominance of private property ownership' as a cause of Britain's economic problems.[3] John McDonnell, Corbyn's Shadow Chancellor of the Exchequer and close ally, has called on Labour to 'oversee a flourishing of…alternative models of ownership, from worker-owned businesses to local energy cooperatives'.[4] With a nod to the 'new revisionist', post-AES left discussed in the previous chapter, McDonnell seeks to draw on 'the best traditions of the labour movement' and show that 'forty years after Eric Hobsbawm wrote of "the forward march of labour halted"', Labour has 'an incredible opportunity to put our economy on a new and better path'.[5]

While many have maintained the radicalism of the Corbyn agenda, others have pointed to its relative moderation. They have argued that the 2017 manifesto represents a limited departure from Ed Miliband's manifesto in 2015 and that its Keynesian proposals are markedly less drastic than those of the manifestos of the AES period.[6] In 2015, Andrew Gamble described 'Corbynomics' as so far representing 'only a very pale reflection' of the AES.[7] Stuart Holland has himself highlighted the differences between his version of the entrepreneurial state and that of Marianna Mazzucato, the UK-based economist who has worked as advisor to Corbyn and whose ideas have had some influence among Corbyn's colleagues. Mazzucato has called on states to acknowledge their entrepreneurial role as leaders of innovation-led economic growth.[8] As Holland points out, however, what distinguishes his AES model of the entrepreneurial state and Mazzucato's is that the latter is not based on state ownership but is 'about sharing knowledge and promoting links between concepts and practice'.[9] Indeed, there has as yet been little in 'Corbynomics' to suggest that a Corbyn government would take state ownership beyond previously nationalised 'key utilities' and 'natural monopolies' like rail, energy and the postal service. As one recent book argues, the Corbyn-led Labour Party has thus far offered 'mild social democratic objectives' to the British electorate, 'a fully costed, tax-and-spend manifesto depicting a return to a mixed economy and a more equitable form of capitalism—in short, Keynesianism'.[10]

The leaders of Corbynism have at times employed radical rhetoric, but they have also expressed an awareness of the limited radicalism of the actual content of their policies. McDonnell has described 'Corbynomics' as having 'floated a number of ideas that weren't politically radical' but which 'demonstrated how you can move the debate forward' in a mainstream British political landscape dominated by 'neoliberalism'.[11] Corbyn has also qualified the radicalism of his economic ideas in the wider context of European capitalism: 'If I was putting forward these ideas in Germany I'd be called depressingly moderate, depressingly old fashioned as they have a national investment bank already and they invest in public services.'[12] This has been one area in which Corbynism's similarity with the AES has been pronounced: as had Holland and other proponents of the AES, Corbynism has taken inspiration from examples of 'best practice' elsewhere in the capitalist world economy, whether Norway, with its nationalised oil industry, or France, Spain and Italy, with their state-backed co-operative sectors.[13] The 'new political mainstream' that Corbynism has sought to establish has not so far expressed an intention to take British politics very far beyond successful models of administration in capitalist countries abroad. 'We'll look to at least double our co-operative sector', McDonnell has stated, 'so that it matches those in Germany and the US.'[14]

There is, however, another area in which Corbynism's parallels with the AES have been marked. Like the old Labour left, Corbynism has stressed the need to foster the closer involvement of workers in a national project for economic revival. In fact, the primary similarity between the AES and Corbynism is arguably found less in their specific proposals than in this general ideological approach that underlies both sets of politics. Yet, as suggested in this brief afterword, a closer reflection on this similarity in ideological approach perhaps also reveals what in fact most fundamentally distinguishes the AES from Corbynism. Corbynism has arisen in an industrial landscape radically different from the one to which the British left had attempted to relate in the 1970s and early 1980s. The kinds of industrial struggles that gave rise to the AES in the early 1970s have not been a feature of the period of Corbyn's rise. The British working class as an organised social force, insofar as it still exists, does not have the political significance today that it possessed in the AES era. It is this difference which perhaps most clearly separates Corbynism from its Labour-left predecessor, and which also raises interesting questions as to the former's political and historical significance as a self-described socialist project. While it is, of course, beyond the scope of this short discussion to attempt to provide any in-depth or comprehensive comparison between Corbynism and the AES, it will aim nevertheless to tentatively highlight a few points of significant divergence between the two Labour projects.

## THE CONTINUED ABSENCE OF CLASS POLITICS

In raising the importance of establishing a new class partnership in the British economy, the new Labour leader has to an extent continued where the previous party leadership had left off. As part of his 'one nation' idea, Ed Miliband had pledged employee representation on committees for company executive remuneration to encourage 'employers and employees to build partnerships for improving both business performance and job quality'.[15] Indeed, on becoming the Conservative Prime Minister in July 2016, albeit with a Corbyn-led Labour Party to her left, and in the context of corporate controversies involving the multi-millionaire retailer Sir Philip Green and alleged tax evasions by Apple and Facebook, Theresa May herself went further than Miliband by announcing plans (later abandoned) for the appointment of employee representatives on company boards, as part of her policy to 'reform capitalism so that it works for everyone'.[16] Corbynism, however, has gone beyond both Miliband and May. It has placed 'economic democracy' at the centre of its policy and rhetoric. As McDonnell told the 2018 party conference,

> at the heart of our programme is the greatest extension of economic democratic rights that this country has ever seen. It starts in the workplace...After decades of talking about industrial democracy, Labour in government will legislate to implement it.[17]

It terms of concrete reforms, this would resemble the Bullock proposals in the 1970s: according to Corbyn's plans, workers at public and private companies with a workforce of 250 or more employees would have the right to elect a third of the seats on the company board.[18] It would also involve, according to the Shadow Chancellor, an 'inclusive ownership fund' to give workers at large companies a stake in the company's returns and 'the same rights as other shareholders to have a say over the direction of their company'.[19] As with the left-wing proponents of the AES, Corbynism has seen this 'democratisation' as key not only for achieving Labour's egalitarian aims but also for the country's future economic vitality. As McDonnell has stated: 'Co-operation and collaboration is how the emerging economy of the future functions', since 'when workers own and manage their companies, those businesses last longer and are more productive'.[20] Corbynism's 'alternative models of ownership' have included an emphasis on the greater incorporation of workers in economic ownership and decision-making as part of their objective to reverse Britain's 'lack of long-term investment and declining rates of productivity'.[21]

This call for better class collaboration has been accompanied by demands for a new progressive British patriotism. McDonnell has embraced the slogan 'patriots pay their taxes', a theme which Corbyn has also endorsed.[22] As one former Labour MP has put it, welcoming the patriotic turn in Corbynism's rhetoric, progressive patriotism could be a way to unite 'disparate interests and communities', as well as hold the powerful to account.[23] Noteworthy here is the so-called Blue Labour tendency that has gained some degree of purchase in and around the Labour Party over the past decade. Launched by the British academic Maurice Glasman in 2009, chief among Blue Labour's ideas is the need to recognise the nation state as the principal entity around which people's identities, interests and solidarities must be formed for a viable strategy to advance traditional Labour objectives ('reciprocity, mutuality and collective democratic decision', as Glasman has put it) against the damaging and undemocratic influences of finance capital and globalisation.[24] Along these lines, Blue Labour proponents have seen in Brexit a left-wing opportunity to break with a politically dominant metropolitan and 'universalist' bourgeois liberalism running contrary to what they believe to be the core preoccupations of the British working class, key among which being mass immigration.[25] They have also linked their call for a renewed left-wing national consciousness closely with an emphasis on the need for improved class collaboration, demanding 'workers on company boards' as part of 'a national economic strategy, developed through negotiation with businesses, unions and citizens throughout the country'.[26] According to Jonathan Rutherford, another academic associated with the Blue Labour project:

> For Blue Labour, the 'we' is not homogenous but a plural that must be brought together in a democratic politics of the common good. Different groups and classes that constitute a polity have interests that require negotiation to explore the possibility of a common good.[27]

In their left-wing critique of Corbynism, Bolton and Pitts argue that Corbyn's politics shares the national focus of Blue Labour, despite the latter's criticism of the Corbyn leadership as subscribing to the same flawed concepts that had constituted the politics of its New Labour predecessors (with their prioritisation of '"abstract values" and universalist principles of equality and rights over the particular communal bonds of mutual reciprocity, local identity, and national, familial and religious ties that characterised "white working class" communities').[28] According to Bolton and Pitts, a key limitation of Corbynism, and what it shares with Blue Labour, is its affirmation of the nation state 'as the irreducible agent of political action' and its positioning of 'the nation against global and international capital'.[29] They point in particular to Corbynism's apparent anti-EU bias, which they see as part of the same kind of protectionist and nation-centred tendency that had characterised 'Bennism' in the 1970s and 1980s. The AES's ideas and analysis thus 'remain of fundamental importance to the Corbyn movement'.[30] Pointing to *Alternative Models of Ownership*, with its call for the state to invest in British production and its view of workers' co-operatives as a potential boon to British productivity and efficiency, Bolton and Pitts argue that this Corbynist document 'is best viewed as an extension or reformulation of the AES itself'.[31]

On the face of it, the ideas Bolton and Pitts highlight do indeed seem lifted directly from the AES. As this book has shown, central to AES analyses was a tendency to view class conflict as a leading obstacle to Britain's economic revitalisation, which would be achieved by increasing the integration of workers with the mechanisms and structures of economic power, wealth and decision-making in order to reduce industrial conflict and increase workers' identification with the aims and interests of Britain's economic growth and productivity. This was also a basis for the AES's emphasis on the need to redress British capitalism's special disadvantages in the global economy: in seeking to provide a solution to the disorder in industrial relations, AES socialists, situated as they were within the ideological boundaries of a Labour socialism tying the interests of the working class to those of the British economy, were compelled to appeal ultimately to the politics of 'the national interest'. The idea, explicitly advanced on the Labour left, was that the 'sectional' interests existing within the British economy—whether those of capital or labour, management or worker—had to be subordinated to the interests of the national economy as a whole, within which the capital-labour relation would continue to exist, albeit on 'improved' terms for the working class.

Yet the political and economic significance of 'sectional' class interests in the AES period presupposed the *assertion* of these interests. The rise of working-class militancy played a crucial role in giving rise to the AES and lending its proposals political pertinence. As discussed in chapter two, the AES informed the politics of a Labour Party whose central pitch to the electorate in the 1970s was that it was uniquely positioned, due to its special links with organised labour, to resolve the disorder in industrial relations and thereby bring the British economy back on to its feet. One commentator has argued that Corbynism has echoes of the AES because the economic problems that it identified in the 1970s—the decline of British manufacturing, under-investment and the power of multinational corporations—remain unresolved.[32] However, this ignores what was arguably a more decisive condition for the AES's rise: the intensification of industrial conflict, together with its increased politicisation, at a time when Labour's ties with its working-class base were weakening. This created greater political space in the Labour Party for alternative policies to those of a previously dominant Labour-right revisionism, policies to re-strengthen Labour's self-identification as a working-class party.

The backdrop to Corbyn's rise was markedly different, since it was unrelated to any upsurge in industrial conflict. The year of Corbyn's election as party leader saw the lowest number of workers on strike in Britain since records began in 1893.[33] That year also saw the unionised portion of total employees drop to a mere 24.7%, its lowest rate since the already low 32.4% recorded in 1995.[34] Despite Corbyn's popularity among trade-union leaders, his Labour leadership has not heralded any resurgence in trade-union membership or militancy, nor a significant trade-union campaign against the Conservative government. The steady process of trade-union decline mentioned in the previous chapter has continued into the Corbyn period. While an average of just over 10 million days a year were lost to strikes in the period between 1968 and 1983, in the four years between 2015 to 2018 that average was around 300,000 (with an average of around 600,000 for the period between 2003 and 2018).[35] In comparison to trade-unionism in the AES period, in which industrial militancy could bring down governments and unions featured as a central concern of state policy, it appears reasonable to say that organised labour in Britain is now a slight shadow of its former self, with a relative lack of significance politically or economically as a social movement.

Labour under Corbyn has to an extent adopted some of the language of class politics, therefore, but it has done so in the absence of a class movement. Labour will now once again be 'the political voice of the working class', Corbyn told a union conference in 2018, after thirty years of claims by 'the media and the establishment...that class doesn't matter anymore'.[36] In its 2017 general-election manifesto, Labour pledged a '20-point plan for security and equality at work', including proposals for banning zero-hour contracts and repealing the Trade Union Act 2016.[37] Yet these proposals, unlike Labour's in the AES period—such as the concessions in its social contract, devised to encourage the unions to accept incomes policy—appear less as a response to demands or pressures from a working-class movement than an attempt to readjust Labour's electoral brand, by invoking past Labour politics, at a time when New Labour is perceived as electorally exhausted. This lack of influence by a real-life class movement seems also reflected in how Corbynism has chosen to present its 'class politics'. Its motto 'for the many, not the few', which was also favoured by Blair, was included in New Labour's rewritten Clause 4 that removed its prior class references. The notion of the '99 per cent'—the idea that, in the words of one Corbyn-supporting Labour MP, 'the fundamental divide in our society remains that between the 99 per cent and the top 1 per cent' of the population[38]—has also gained traction, seemingly rendering unnecessary any serious analysis of contemporary class forces and their configuration. Bolton and Pitts have ascribed this to Corbynism's left-wing populism, in which 'class as a constitutive social relation...disappears from sight altogether'.[39] Yet it could perhaps be added that the lack of precision and seriousness with which Corbynism has approached class divisions reflects the fact that class conflict has not been an impetus for its rise.

There are those on the left who, of course, argue to the contrary, posing the rise of Corbynism as a response to social pressures against neo-liberalism and austerity, or, as Simon Hannah contends, a product of the increasing unsustainability of 'the class compromise on which Labour was founded in 1900'.[40] According to another left-wing author, Richard Seymour, Corbyn's election as party leader owed to the fact that he was seen 'as a man of the movements, not of the markets', and the 2017 Labour manifesto 'completely changed the terrain, so that class was as important as nation to the final outcome'.[41] However, Seymour also acknowledges the 'secular crisis of the labour movement and its grass roots', i.e. the long-term process of working-class electoral desertion of the Labour Party, the reversal of which he sees as one of the main challenges facing Corbyn.[42] The hope here, common among the 'far left' in and around Corbynism, is that a Corbyn-led Labour Party can broaden the political debate, radicalise it, help revive the labour movement, and return workers' loyalties to Labour as the reconstituted party of the left.[43] Hannah points to the need for the Labour left to finally do 'something it has always talked about but never done—building a mass extra-parliamentary movement'.[44] According to such formula, it is not so much 'pressure from below' which compels Labour to adopt left-wing policies, but the Labour Party itself which may help give birth to the mass social movement seen as necessary for radical social change. While this may not be impossible, it is also, given Labour's history, improbable. Corbyn's 'far left' supporters are certainly not unaware of Labour's historical limitations, and their optimism about Corbynism is often combined with an acute understanding of Labour's past as a moderating if not outrightly detrimental influence on socialist politics in Britain.[45] Their hope, however, is that, in the given circumstances, in the restricted parameters currently confronting socialist politics, Corbynism can play a different role, opening up possibilities for a radicalism that may, in the process, even lead to an unprecedented socialist transformation of Labour itself. In this, the 'far left' around Corbyn seem to have something in common with the left-wing proponents of the AES in the 1970s and early 1980s: the belief, as mentioned in chapter six, that Labour may be able to defy its origins, traditions and long-established practices to finally become a force for socialist radicalisation in Britain. But if this was unrealistic in the 1970s, a time of considerable class unrest, it is arguably even more so in the present period of relative class calm.

This unlikelihood was perhaps confirmed by Corbynism's response to an issue in contemporary British politics in which class arguably *did* play a significant role: the 2016 referendum on the UK's membership of the EU, in which millions of working-class people voted to leave an institution that has, in its various forms, represented the framework for British capitalism for over four decades. The class composition of the Leave vote was, of course, varied, and many working-class people also voted Remain, including majorities against Brexit in Scotland, Northern Ireland and among black and Asian voters. As concluded by a 2016 NatCen study, however, those most likely to vote Leave were those from the working class, and in particular its poorer sections—voters earning less than £1200 per month, living in social housing, and without university qualifications.[46] From the perspective of class politics and class analysis, it was not insignificant that a very high number of the country's least well-off citizens rejected the advice of the vast majority of the political and business establishment in Britain—including the leaders of the three main political parties—and voiced their opposition to the transnational organisation of the powerful capitalist states of Europe.

The fact that the bulk of the left around Corbyn, including the leaders of most British trade unions, sided with Remain appears to demonstrate that Corbynism has not broken with the New Labour view of the EU as a bulwark for social-democratic and progressive politics. This is perhaps most clearly seen in the frequent left-wing assertion that the EU's laws and institutions are a means to protect workers' rights and British jobs and wages.[47] By continuing to assert this idea—established on the British left with the demise of the AES and the decline of organised labour—the British labour movement conveys its lack of confidence in its own ability to fight for and secure its own interests. In addition, Corbynism's support for the EU appears to express its reluctance to carry out its stated aim of building a grassroots extra-parliamentary movement against the status quo. Instead, by demanding and marching for a second referendum with Remain as one of the ballot options,[48] Corbyn's supporters have risked appearing as advocates for the status quo, and as among the ranks of those who see in Brexit an expression of led-astray masses initially oblivious to their true interests.[49] Furthermore, by rejecting the Leave vote on the grounds that its campaign was led by right-wingers like Boris Johnson, Michael Gove and Nigel Farage, they not only discount the fact that Remain had the backing of a much larger portion of the British ruling class (of the 'one per cent'), but also that it was perhaps precisely the absence of a significant left leadership that caused the politics of anti-immigration and British and English nationalism to feature in the Brexit cause as prominently as they did in the first place.

In a sense, of course, it was to be expected that Corbynism, whatever Corbyn's own history as an opponent of the EU, should have continued on the path of transnationalism laid down by the left in the aftermath of the defeat and decline of organised labour in the 1980s, since that condition for its rise has yet to be reversed. The aim of this brief discussion has been to indicate that Corbynism and the AES grew out of two very different historical contexts. As to where Corbynism will lead, that remains to be seen; whatever its current politics, the oft-cited political uncertainty and 'anti-establishment' populist mood of our present period seem likely to produce further political surprises in the years ahead. Yet, whatever the impetus behind Corbyn's rise, it was distinct from that which helped give rise to the AES in the early 1970s. Despite any parallels in policy ideas with Corbyn's manifesto, the AES remains distinguished by its social context and core raison d'être: to incorporate an increasingly militant workforce into a strategy for Britain's economic recovery—a strategy that would need to involve, according to its proponents, 'a fundamental and irreversible shift in the balance of power and wealth in favour of working people and their families'.

## NOTES

1. See Perryman (ed.), *The Corbyn Effect*; Seymour, *Corbyn*; McDonnell (ed.), *Economics for the Many*, Hannah, *A Party with Socialist in It*.
2. Labour Party, *For the Many, Not the Few*, p. 13.
3. Labour Party, *Alternative Models of Ownership*, p. 5.
4. McDonnell, 'Introduction', p. xvi.
5. Ibid., pp. xv, xviii.
6. Bush, 'Jeremy Corbyn's Policies Aren't that Different from Ed Miliband's or Even New Labour?'; Rawnsley, 'The Really Scary Thing About Corbyn?'
7. Gamble, 'Corbynomics: Part 1'.
8. Mazzucato, *The Entrepreneurial State*.
9. Holland, 'Interview: Hope Amidst Despair?' p. 92.
10. Hannah, *A Party with Socialists in It*, pp. 234–5.
11. Cited in Nunns, *The Candidate*, p. 359.
12. Ibid., pp. 358–9.
13. Labour Party, *Alternative Models of Ownership*, pp. 29, 14–7.
14. McDonnell, Speech to Labour Annual Conference 2016.
15. Labour Party, *Britain Can Be Better*, p. 21.
16. Mason, 'Theresa May to "Reform Capitalism"'; Pratley, 'Theresa May's Plan to Put Workers in Boardrooms'.
17. McDonnell, Speech to Labour Annual Conference 2018.
18. Corbyn, Speech to Labour Annual Conference 2018.
19. McDonnell, Speech to Labour Annual Conference 2018.
20. McDonnell, Speech to Labour Annual Conference 2016.
21. Labour Party, *Alternative Models of Ownership*, p. 5.
22. McDonnell, Speech to Labour Annual Conference 2016; Corbyn, Speech to Labour Annual Conference 2016.
23. Denham, 'Slowly But Surely, the Patriotism Question Is Making Its Way into Labour'.
24. Glasman, 'Brexit Offers the Possibility for Socialists to Lead a Political Transformation'.
25. Rutherford, 'Nigel Farage and Our Democratic Nation'.
26. 'What We Support', Blue Labour website, https://www.bluelabour.org/blue-labour-in-practice/ (accessed August 2019).
27. Rutherford, 'Why Blue Labour Is Still Relevant Under Corbyn'.
28. Bolton and Pitts, *Corbynism*, p. 15.
29. Ibid., pp. 113, 148.

30. Ibid., p. 132.
31. Ibid., p. 133.
32. Elliott, 'G20: Is It Time to Go Back to the Future, Before Globalisation?'
33. Ruddick, 'Number of Striking Workers Now Lower Than Ever'.
34. Department for Business, Innovation and Skills, *Trade Union Membership 2015*, p. 3.
35. Office for National Statistics, *Labour Disputes in the UK: 2018*.
36. Labour Party, 'Labour Is Back as the Political Voice of the Working Class—Corbyn'.
37. Labour Party, *For the Many, Not the Few*, pp. 47–50.
38. Burgon, 'Only a Socialist Labour Government Can Resolve Britain's Deepening Crises'.
39. Bolton and Pitts, *Corbynism*, p. 167.
40. Hannah, *A Party with Socialists in It*, p. 242.
41. Seymour, *Corbyn*, pp. 7, xxiii–iv.
42. Ibid., p. 61.
43. Ibid., pp. 248–51.
44. Hannah, *A Party with Socialists in It*, p. 242.
45. For example: Seymour, *Corbyn*, pp. 89–137; Hannah, *A Party with Socialists in It*.
46. NatCen, *Understanding the Leave Vote*, p. 7.
47. O'Grady, 'Is the European Union Good or Bad for British Workers?'
48. Cooper, 'Jeremy Corbyn's Momentum Movement to Mobilise Its 100,000 Supporters Behind Remain in the EU Referendum'; Jones, "Soft' Brexit Is Dead'.
49. For a discussion, see Winlow et al., *The Rise of the Right*, pp. 197–208.

# Bibliography

Aaronovitch, Sam, ed. *The American Threat to British Culture*. London: Arena, Fore Publications Ltd., 1951.

Aaronovitch, Sam. *The Road from Thatcherism: The Alternative Economic Strategy*. London: Lawrence and Wishart, 1981.

Aaronovitch, Sam. 'The Alternative Economic Strategy: Goodbye to All that?' *Marxism Today*, February 1986.

Abrams, Mark, and Richard Rose. *Must Labour Lose?* London: Penguin Books, 1960.

A Group of Sheffield Steel Workers. *Steel Workers Next Step*. IWC Pamphlet no. 7. Nottingham: Institute for Workers' Control, undated pamphlet.

Alford, Robert. 'Class Voting in Anglo-American Political Systems'. In Seymour Martin Lipset and Stein Rokkan, eds. *Party Systems and Voter Alignments: Cross-National Perspectives*. New York: The Free Press, 1967.

Allen, V.L. *Militant Trade Unionism*. London: Merlin Press, 1966.

Amalgamated Engineering and Foundry Workers' Union. 'Industrial Democracy in Great Britain'. *ICF International Conference on Industrial Democracy*, November 1968.

Anderson, Perry. 'Problems of Socialist Strategy'. In Perry Anderson and Robin Blackburn, eds. *Towards Socialism*. London: Collins, 1966.

Anderson, Perry. 'Renewals'. *New Left Review*, January–February 2000.

Andrews, David R. *Keynes and the British Humanist Tradition: The Moral Purpose of the Market*. Abingdon: Routledge, 2010.

Andrews, Geoff. *Endgames and New Times: The Final Years of British Communism 1964–1991*. London: Lawrence and Wishart, 2004.

© The Editor(s) (if applicable) and The Author(s), under exclusive license to Springer Nature Switzerland AG 2020
B. Tufekci, *The Socialist Ideas of the British Left's Alternative Economic Strategy*,
https://doi.org/10.1007/978-3-030-34998-1

Archibugi, Franco. 'Capitalist Planning in Question'. In Stuart Holland, ed. *Beyond Capitalist Planning*. Oxford: Basil Blackwell, 1978.

Archibugi, Franco, Jacques Delors, and Stuart Holland. 'Planning for Development'. In Stuart Holland, ed. *Beyond Capitalist Planning*. Oxford: Basil Blackwell, 1978.

Archibugi, Franco, Jacques Delors, and Stuart Holland. 'The International Crisis'. In Stuart Holland, ed. *Beyond Capitalism Planning*. Oxford: Basil Blackwell, 1978.

Bailey, Alan. 'Not All "the Bad Old Days": Revisiting Labour's 1970s Industrial Strategy'. The Progressive Policy Think Tank (accessed in May 2016 from https://www.ippr.org/juncture/not-all-the-bad-old-days-revisiting-labours-1970s-industrial-strategy).

Barratt Brown, Michael. *After Imperialism*. London: Merlin Press, 1970.

Barratt Brown, Michael. *UCS: The Social Audit*. IWC pamphlet. Nottingham: Institute for Workers' Control, 1971.

Barratt Brown, Michael. *From Labourism to Socialism: The Political Economy of Labour in the 1970's*. Nottingham: Spokesman Books, 1972.

Barratt Brown, Michael. 'The Growth and Distribution of Income and Wealth'. In Ken Coates, ed. *What Went Wrong: Explaining the Fall of the Labour Government*. Nottingham: Spokesman Books, 1979.

Barratt Brown, Michael. *Labour and Sterling*. IWC Pamphlet no. 3. Nottingham: Institute for Workers' Control, undated pamphlet.

Barratt Brown, Michael. *Opening the Books*. IWC pamphlet no. 4. Nottingham: Institute for Workers' Control, undated pamphlet.

Barratt Brown, Michael, and Stuart Holland. *Public Ownership and Democracy*. IWC Pamphlet no. 38. Nottingham: Institute for Workers' Control, undated pamphlet.

Barratt Brown, Michael, Ken Coates, and Tony Topham. 'Workers' Control Versus "Revolutionary" Theory'. In *Socialist Register 1975*. London: Merlin Press, 1975.

Bearman, Jonathan. 'Anatomy of the Bennite Left'. *International Socialism*, Autumn 1979 (accessed in February 2015 from https://www.marxists.org/history/etol/newspape/isj2/1979/isj2-006/bearman.html).

Beer, Samuel H. *Modern British Politics: A Study of Parties and Pressure Groups*. London: Faber and Faber, 1969.

Bell, Daniel. *The End of Ideology: On the Exhaustion of Political Ideas in the Fifties*. New York: Harvard University Press, 1960.

Ben-Ami, Daniel. *Ferraris for All: In Defence of Economic Progress*. Bristol: The Policy Press, 2010.

Benn, Tony. *Fighting Back: Speaking Out for Socialism in the Eighties*. London: Hutchinson, 1988.

Benn, Tony. *Industrial Democracy: Tony Benn at the IWC Debate—An Account of the Institute for Workers' Control Meeting at the Labour Party Conference, November 1974.* IWC Pamphlet no. 45. Nottingham: Institute for Workers' Control, 1975.

Benn, Tony. *Parliament, People and Power: Agenda for a Free Society.* London: Verso, 1982.

Benn, Tony (Anthony Wedgwood). 'Preface'. In Inigo Bing, ed. *The Labour Party: An Organisational Study.* Fabian Tract 407. London: Fabian Society, 1971.

Benn, Tony. *The Case for a Constitutional Civil Service.* IWC Pamphlet no. 69. Nottingham: Institute for Workers' Control, undated pamphlet.

Benn, Tony. 'The Industrial Context'. In Ken Coates, ed. *The New Worker Co-operatives.* Nottingham: Spokesman Books for the IWC, 1976.

Benn, Tony (Anthony Wedgewood). *The New Politics: A Socialist Reconnaissance.* Fabian Tract 402. London: Fabian Society, 1970.

Benn, Tony. *The Speaker, the Commons and Democracy.* Nottingham: Spokesman Books, 2000.

Benn, Tony. 'Who Dares Wins'. *Marxism Today,* January 1985.

Benn, Tony, Frances Morrell, and Francis Cripps. *A Ten Year Industrial Strategy for Britain.* IWC Pamphlet no. 49. Nottingham: Institute for Workers' Control, undated pamphlet.

Black, Lawrence, and Hugh Pemberton. 'Introduction. The Benighted Decade? Reassessing the 1970s'. In Lawrence Black, Hugh Pemberton, and Pat Thane, eds. *Reassessing 1970s Britain.* Manchester: Manchester University Press, 2013.

Blackledge, Paul. *Perry Anderson, Marxism and the New Left.* London: Merlin Press, 2004.

Blair, Tony. 'Forging a New Agenda'. *Marxism Today,* October 1991.

Bolton, Matt, and Frederick Harry Pitts. *Corbynism: A Critical Approach.* Bingley: Emerald Publishing Limited, 2018.

Boyd, John M. *Is Industrial Democracy Compatible with Efficiency?* The 1967 E.W. Hancock Paper. The Institution of Production Engineers, 1967.

Bradley, Ian. 'Master Plan for a Master Race: The National Front's Vision of Greater Britain'. *Times* (London), 30 August 1977.

British Institute of Management. *Employee Participation: A Management View—Report of a BIM Working Party.* London: BIM, 1975.

British Institute of Management. *Industrial Democracy: Some Implications for Management.* London: BIM Occasional Papers (New Series), 1968.

Budge, Ian. 'Relative Decline as a Political Issue: Ideological Motivations of the Politico-Economic Debate in Post-war Britain'. *Contemporary Record,* 7:1, 1993.

Burgon, Richard. 'Only a Socialist Labour Government Can Resolve Britain's Deepening Crises'. *Morning Star,* 21 March 2019 (accessed in August

2019 from https://morningstaronline.co.uk/article/f/only-socialist-labour-government-can-resolve-britains-deepening-crises).

Burton-Cartledge, Phil. 'Marching Separately, Seldom Together: The Political History of Two Principal Trends in British Trotskyism, 1945–2009'. In Evan Smith and Matthew Worley, eds. *Against the Grain: The British Far Left from 1956*. Manchester: Manchester University Press, 2014.

Bush, Stephen. 'Jeremy Corbyn's Policies Aren't that Different from Ed Miliband's or Even New Labour. So why Is He Being Attacked?' *New Statesman*, 11 April 2017 (accessed in July 2019 from https://www.newstatesman.com/politics/welfare/2017/04/jeremy-corbyns-policies-arent-different-ed-milibands-or-even-new-labour-so).

Butler, David, and Donald Stokes. *Political Change in Britain: The Evolution of Electoral Change*. London: Macmillan Press, 1974.

Callaghan, John. 'Rise and Fall of the Alternative Economic Strategy: From Internationalisation of Capital to "Globalisation"'. *Contemporary British History*, 14:3, 2000.

Callinicos, Alex. 'The Politics of *Marxism Today*'. *International Socialism*, Summer 1985 (accessed in January 2017 from https://www.marxists.org/history/etol/writers/callinicos/1985/xx/marxtoday.html#n31).

Cawood, Ian. 'Crisis? What Crisis? The Callaghan Government and the British "Winter of Discontent"', January 2015 (accessed in May 2017 from http://www.history.ac.uk/reviews/review/1711).

Chiplin, Brian, John Coyne, and Ljubo Sirc. *Can Workers Manage?* Institute of Economic Affairs. Hobart Paper 77, Sussex: IAE, 1977.

Christensen, John, Nick Shaxson, and Duncan Wigan. 'The Finance Curse: Britain and the World Economy'. *British Journal of Politics and International Relations*, 18:1, 2016.

City Company Law Committee. *A Reply to Bullock*, 1977.

Cliff, Tony. *The employers' offensive*, 1970 (accessed in May 2016 from https://www.marxists.org/archive/cliff/works/1970/offensive/index.htm).

Coates, David. *Crisis of Labour: Industrial Relations and the State in Contemporary Britain*. Oxford: Philip Allan Publishers Ltd., 1989.

Coates, David, and John Hillard, eds. *The Economic Decline of Modern Britain*. Sussex: Wheatsheaf Books Ltd., 1986.

Coates, Ken. 'Democracy and Workers' Control'. In Perry Anderson and Robin Blackburn, eds. *Towards Socialism*. New York: Cornell University Press, 1966.

Coates, Ken. 'Socialists and the Labour Party'. In *Socialist Register 1973*. London: Merlin Press, 1973.

Coates, Ken. 'What Went Wrong?' In Ken Coates, ed. *What Went Wrong: Explaining the Fall of the Labour Government*. Nottingham: Spokesman Books, 1979.

Coates, Ken. 'Whatever Happened to Industrial Democracy?' In Ken Coates, ed. *What Went Wrong: Explaining the Fall of the Labour Government.* Nottingham: Spokesman Books, 1979.

Coates, Ken, and Tony Topham. 'Participation or Control?' In Ken Coates, ed. *Can the Workers Run Industry?* London: Sphere Books Ltd., 1968.

Coates, Ken, and Tony Topham. *The New Unionism: Case for Workers' Control.* London: Peter Owen Ltd., 1972.

Cole, G.D.H. *Socialist Thought: Marxism and Anarchism, 1850–1890.* London: Macmillan and Co Ltd., 1961.

Cole, G.D.H., and Mellor, William. *Workers' Control and Self-government in Industry.* London: New Fabian Research Bureau and Messrs. Victor Gollancz Ltd., 1933.

Communist International. *Manifesto of the Second World Congress* (accessed in March 2015 from https://www.marxists.org/archive/trotsky/1924/ffyci-1/ch12b.htm).

Confederation of British Industry. *Guidelines for Action on Employee Involvement.* London: CBI, 1979.

Confederation of British Industry. *In Place of Bullock.* London: CBI, 1977.

Conrad, Jack. *In the Enemy Camp: Using Parliament for Revolution.* London: November Publications Ltd., 1993.

Conservative Trade Unionists. *Participation—A New Way Ahead,* 1976.

Cook, Dave. 'The British Road to Socialism and the Communist Party'. *Marxism Today,* December 1978.

Cooley, Mike. *A Debate on Workers Control.* IWC Pamphlet no. 64. Nottingham: Institute for Workers' Control, 1978.

Cooper, Charlie. 'Jeremy Corbyn's Momentum Movement to Mobilise Its 100,000 Supporters Behind Remain in the EU Referendum'. *Independent* (accessed in August 2019 from https://www.independent.co.uk/news/jeremy-corbyn-s-momentum-movement-to-mobilise-its-100000-supporters-behind-remain-in-the-eu-a7047076.html).

Corbyn, Jeremy. Speech to Labour Annual Conference 2018 (accessed in July 2019 from https://labour.org.uk/press/jeremy-corbyn-speaking-labour-party-conference-today/).

Corbyn, Jeremy. Speech to the TUC, 15 September 2015 (accessed in September 2016 from http://jeremycorbyn.org.uk/articles/jeremy-corbyns-speech-to-the-tuc/).

CPGB. *Draft Programme of the C.P.G.B. to the Comintern,* 1924 (accessed in October 2015 from https://www.marxists.org/history/international/comintern/sections/britain/periodicals/communist_review/1924/02/draft_programme.htm).

CPGB. *Manifesto for New Times: A Strategy for the 1990s.* London: CPGB, 1990.

CPGB. *Solidarity with the Miners: A Communist Party Broadsheet*, undated (c. 1984).

CPGB. *The British Road to Socialism*, 1951 (accessed in July 2015 from https://www.marxists.org/history/international/comintern/sections/britain/brs/1951/51.htm#6).

CPGB. *The British Road to Socialism*, 1977 (accessed in July 2015 from https://www.marxists.org/history/international/comintern/sections/britain/brs/1977/index.htm).

Crewe, Ivor, Bo Sarlvik, and James Alt. 'Partisan Dealignment in Britain 1964–1974'. *British Journal of Political Science*, 7:2, 1977.

Cripps, Francis, and Wynne Godley. 'A Formal Analysis of the Cambridge Economic Policy Group Model'. *Economica*, 43:172, 1976.

Cripps, Francis, and Wynne Godley. 'Control of Imports as a Means to Full Employment and the Expansion of World Trade: The UK's Case'. *Cambridge Journal of Economics*, 2:3, 1978.

Cronin, James. *New Labour's Pasts: The Labour Party and Its Discontents*. Harlow: Pearson Education Ltd., 2004.

Crosland, Anthony. *Socialism Now and Other Essays*. London: Jonathan Cape Ltd., 1975.

Crosland, Anthony. *The Future of Socialism*. London: Jonathan Cape, 1956.

Crossman, Richard. 'Introduction'. In Walter Bagehot, *The English Constitution*. London: Fontana, 1964.

Darlington, Ralph, and Dave Lyddon. *Glorious Summer: Class Struggle in Britain 1972*. London: Bookmarks, 2001.

Davies, Jonathan S. *Challenging Governance Theory: From Networks to Hegemony*. Bristol: The Policy Press, 2011.

Denham, John. 'Slowly But Surely, the Patriotism Question Is Making Its Way into Labour'. *New Statesman*, 29 September 2016 (accessed in October 2016 from http://www.newstatesman.com/politics/staggers/2016/09/slowly-surely-patriotism-question-making-its-way-labour).

Department for Business, Innovation and Skills. *Trade Union Membership 2015*, May 2016 (accessed in July 2019 from https://assets.publishing.service.gov.uk/government/uploads/system/uploads/attachment_data/file/525938/Trade_Union_Membership_2015_-_Statistical_Bulletin.pdf).

Deutscher, Isaac. 'On Internationals and Internationalism', 1964 (accessed in October 2015 from https://www.marxists.org/archive/deutscher/1964/internationals-internationalism.htm).

Diamond, Patrick. *The Crosland Legacy: The Future of British Social Democracy*. Bristol: Policy Press, 2016.

Dix, Bernard. Review of Sam Aaronovitch's *The Road from Thatcherism*. *Marxism Today*, May 1981.

Dostaler, Gilles. *Keynes and His Battles*. Cheltenham: Edward Elgar Publishing Ltd., 2007.

Driver, Stephen. *Understanding British Political Parties*. Cambridge: Polity Press, 2011.

East, Robert, Helen Power, and Philip A. Thomas. 'The Death of Mass Picketing'. *Journal of Law and Society*, 12:3, 1985.

Eaton, John, John Hughes, and Ken Coates. *UCS: Workers' Control: The Real Defence Against Unemployment Is Attack*. IWC Pamphlet no. 25. Nottingham: Institute for Workers' Control, undated pamphlet.

Ellen, Geoff. 'Labour and Strike-Breaking 1945–1951'. *International Socialism*, Summer 1984 (accessed in August 2017 from https://www.marxists.org/history/etol/newspape/isj2/1984/isj2-024/ellen.html).

Elliott, Larry. 'G20: Is It Time to Go Back to the Future, Before Globalisation?' *Guardian*, 4 September 2016 (accessed in July 2019 from https://www.theguardian.com/business/2016/sep/04/g20-is-it-time-to-go-back-to-the-future-before-globalisation).

Ellison, Nick. *Egalitarian Thought and Labour Politics: Retreating Visions*. London: Routledge, 1994.

Ellison, Nick, and Sarah Ellison. 'Creating "Opportunity for All"? New Labour, New Localism and the Opportunity Society'. *Social Policy and Society*, 5:3, 2006.

Engels, Friedrich. 'On the Question of Free Trade', 1888 (accessed in October 2015 from https://www.marxists.org/archive/marx/works/1888/free-trade/).

Engels, Friedrich. 'Socialism in Germany', 1892 (accessed from https://www.marxists.org/archive/marx/works/1892/01/socialism-germany.htm).

*Express*. 'Labour's Leaked Manifesto Reveals Jeremy Corbyn Pushing Party Back to the 1970s', 11 May 2017 (accessed in September 2017 from http://www.express.co.uk/news/politics/803002/Labour-manifesto-leaked-Jeremy-Corbyn-General-Election-2017).

Evans, Geoffrey. 'Class and Vote: Disrupting the Orthodoxy'. In Geoffrey Evans, ed. *The End of Class Politics? Class Voting in Comparative Context*. Oxford: Oxford University Press, 1999.

Evans, Geoffrey, Anthony Heath, and Clive Payne. 'Modelling Trends in the Class/Party Relationship 1964–87'. *Electoral Studies*, 10:2, 1991.

Fairclough, Norman. *New Labour, New Language*. London: Routledge, 2000.

Fielding, Steven, and Declan McHugh. 'The Progressive Dilemma and the Social Democratic Perspective'. In John Callaghan, Steve Fielding, and Steve Ludlam, eds. *Interpreting the Labour Party: Approaches to Labour Politics and History*. Manchester: Manchester University Press, 2003.

Fine, Ben, Laurence Harris, Marjorie Mayo, Angela Weir, and Elizabeth Wilson. *Class Politics: An Answer to Its Critics*. London: Leftover Pamphlets, undated pamphlet (c. mid-1980s).

Fishman, Nina. '1951–1960' (accessed in August 2017 from http://www.unionhistory.info/timeline/1945_1960_2.php).

Foote, Geoffrey. 'Interview with Tony Benn'. *Capital and Class*, issue 17, Summer 1982.

Foote, Geoffrey. *The Labour Party's Political Thought: A History*. London: Macmillan Press, 1986.

Forester, Tom. 'Neutralising the Industrial Strategy'. In Ken Coates, ed. *What Went Wrong: Explaining the Fall of the Labour Government*. Nottingham: Spokesman Books, 1979.

Forester, Tom. *The Labour Party and the Working Class*. London: Heinemann Educational, 1976.

Franklin, Mark N. *The Decline of Class Voting in Britain: Changes in the Basis of Electoral Change 1964–1983*. Oxford: Oxford University Press, 1985.

Furedi, Frank. *The Politics of Fear: Beyond Left and Right*. London: Continuum, 2005.

Gaitskell, Hugh. Speech Against UK Membership of the Common Market, 3 October 1962 (accessed in September 2015 from https://www.cvce.eu/content/publication/1999/1/1/05f2996b-000b-4576-8b42-8069033a16f9/publishable_en.pdf).

Gamble, Andrew. *Britain in Decline: Economic Policy, Political Strategy and the British State*. London: Macmillan Press Ltd., 1981.

Gamble, Andrew. 'Corbynomics: Part 1'. *SPERI*, 3 November 2015 (accessed in July 2019 from http://speri.dept.shef.ac.uk/2015/11/03/corbynomics-part-1/).

Gamble, Andrew. *The Free Economy and the Strong State: The Politics of Thatcherism*. Hampshire: Palgrave, 1994.

Gardiner, Jean, and Sheila Smith. 'Feminism and the Alternative Economic Strategy'. *Marxism Today*, October 1981.

George, Stephen. *Britain and European Integration Since 1945*. Oxford: Blackwell, 1991.

Giddens, Anthony. *Beyond Left and Right: The Future of Radical Politics*. Cambridge: Polity Press, 1994.

Glasman, Maurice. 'Brexit Offers the Possibility for Socialists to Lead a Political Transformation'. *Morning Star*, 22 December 2018 (accessed in May 2019 from https://morningstaronline.co.uk/article/brexit-offers-possibility-socialists-lead-political-transformation).

Glyn, Andrew. *Capitalist Crisis: Tribune's 'Alternative Strategy' or a Socialist Plan*. London: Militant, undated.

Glyn, Andrew. 'Review Article: Capitalism, Conflict and Inflation'. *Marxism Today*, June 1980.

Glyn, Andrew. *The Economic Case Against Pit Closures*. Yorkshire: NUM, undated.

Gorz, André. *Farewell to the Working Class: An Essay on Post-industrial Socialism.* London: Pluto, 1997.

Grafton, Frank. 'The Road from Thatcherism, or the Road from Marxism?' *Leninist*, Winter 1981–1982 (accessed in May 2016 from http://cpgb.org.uk/assets/files/leninistpdf/The%20Leninist%20(1).pdf).

Graham, Alistair. *The Workers' Next Step.* London: Independent Labour Party, 1973.

*Guardian.* 'Labour Breaks Taboo on Ownership', 28 November 1983.

Hain, Peter. *The Democratic Alternative: A Socialist Response to Britain's Crisis.* Middlesex: Penguin Books, 1983.

Hain, Peter, and Simon Hebditch. *Radicals and Socialism.* IWC Pamphlet no. 58, Nottingham: IWC.

Hall, Peter A. 'Policy Paradigms, Social Learning, and the State: The Case of Economic Policymaking in Britain'. *Comparative Politics*, 25:3, 1993.

Hall, Stuart. 'Faith, Hope or Clarity'. *Marxism Today*, January 1985.

Hall, Stuart. 'Realignment—For What?' *Marxism Today*, December 1985.

Hall, Stuart. 'Redrawing the Political Map'. *Marxism Today*, December 1982.

Hall, Stuart. 'The Great Moving Nowhere Show'. *Marxism Today*, November–December 1998.

Hall, Stuart. 'The Great Moving Right Show'. In Stuart Hall and Martin Jacques, eds. *The Politics of Thatcherism.* London: Lawrence and Wishart, 1983.

Hannah, Simon. *A Party with Socialists in It: A History of the Labour Left.* London: Pluto Press, 2018.

Harmon, Mark D. *The British Labour Government and the 1976 IMF Crisis.* Houndmills: Macmillan Press, 1997.

Harris, John. '"If You've Got Money, You Vote in...if You Haven't Got Money, You Vote Out"'. *Guardian*, 24 June 2016 (accessed in January 2017 from https://www.theguardian.com/politics/commentisfree/2016/jun/24/divided-britain-brexit-money-class-inequality-westminster).

Harris, John. 'Marxism Today: The Forgotten Visionaries Whose Ideas Could Save Labour'. *Guardian*, 29 September 2015 (accessed in January 2017 from https://www.theguardian.com/politics/2015/sep/29/marxism-today-forgotten-visionaries-whose-ideas-could-save-labour).

Harrison, John. 'The Politics of the Alternative Economic Strategy'. *Marxism Today*, May 1981.

Hassan, Gerry, and Eric Shaw, *The People's Flag and the Union Jack: An Alternative History of Britain and the Labour Party.* London: Biteback Publishing Ltd., 2019.

Hatfield, Michael. *The House the Left Built: Inside Labour Policy-Making, 1970–75.* London: Victor Gollancz Ltd., 1978.

Hattersley, Roy. 'It's No Longer My Party'. *Guardian*, 24 June 2001 (accessed in May 2017 from https://www.theguardian.com/politics/2001/jun/24/labour2001to2005.news).

Hattersley, Roy. 'Trustee of Keir Hardie's Cloth Cap'. *Guardian*, 5 June 2000 (accessed in May 2017 from https://www.theguardian.com/politics/2000/jun/05/labour.labour1997to991).

Hay, Colin. 'Narrating the Crisis: The Discursive Construction of the "Winter of Discontent"'. *Sociology*, 30:2, 1996.

Hay, Colin. 'The Winter of Discontent Thirty Years on'. *The Political Quarterly*, 80:4, 2009.

Heartfield, James. *Green Capitalism: Manufacturing Scarcity in an Age of Abundance*. London, 2008.

Heartfield, James. *The 'Death of the Subject' Explained*. Sheffield: Sheffield Hallam Press, 2002.

Heartfield, James. *The European Union and the End of Politics*. Winchester: Zero Books, 2013.

Heath, Anthony, Roger Jowell, and John Curtice. *How Britain Votes*. Oxford: Pergamon Press, 1985.

Heffer, Eric. *Class Struggle in Parliament: Socialist View of Industrial Relations*. Littlehampton Book Services Ltd., 1973.

Hindess, Barry. *The Decline of Working-Class Politics*. London: Granada Publishing Limited, 1971.

Hobsbawm, Eric. 'Labour's Lost Millions'. In Eric Hobsbawm, *Politics for a Rational Left: Political Writing 1977–1988*. London: Verso, 1989.

Hobsbawm, Eric. 'Preface'. In Eric Hobsbawm, *Politics for a Rational Left: Political Writing 1977–1988*. London: Verso, 1989.

Hobsbawm, Eric. 'Snatching Victory from Defeat'. In Eric Hobsbawm, *Politics for a Rational Left: Political Writing 1977–1988*. London: Verso, 1989.

Hobsbawm, Eric. *The Age of Capital, 1848–1875*. London: Weidenfeld and Nicholson, 1975.

Hobsbawm, Eric. 'The Beginnings of Decline'. In David Coates and John Hillard, eds. *The Economic Decline of Modern Britain: The Debate Between Left and Right*. Sussex: Wheatsheaf Books Ltd., 1986.

Hobsbawm, Eric. 'The Debate on "The Forward March of Labour Halted?"' In Eric Hobsbawm, *Politics for a Rational Left: Political Writing 1977–1988*. London: Verso, 1989.

Hobsbawm, Eric. 'The Forward March of Labour Halted?' In Eric Hobsbawm, *Politics for a Rational Left: Political Writing 1977–1988*. London: Verso, 1989.

Hobsbawm, Eric. 'The Retreat into Extremism'. In Eric Hobsbawm, *Politics for a Rational Left: Political Writing 1977–1988*. London: Verso, 1989.

Hodgson, Geoffrey. *'Militant' and the Alternative Economic Strategy*. London: Clause 4 Publications, 1979.

Hodgson, Geoffrey. *Socialist Economic Strategy*. Labour Party Discussion Series no. 2, 1979.

Hodgson, Geoffrey. 'Britain's Crisis and the Road to International Socialism: A Reply to Jonathan Bearman'. *International Socialism*, Winter 1980.

Hodgson, Geoffrey. *Labour at the Crossroads*. Oxford: Martin Robertson, 1981.

Hodgson, Geoffrey. 'Socialist Economic Strategy: A Reply to Donald Swartz'. *Capital and Class*, Spring 1982.

Hodgson, Geoffrey. *The Democratic Economy: A New Look at Planning, Markets and Power*. Middlesex: Penguin Books, 1984.

Hodgson, Geoffrey. 'When I Tried to Rewrite Labour's Clause Four' (accessed in September 2017 from http://newpolitics.apps-1and1.net/when-i-tried-to-rewrite-labours-clause-four).

Holland, Stuart. 'Adoption and Adaptation of the IRI Formula: Britain, France, Canada, Australia, Sweden, West Germany'. In Stuart Holland, ed. *The State as Entrepreneur: New Dimensions for Public Enterprise—The IRI State Shareholding Formula*. London: Weidenfeld and Nicolson, 1972.

Holland, Stuart. 'Alternative European and Economic Strategies'. In Lawrence Black, Hugh Pemberton, and Pat Thane, eds. *Reassessing 1970s Britain*. Manchester: Manchester University Press, 2013.

Holland, Stuart. 'Capital, Labour and the State'. In Ken Coates, ed. *What Went Wrong: Explaining the Fall of the Labour Government*. Nottingham: Spokesman Books, 1979.

Holland, Stuart. *Capital Versus the Regions*. London: The Macmillan Press, 1976.

Holland, Stuart. 'Demythologising "Old Labour"'. *The Spokesman* (accessed in June 2015 from http://www.spokesmanbooks.com/Spokesman/PDF/110Holland.pdf).

Holland, Stuart. 'Eurobonds: An Open Letter to Martin Schulz'. *Social Europe*, 18 May 2017 (accessed in June 2017 from https://www.socialeurope.eu/eurobonds-without-mutualisation-national-guarantees-fiscal-transfers-open-letter-martin-schulz).

Holland, Stuart. 'Interview: Hope Amidst Despair?' *Renewal: A Journal of Social Democracy* (accessed in July 2019 from http://www.renewal.org.uk/articles/hope-amidst-despair).

Holland, Stuart, ed. 'Introduction'. In *Beyond Capitalist Planning*. Oxford: Basil Blackwell, 1978.

Holland, Stuart, ed. *Out of Crisis: A Project for European Recovery*. Nottingham: Spokesman Books, 1983.

Holland, Stuart. 'Planning Disagreements'. In Stuart Holland, ed. *Beyond Capitalist Planning*. Oxford: Basil Blackwell, 1978.

Holland, Stuart. 'State Entrepreneurship and State Intervention'. In Stuart Holland, ed. *The State as Entrepreneur: New Dimensions for Public Enterprise—The IRI State Shareholding Formula*. London: Weidenfeld and Nicolson, 1972.

Holland, Stuart. *Strategy for Socialism: The Challenge of Labour's Programme.* Nottingham: Spokesman Books, 1975.

Holland, Stuart. *The European Imperative: Economic and Social Cohesion in the 1990s.* Nottingham: Spokesman Books, 1993.

Holland, Stuart. *The Global Economy: From Meso to Macroeconomics.* London: Weidenfeld and Nicolson, 1987.

Holland, Stuart. *The Market Economy: From Micro to Mesoeconomics.* New York: St. Martin's Press, 1987.

Holland, Stuart. 'The National Context'. In Stuart Holland, ed. *The State as Entrepreneur: New Dimensions for Public Enterprise—The IRI State Shareholding Formula.* London: Weidenfeld and Nicolson, 1972.

Holland, Stuart. 'The New Communist Economics'. In Paolo Filo della Torre, Edward Mortimer, and Jonathan Story, eds. *Eurocommunism: Myth or Reality?* Middlesex: Penguin Books, 1979.

Holland, Stuart. *The Regional Problem.* London: The Macmillan Press, 1976.

Holland, Stuart. *The Socialist Challenge.* London: Quartet Books, 1975.

Holland, Stuart. *Uncommon Market: Capital, Class and Power in the European Community.* London: The Macmillan Press, 1980.

Holmes, Martin. *The Labour Government, 1974–79: Political Aims and Economic Reality.* Hampshire: The Macmillan Press, 1985.

Hull and London Port Workers' Control Groups. *The Dockers' Next Step.* IWC Pamphlet no. 12. Nottingham: Institute for Workers' Control, undated pamphlet.

Hyman, Richard. 'Andre Gorz and His Disappearing Proletariat'. In *Socialist Register 1983.* London: Merlin Press, 1983.

Hyman, Richard. *Industrial Relations: A Marxist Introduction.* Basingstoke: Palgrave Macmillan.

Hyman, Richard. 'Workers' Control and Revolutionary Theory: An Appraisal of the Publications of the Institute for Workers' Control'. In *Socialist Register 1974.* London: Merlin Press, 1974.

Industrial Participation Association. *Works Councils, Employee Directors, Supervisory Boards: A Guide to the Debate.* IPA Study Paper no. 2, 1973.

Industrial Relations Services. *Special Supplement: The Bullock Report,* undated (c. 1977).

ITV News. 'The Queen at 90: Tony Blair on the Week that Threatened to Topple the Monarch', 18 April 2016 (accessed in January 2017 from http://www.itv.com/news/2016-04-18/the-week-that-threatened-to-topple-the-queen/).

Jacques, Martin. 'Good to Be Back'. *Marxism Today,* November–December 1998.

Jacques, Martin. 'Thatcherism—Breaking Out of the Impasse'. In Stuart Hall and Martin Jacques, eds. *The Politics of Thatcherism.* London: Lawrence and Wishart, 1983.

Johnson, Carol. 'Relations with Government and Parliament'. In Stuart Holland, ed. *The State as Entrepreneur: New Dimensions for Public Enterprise—The IRI State Shareholding Formula*. London: Weidenfeld and Nicolson, 1972.

Jones, Barry, and Michael Keating. *Labour and the British State*. Oxford: Clarendon Press, 1985.

Jones, Bryn. 'Those Crazy Days of "Socialism": The 1970s and the Strange Death of Social Democracy'. *New Left Project* (accessed in January 2017 from http://www.newleftproject.org/index.php/site/article_comments/those_crazy_days_of_socialism_the_1970s_and_the_strange_death_of_social_dem).

Jones, Owen. 'Class War: Thatcher's Attack on Trade Unions, Industry and Working-Class Identity'. *Verso*, 8 April 2013 (accessed in May 2017 from https://www.versobooks.com/blogs/1274-class-war-thatcher-s-attack-on-trade-unions-industry-and-working-class-identity).

Jones, Owen. '"Soft" Brexit Is Dead. Now Labour Must Really Embrace a People's Vote'. *Guardian*, 27 June 2019 (accessed in July 2019 from https://www.theguardian.com/commentisfree/2019/jun/27/soft-brexit-dead-labour-peoples-vote-referendum-remain).

Jones, Tudor. *Remaking the Labour Party: From Gaitskell to Blair*. London: Routledge, 1996.

Kahler, Miles. 'European Protectionism in Theory and Practice'. *World Politics*, 37: 4, 1985.

Kennet, Wayland, Larry Whitty, and Stuart Holland. *Sovereignty and Multinational Companies*. Fabian Tract 409. London: Fabian Society, 1971.

Keynes, John Maynard. *The General Theory of Employment, Interest and Money*. Hampshire: Palgrave Macmillan, 2007.

LCC (Labour Co-ordinating Committee). *The Realignment of the Right: The Real Face of the SDP*. London: Blackrose Press, 1982.

LCC (Labour Co-ordinating Committee). *There Is an Alternative: Policies for prosperity in the Eighties*, undated pamphlet (c. 1980).

Labour Party. *Alternative Models of Ownership*, 2017 (accessed in July 2019 from https://labour.org.uk/wp-content/uploads/2017/10/Alternative-Models-of-Ownership.pdf).

Labour Party. *Ambitions for Britain*—2001 General Election Manifesto (accessed in January 2017 from http://www.politicsresources.net/area/uk/e01/man/lab/ENG1.pdf).

Labour Party. *Britain Can Be Better*—2015 General Election Manifesto (accessed in July 2019 from https://b.3cdn.net/labouruk/e1d45da42456423b8c_vwm6brbvb.pdf).

Labour Party. *Britain Will Win*—1987 General Election Manifesto (accessed in January 2017 from http://www.politicsresources.net/area/uk/man/lab87.htm).

Labour Party. *Britain Will Win with Labour*—1974 October General Election Manifesto (accessed in March 2015 from http://www.politicsresources.net/area/uk/man/lab74oct.htm).

Labour Party. *For the Many, Not the Few*—2017 General Election Manifesto (accessed in July 2019 from https://labour.org.uk/wp-content/uploads/2017/10/labour-manifesto-2017.pdf).

Labour Party. 'Labour Is Back as the Political Voice of the Working Class—Corbyn', 3 July 2018 (accessed in August 2019 https://labour.org.uk/press/labour-back-political-voice-working-class-corbyn/).

Labour Party. *Labour's Call to Action: The Nation's Opportunity*—1931 General Election Manifesto (accessed in March 2015 from http://labourmanifesto.com/1931/1931-labour-manifesto.shtml).

Labour Party. 'Labour's Call to the People—1922 General Election Manifesto'. In Iain Dale, ed. *Labour Party General Election Manifestos, 1900–1997.* London: Routledge, 2000.

Labour Party. *Labour's Programme 1973.* London, 1973.

Labour Party. *Labour's Programme 1976.* London, 1976.

Labour Party. *Let Us Win Through Together*—1950 General Election Manifesto (accessed in March 2015 from http://www.politicsresources.net/area/uk/man/lab50.htm).

Labour Party. *Let Us Work Together—Labour's Way Out of the Crisis*—1974 February General Election Manifesto (accessed in March 2015 from: http://www.politicsresources.net/area/uk/man/lab74feb.htm).

Labour Party. *New Labour Because Britain Deserves Better*—1997 General Election Manifesto (accessed in January 2017 from http://www.politicsresources.net/area/uk/man/lab97.htm).

Labour Party. *Now Britain's Strong—Let's Make It Great to Live in*—1970 General Election Manifesto (accessed in March 2015 from http://www.politicsresources.net/area/uk/man/lab70.htm).

Labour Party. *The Dilemma of Eurocommunism.* London, 1980.

Labour Party. *The Labour Way Is the Better Way*—1979 General Election Manifesto (accessed in March 2015 from http://www.politicsresources.net/area/uk/man/lab79.htm).

Labour Party. *The New Hope for Britain*—1983 General Election Manifesto (accessed in March 2015 from http://www.politicsresources.net/area/uk/man/lab83.htm).

Labour Party. *The Regeneration of British Industry*, August 1974 (accessed in July 2015 from http://filestore.nationalarchives.gov.uk/pdfs/small/cab-129-178-c-74-90-15.pdf).

Labour Party. *Time for Decision*—1966 General Election Manifesto (accessed in March 2015 from http://www.politicsresources.net/area/uk/man/lab66.htm).

Labour Party Young Socialists. *Programme for Britain*. London: Labour Party, 1973.

Labour Research Department. *The Miners' Case*. London: LRD Publications Ltd., undated.

Laclau, Ernesto. 'Debate: Roads from Socialism'. *Marxism Today*, October 1989.

Laclau, Ernesto, and Chantal Mouffe. *Hegemony and Socialist Strategy: Towards a Radical Democratic Politics*. London: Verso, 2001.

Laclau, Ernesto, and Chantal Mouffe. 'Socialist Strategy: Where Next?' *Marxism Today*, January 1981.

Laybourn, Keith. *A History of British Trade Unionism, c. 1770–1990*. Gloucestershire: Alan Sutton Publishing Ltd., 1992.

Layton, Christopher. 'State Entrepreneurship in a Market Environment'. In Stuart Holland, ed. *The State as Entrepreneur: New Dimensions for Public Enterprise—The IRI State Shareholding Formula*. London: Weidenfeld and Nicolson, 1972.

Leadbeater, Charlie. 'Power to the Person'. *Marxism Today*, October 1988.

Lenin, V.I., '"Left-Wing" Childishness', April 1918 (accessed in March 2015 from https://www.marxists.org/archive/lenin/works/1918/may/09.htm).

Lenin, V.I. *'Left-Wing' Communism: An Infantile Disorder*, 1920 (accessed in March 2015 from https://www.marxists.org/archive/lenin/works/1920/lwc/ch10.htm).

Lenin, V.I. 'Meeting of the International Socialist Bureau', 1908 (accessed in March 2015 from https://www.marxists.org/archive/lenin/works/1908/oct/16b.htm).

Lenin, V.I. 'Report of the Second Congress of the Communist International', 1920 (accessed in March 2015 from https://www.marxists.org/archive/lenin/works/1920/jul/x03.htm).

Lenin, V.I. 'The Discussion on Self-determination Summed Up', 1916 (accessed in October 2015 from https://www.marxists.org/archive/lenin/works/1916/jul/x01.htm).

Lenin, V.I. 'The New Economic Policy and the Tasks of the Political Education Departments: Report to The Second All-Russia Congress of Political Education Departments', 17 October 1921 (accessed in May 2015 from https://www.marxists.org/archive/lenin/works/1921/oct/17.htm).

Lenin, V.I. 'The Right of Nations to Self-determination', 1914 (accessed in August 2016 from https://www.marxists.org/archive/lenin/works/1914/self-det/ch05.htm).

Lenin, V.I. 'The Socialist Revolution and the Right of Nations to Self-Determination', 1916 (accessed in October 2015 from https://www.marxists.org/archive/lenin/works/1916/jan/x01.htm).

Lenin, V.I. 'What Is to Be Done?' In Henry M. Christman, ed. *Essential Works of Lenin: 'What Is to Be Done?' and Other Writings*. New York: Dover Publications, Inc., 1987.

Leys, Colin. *Politics in Britain: From Labourism to Thatcherism.* London: Verso, 1989.

Liberal Industrial Inquiry. *Britain's Industrial Future: Being the Report of the Liberal Industrial Inquiry.* London: Ernest Benn Ltd., 1928.

Liberal Party. *The Nation's Task*—1951 General Election Manifesto (accessed in November 2015 from http://www.politicsresources.net/area/uk/man/lib51.htm).

Liberal Party. *What a Life!*—1970 General Election Manifesto (accessed in November 2015 from http://www.libdemmanifesto.com/1970/1970-liberal-manifesto.shtml).

Liberal Party Research and Information Department. 'Employee Participation'. *Current Topics,* 3:5, 1964.

Lipset, Seymour Martin. *Political Man: The Social Bases of Politics.* London: Heinemann, 1983.

Llorente, Renzo. 'Marx's Concept of "Universal Class": A Rehabilitation'. *Science and Society* (Special Issue: *New Dimensions in Political Economy*), 77, 2013.

London CSE (Conference of Socialist Economists) Group. 'Crisis, the Labour Movement and the Alternative Economic Strategy'. *Capital and Class,* Summer 1979.

London CSE (Conference of Socialist Economists Group) and the LCC (Labour Co-ordinating Committee). *The Alternative Economic Strategy: A Response by the Labour Movement to the Economic Crisis.* London: Blackrose Press (TU) Ltd., 1980.

Looker, Robert. 'A Golden Past? The Labour Party and the Working Class in 1945'. In Jim Fyrth, ed. *Labour's Promised Land? Culture and Society in Britain 1945–51.* London: Lawrence and Wishart, 1995.

Lukacs, Georg. *History and Class Consciousness.* London: Merlin Press, 1971.

Luxemburg, Rosa. *Reform or Revolution and Other Writings.* New York: Dover Publications, Inc., 2006.

*Mail Online,* 'The NEW Longest Suicide Note: Leaked Labour Manifesto Reveals Plans to Take Britain Back to the 1970s by Renationalising Railways, Scrapping Strike Laws and £6bn Tax Raid', 11 May 2017 (accessed in September 2017 from http://www.dailymail.co.uk/news/article-4494728/Labour-manifesto-plans-r eturn-Britain-1970s.html).

Mandel, Ernest. A Socialist Strategy for Western Europe. IWC Pamphlet no. 10. Nottingham: Institute for Workers' Control, undated pamphlet.

Mandel, Ernest. *From Stalinism to Eurocommunism: The Bitter Fruits of 'Socialism in One Country'.* London: NLB, 1978.

Marx, Karl. 'Class Struggle and the Mode of Production'. In Robert Tucker, ed. *The Marx-Engels Reader.* New York: W. W. Norton & Company, 1978.

Marx, Karl. *Critique of the Gotha Programme.* Peking: Foreign Languages Press, 1972.

Marx, Karl. *Grundrisse*. New York: Vintage Books, 1973.

Marx, Karl. 'Preface to the First Edition'. *Capital: A Critique of Political Economy*. London: Penguin Books, 1990.

Marx, Karl. 'Speech on the Question of Free Trade' In Marx and Engels, *Collected Works*, vol. 6. London: Lawrence and Wishart, 1976.

Marx, Karl. 'The Civil War in France'. In Robert Tucker, ed. *The Marx-Engels Reader*. New York: W. W. Norton & Company, 1978.

Marx, Karl. 'The Protectionists, the Free Traders and the Working Class'. In Marx and Engels, *Collected Works*, vol. 6. London: Lawrence and Wishart, 1976.

Marx, Karl and Friedrich Engels. 'Manifesto of the Communist Party'. In Robert Tucker, ed. *The Marx-Engels Reader*, New York: W. W. Norton & Company, 1978.

Marx, Karl, and Friedrich Engels. Preface to the 1872 German edition of the *Communist Manifesto* (accessed in May 2015 from https://www.marxists.org/archive/marx/works/1848/communist-manifesto/preface.htm).

Mason, Rowena. 'Theresa May to "Reform Capitalism" After Philip Green BHS Scandal'. *Guardian*, 25 July 2016 (accessed in September 2016 from https://www.theguardian.com/politics/2016/jul/25/theresa-may-reform-capitalism-philip-green-bhs-scandal).

Mattick, Paul. 'Marx and Keynes', 1955 (accessed in July 2015 from https://www.marxists.org/archive/mattick-paul/1955/keynes.htm).

Mazzucato, Mariana. *The Entrepreneurial State: Debunking Public vs. Private Sector Myths*. London: Anthem Press, 2013.

McDonnell, John, ed. *Economics for the Many*. London: Verso, 2018.

McDonnell, John, 'Introduction'. In John McDonnell, ed. *Economics for the Many*. London: Verso, 2018.

McDonnell, John. Speech to Labour Annual Conference 2016. *Spectator*, 26 September 2016 (accessed in September 2016 from https://blogs.spectator.co.uk/2016/09/full-speech-john-mcdonnell-labour-conference/).

McDonnell, John. Speech to Labour Annual Conference 2018 (accessed in July 2019 from https://labour.org.uk/press/john-mcdonnells-full-speech-labour-conference-2018/).

McIlroy, John. 'Notes on the Communist Party and Industrial Politics'. In John McIlroy, Nina Fishman, and Alan Campbell, eds. *The High Tide of British Trade Unionism: Trade Unions and Industrial Politics, 1964–79*. Monmouth: Merlin Press, 2007.

McKenzie, Robert, and Allan Silver. *Angels in Marble: Working Class Conservatives in Urban England*. London: Heinemann, 1968.

Meacher, Michael. *Socialism with a Human Face: The political economy of Britain in the 1980s*. London: George Allen and Unwin, 1982.

Medhurst, John. *That Option No Longer Exists: Britain 1974–76*. Winchester: Zero Books, 2014.

Medhurst, John. 'The Myth of the 1970s'. *Red Pepper*, 23 October 2014 (accessed in January 2016 from http://www.redpepper.org.uk/the-myth-of-the-1970s/).

Meredith, Stephen. 'Mr Crosland's Nightmare? New Labour and Equality in Historical Perspective'. *British Journal of Politics and International Relations*, 8:2, 2006.

Miliband, Ralph. *Parliamentary Socialism: A Study in the Politics of Labour*. London: Merlin Press, 1972.

Miliband, Ralph. 'Moving on'. In *Socialist Register 1976*. London: Merlin Press, 1976.

Miliband, Ralph. 'A State of De-subordination'. *British Journal of Sociology*, 29:4, 1978.

Miliband, Ralph. *Capitalist Democracy in Britain*. Oxford: Oxford University Press, 1982.

Miliband, Ralph. 'The New Revisionism in Britain'. *New Left Review*, March–April 1985.

Miliband, Ralph. 'Postscript'. In David Coates, ed. *Paving the Third Way: The Critique of Parliamentary Socialism*. London: Merlin Press, 2003.

Minkin, Lewis. *The Contentious Alliance: Trade Unions and the Labour Party*. Edinburgh: Edinburgh University Press, 1991.

Monbiot, George. 'In This Age of Diamond Saucepans, Only a Recession Makes Sense'. *Guardian*, 9 October 2007 (accessed in January 2017 from https://www.theguardian.com/commentisfree/2007/oct/09/comment.economy).

Monds, Jean. 'Workers Control and the Historians: A New Economism'. *New Left Review*, May–June 1976.

Morrow, Felix. *The First Phase of the Coming European Revolution: A Criticism of the International Resolution of the Fifteenth Anniversary Plenum*, 1943 (accessed in May 2016 from https://www.marxists.org/archive/morrow-felix/1943/12/criticism.htm).

Nairn, Tom. 'The Modern Janus'. *New Left Review*, 94, November–December 1975.

Nairn, Tom. 'The Twilight of the British State'. *New Left Review*, January–April 1977 (accessed in September 2015 from https://newleftreview.org/I/101-102/tom-nairn-the-twilight-of-the-british-state).

Napolitano, Giorgi, Gordon Brown, and Cynthia Cockburn. 'Debate: Smaller Worlds'. *Marxism Today*, November 1989.

NatCen. *Understanding the Leave Vote*, 2016 (accessed in July 2019 from http://natcen.ac.uk/media/1319222/natcen_brexplanations-report-final-web2.pdf).

Nichols, Brian. 'The Politics of the Alternative Economy Strategy'. *Marxism Today*, June 1981.

Nisbet, Robert. 'The Decline and Fall of Social Class'. *The Pacific Sociological Review*, 2:1, 1959.

Norman, Jesse, and Janan Ganesh. *Compassionate Conservatism: What It Is, Why We Need It.* London: Policy Exchange, 2006.

Norman, William. 'Signposts for the 60's'. *New Left Review*, September–October 1961.

Nowzad, Bahram. 'The Resurgence of Protectionism'. *Finance and Development*, 15:3, 1978.

Nunns, Alex. *The Candidate: Jeremy Corbyn's Improbable Path to Power.* London: OR Books, 2018.

O'Grady, Frances. 'Is the European Union Good or Bad for British Workers?' *Guardian*, 6 June 2016 (accessed in July 2019 from https://www.theguardian.com/commentisfree/2016/jun/06/should-uk-brexit-trade-union-views).

Office for National Statistics. *Labour Disputes in the UK: 2018*, 17 May 2019 (accessed in June 2019 from: https://www.ons.gov.uk/employmentandlabourmarket/peopleinwork/workplacedisputesandworkingconditions/articles/labourdisputes/2018).

Palmer, John. 'Ken Coates Obituary'. *Guardian*, 29 June 2010 (accessed in May 2016 from https://www.theguardian.com/politics/2010/jun/29/ken-coates-obituary).

Panitch, Leo. *Social Democracy and Industrial Militancy: The Labour Party, the Trade Unions and Incomes Policy, 1945–1974.* Cambridge: Cambridge University Press, 1976.

Panitch, Leo. 'Socialist Renewal and the Labour Party'. In *Socialist Register 1988*. London: Merlin Press, 1988.

Panitch, Leo. *Working-Class Politics in Crisis: Essays on Labour and the State.* London: Verso, 1986.

Panitch, Leo, and Colin Leys. *The End of Parliamentary Socialism: From New Left to New Labour.* London: Verso, 2001.

Pasic, Najdan, Stanislav Grozdanic, and Milorad Radevic, eds. *Workers' Management in Yugoslavia: Recent Developments and Trends.* Geneva: International Labour Office, 1982.

Perryman, Mark, ed. *The Corbyn Effect.* London: Lawrence and Wishart, 2017.

Pimlott, Ben. 'Are CLPs Necessary?' In Inigo Bing, ed. *The Labour Party: An Organisational Study.* Fabian Tract 407, June 1971. London: Fabian Society.

Pimlott, Ben. 'From "Old Left" to "New Labour"? Eric Hobsbawm and the Rhetoric of "Realistic Marxism"'. *Labour/Le Travail*, 56, 2005.

Pimlott, Ben. 'The Labour Left'. In Chris Cook and Ian Taylor, eds. *The Labour Party: An Introduction to Its History, Structure and Politics.* London: Longman, 1980.

Pratley, Nils. 'Theresa May's Plan to Put Workers in Boardrooms Is Extraordinary'. *Guardian*, 11 July 2016 (accessed in September 2016 from https://www.theguardian.com/politics/nils-pratley-on-finance/2016/jul/11/theresa-may-plan-workers-boardroom-reform-extraordinary-tories).

Preobrazhensky, Eugene. *The New Economics*. London: Oxford University Press, 1965.

Pulzer, Peter G.J. *Political Representation and Elections in Britain*. London: Allen & Unwin, 1967.

Radice, Giles, ed. *Working Power: Policies for Industrial Democracy*. Fabian Tract 431, 1974.

Ramelson, Bert. *Bury the Social Contract: The Case for an Alternative Policy*. London: Farleigh Press Ltd., 1977.

Ramelson, Bert. 'Gospel According to Sam'. *Marxism Today*, March 1986.

Rawnsley, Andrew. 'The Really Scary Thing About Corbyn? He's Not Radical at All'. *Guardian*, 14 May 2017 (accessed in May 2017 from https://www.theguardian.com/commentisfree/2017/may/13/scary-jeremy-corbyn-not-radical-at-all-labour-manifesto).

Report of the Committee of Inquiry on Industrial Democracy ('Bullock Report'). London, 1977.

Report of the Royal Commission on Trade Unions and Employers' Associations 1965–68 ('Donovan Report'). London, 1968.

Reynolds, Justin. 'Labour's Alternative Economic Strategy, 40 Years on'. *New Left Project* (accessed in May 2016 from http://www.newleftproject.org/index.php/site/article_comments/labours_alternative_economic_strategy_40_years_on).

Richards, Frank. *The Miners' Next Step*. London: Junius, 1984.

Roberts, David. 'Labour in Office: 1924, 1929–31'. In Chris Cook and Ian Taylor, eds. *The Labour Party: An Introduction to Its History, Structure and Politics*. London: Longman, 1980.

Roberts, Geoff. 'The CP, the SWP and the Strategy for Socialism in Britain'. *International Socialism*, June 1977.

Roberts, Richard. 'How One Man Changed How British Politicians Felt About Europe—Forever'. *New Statesman*, 29 February 2016 (accessed in May 2017 from http://www.newstatesman.com/politics/staggers/2016/02/how-one-man-changed-how-british-politicians-felt-about-europe-forever).

Rose, Richard, and Ian McAllister. *Voters Begin to Choose: From Closed Class to Open Elections in Britain*. London: Sage, 1986.

Ross, George, and Jane Jenson, 'Post-war Class Struggle and the Crisis of Left Politics'. In *Socialist Register 1985–6*. London: Merlin Press, 1986.

Rowthorn, Bob. *Capitalism, Conflict and Inflation: Essays in Political Economy*. London: Lawrence and Wishart, 1980.

Rowthorn, Bob. 'No Such Miracle'. *Marxism Today*, November 1989.

Rowthorn, Bob. 'The Alternative Economic Strategy'. *International Socialism*, Spring 1980 (accessed in July 2015 from https://www.marxists.org/history/etol/newspape/isj2/1980/no2-008/rowthorn.html).

Rowthorn, Bob. 'The Politics of the Alternative Economic Strategy'. *Marxism Today*, January 1981.

Ruddick, Graham. 'Number of Striking Workers Now Lower Than Ever'. *Guardian*, 2 August 2016 (accessed in May 2017 from https://www.theguardian.com/uk-news/2016/aug/02/number-of-striking-workers-now-lower-than-ever).

Rutherford, Jonathan. 'Nigel Farage and Our Democratic Nation'. *Blue Labour*, 18 May 2019 (accessed in July 2019 from https://www.bluelabour.org/2019/05/18/nigel-farage-and-our-democratic-nation/).

Rutherford, Jonathan. 'Why Blue Labour Is Still Relevant Under Corbyn'. Labour List, 2 April 2019 (accessed in July 2019 from https://labourlist.org/2019/04/why-blue-labour-is-still-relevant-under-corbyn/).

Ryan, Linda. 'Labour or the Red Front'. *Confrontation*, no. 2, Summer 1987.

Salisbury, Brian. 'Story of the Lucas Plan' (accessed in June 2016 from http://lucasplan.org.uk/story-of-the-lucas-plan/).

Sassoon, Donald. *One Hundred Years of Socialism: The West European Left in the Twentieth Century*. London: I.B. Tauris and Co. Ltd, 2014.

Saville, John. 'Britain: Prospects for the Seventies'. In *Socialist Register 1970*. London: Merlin Press, 1970.

Scanlon, Hugh. *The Way Forward for Workers' Control*. IWC Pamphlet no. 1. Nottingham: Institute for Workers' Control, undated pamphlet.

Scargill, Arthur. *A Debate on Workers Control*. IWC Pamphlet no. 64. Nottingham: Institute for Workers' Control, 1978.

Scargill, Arthur, and Peggy Kahn. *The Myth of Workers' Control*. Occasional Papers in Industrial Relations: University of Leeds and University of Nottingham, 1980.

Scargill, Arthur, *The Harrogate Debate: The Miners Debate Workers' Control*. London: The Ernest Bevin Society, 1984.

Scargill, Arthur. 'In His Own Words'. Socialist Labour Party (accessed in May 2017 from http://www.socialist-labour-party.org.uk/Scargill%20Own%20Words.pdf).

Sedgemore, Brian. *The How and Why of Socialism*. Nottingham: Spokesman Books, 1977.

SERTUC, and Kent NUM. *Winning the Argument: Speaker's Note* (undated document).

Seyd, Patrick. *The Rise and Fall of the Labour Left*. London: Macmillan Education Ltd., 1987.

Seymour, Richard. *Corbyn: The Strange Rebirth of Radical Politics*. London: Verso, 2017.

Sharples, Adam. 'The Politics of the Alternative Economic Strategy'. *Marxism Today*, April 1981.

Shaw, Eric. *Discipline and Discord in the Labour Party: The Politics of Managerial Control in the Labour Party, 1951–87*. Manchester: Manchester University Press, 1988.

Shaw, Eric. *The Labour Party Since 1945: Old Labour—New Labour*. Oxford: Blackwell, 1996.

Shaw, Eric. *The Labour Party Since 1979: Crisis and Transformation*. London: Routledge, 1994.

Singleton, Frederick, and Anthony Topham. *Workers' Control in Yugoslavia*. Fabian Research Series 233. London: The Fabian Society, 1963.

Slater, Montagu. 'Literature'. In Sam Aaronovitch et al., *The American Threat to British Culture*. London: Arena, Fore Publications Ltd., 1951.

Smith, Adrian. 'The Lucas Plan: What Can It Tell Us About Democratising Technology Today?' *Guardian*, 22 January 2014 (accessed in June 2016 from https://www.theguardian.com/science/political-science/2014/jan/22/remembering-the-lucas-plan-what-can-it-tell-us-about-democratising-technology-today).

Smith, Mark. 'The Truth Behind that Speech that Saved Clyde yards'. *The Herald*, 28 July 2011 (accessed in June 2016 from http://www.heraldscotland.com/news/13033740.The_truth_behind_speech_that_saved_Clyde_yards/).

Snowden, Philip. 'Free Trade'. In Frank Bealey, ed. *The Social and Political Thought of the British Labour Party*. London: Weidenfeld and Nicolson, 1970.

Sparks, Colin. 'The Reformist Challenge'. *International Socialism*, April 1977 (accessed from https://www.marxists.org/history/etol/newspape/isj/1977/no097/sparks.htm).

*Spectator*. 'Industry and Society', 18 July 1957 (accessed in July 2015 from http://archive.spectator.co.uk/article/19th-july-1957/4/industry-and-society).

Standing, Guy. *The Precariat: The New Dangerous Class*. London: Bloomsbury Academic, 2011.

Stewart, Michael. *Keynes and After*. London: Penguin Books, 1986.

Strange, Susan. 'The Management of Surplus Capacity: Or How Does Theory Stand Up to Protectionism 1970s Style?' *International Organization*, 33:3, 1979.

Swartz, Donald. 'The Eclipse of Politics: The Alternative Economic Strategy as Socialist Strategy'. *Capital and Class*, Spring 1981.

Taylor, Robert. *The TUC: From the General Strike to New Unionism*. Hampshire: Palgrave, 2000.

*Telegraph*. 'Death of New Labour as Jeremy Corbyn's Socialist Party Begins a Period of Civil War', 12 September 2015 (accessed in May 2016 from http://www.telegraph.co.uk/news/politics/Jeremy_Corbyn/11861327/jeremy-corbyn-victory-new-labour-death.html).

*Telegraph*. 'Revealed: Corbyn's Manifesto to Take Britain Back to the 1970s', 11 May 2017 (accessed in September 2017 from https://www.pressreader.com/uk/the-daily-telegraph/20170511/281479276333009).

*Telegraph*. 'The Full Text of Tony Blair's Letter to Michael Foot Written in July 1982', 16 June 2006 (accessed in May 2017 from http://www.telegraph.co. uk/news/uknews/1521418/The-full-text-of-Tony-Blairs-letter-to-Michael-Foot-written-in-July-1982.html).

Thompson, Noel. *Left in the Wilderness: The Political Economy of British Democratic Socialism since 1979*. Chesham: Acumen, 2002.

Thompson, Noel. *Political Economy and the Labour Party: The Economics of Democratic Socialism, 1884–2005*. London: Routledge, 2006.

Thompson, Noel. 'Supply Side Socialism: The Political Economy of New Labour'. *New Left Review*, March–April 1996.

Thorpe, Andrew. *A History of the British Labour Party*. Hampshire: Palgrave Macmillan, 2008.

Thorpe, Andrew. 'The Communist Party and the New Party'. *Contemporary British History*, 23:4, 2009.

Thorpe, Andrew. 'The Labour Party and the Trade Unions'. In John McIlroy, Nina Fishman, and Alan Campbell, eds. *The High Tide of British Trade Unionism: Trade Unions and Industrial Politics, 1964–79*. Monmouth: Merlin Press, 2007.

Tinker, Jon. 'The Environment: No Parsnips from Labour'. *New Scientist*, 20 September 1973.

Titmuss, R.M. 'Social Welfare and Art of Giving'. In Deakin, Nicholas, Catherine Jones-Finer, and Bob Matthews, eds. *Welfare and the Capitalist State: Critical Concepts in Political Science*, vol. 2. London: Routledge, 2004.

Tito, Marshal. *Workers Manage Factories in Yugoslavia*. Belgrade: Jugostampa, 1950.

Tomlinson, Jim. 'Economic Policy: Lessons from Past Labour Governments'. In Brian Brivati and Tim Bale, eds. *New Labour in Power: Precedents and Prospects*. London: Routledge, 1997.

Tomlinson, Jim. 'Labour and the Economy'. In Duncan Tanner, Pat Thane and Nick Tiratsoo, eds. *Labour's First Century*. Cambridge: Cambridge University Press, 2000.

TUC (Trades Union Congress). *Evidence to the Royal Commission on Trade Unions and Employers' Associations*. London: TUC, 1966.

TUC (Trades Union Congress). *Industrial Democracy: Report by the TUC General Council to the 1974 Trades Union Congress*. London: TUC, 1974.

Trotsky, Leon. 'Revisionism and Planning: The Revolutionary Struggle Against Labor Fakers', 1934 (accessed in March 2015 from https://www.marxists.org/archive/trotsky/1934/01/planning.htm).

Trotsky, Leon. *The Death Agony of Capitalism and the Tasks of the Fourth International: The Mobilization of the Masses Around Transitional Demands to Prepare the Conquest of Power*, 1938 (accessed in May 2016 from https://www.marxists. org/archive/trotsky/1938/tp/).

Tufekci, Baris. '"Politics of Containment": The (Ralph) Milibandian Critique of the Labour Party'. *Socialist History Journal*, 51, 2017.

Unofficial Reform Committee. *The Miners' Next Step: Being a Suggested Scheme for the Reorganisation of the Federation*. Tonypandy, 1912.

UK Government. *Securing the Future: Delivering UK Sustainable Development Strategy*, March 2005 (accessed in January 2017 from https://www.gov.uk/government/uploads/system/uploads/attachment_data/file/69412/pb10589-securing-the-future-050307.pdf).

Varoufakis, Yanis, Stuart Holland, and James K. Galbraith. *A Modest Proposal for Resolving the Eurozone Crisis, Version 4.0*, July 2013 (accessed in May 2017 from https://varoufakis.files.wordpress.com/2013/07/a-modest-proposal-for-resolving-the-eurozone-crisis-version-4-0-final1.pdf).

*Wales Online*. '"I Felt Helpless During Miners' Strike" Admits Former Labour Leader Neil Kinnock', 6 October 2014 (accessed in May 2017 from http://www.walesonline.co.uk/news/wales-news/i-felt-helpless-during-miners-7891594).

Warde, Alan. *Consensus and Beyond: Development of Labour Party Strategy Since the Second World War*. Manchester: Manchester University Press, 1982.

Warren, Bill. '"The British Road to Socialism"', *New Left Review*, September–October 1970 (accessed in September 2015 from https://newleftreview.org/I/63/bill-warren-the-british-road-to-socialism).

Warren, Bill, and Mike Prior. *Advanced Capitalism and Backward Socialism*. Spokesman, 1975 (accessed in September 2015 from http://www.hegemonics.co.uk/docs/Advanced-Capitalism-Backward%20Socialism.pdf).

White, Eirene. *Workers' Control?* London: Fabian Publications Ltd., 1949.

Whiteley, Paul. *The Labour Party in Crisis*. London: Methuen, 1983.

Wickham-Jones, Mark. *Economic Strategy and the Labour Party: Politics and Policy-Making, 1970–83*. London: Macmillan Press Ltd., 1996.

Wickham-Jones, Mark. 'The Challenge of Stuart Holland: The Labour Party's Economic Strategy During the 1970s'. In Lawrence Black, Hugh Pemberton, and Pat Thane, eds. *Reassessing 1970s Britain*. Manchester: Manchester University Press, 2013.

Wickham-Jones, Mark. 'The New Left'. In Raymond Plant, Matt Beech, and Kevin Hickson, eds. *The Struggle for Labour's Soul: Understanding Labour's Political Thought Since 1945*. London: Routledge, 2004.

Williams, Mike. 'Review Article: "The Alternative Economics Strategy: A Labour Movement Response to the Economics Crisis", by The London CSE Group'. *Capital and Class*, Summer 1981.

Williams, Raymond. *Problems in Materialism and Culture: Selected Essays*. London: Verso, 1980.

Williamson, Adrian. 'The Bullock Report on Industrial Democracy and the Post-war Consensus'. *Contemporary British History*, 30:1, 2016.

Winlow, Simon, Steve Hall, and James Treadwell. *The Rise of the Right: English Nationalism and the Transformation of Working-Class Politics.* Bristol: Policy Press, 2016.

Wintour, Patrick, and Michael White. 'Blair Pins Hopes on Sweeping Changes to Reinvigorate Policy Thinking'. *Guardian*, 4 September 2003 (accessed in June 2017 from https://www.theguardian.com/politics/2003/sep/04/uk.society1).

Wood, Ellen Meiksins. 'Debate on the Manifesto for New Times'. *Marxism Today*, August 1989.

Wood, Ellen Meiksins. *The Retreat from Class: A New 'True' Socialism.* London: Verso, 1998.

Wrigley, Chris. *British Trade Unions Since 1933.* Cambridge: Cambridge University Press, 2002.

Yaffe, David. 'The Crisis of Profitability: A Critique of the Glyn-Sutcliffe Thesis'. *New Left Review*, July–August 1973.

# Index

**A**

Aaronovitch, Sam, 42, 46, 61, 92–94,
 99, 120, 127, 130, 179, 200, 204
Anderson, Perry, 39, 61, 199, 205

**B**

Barratt Brown, Michael, 40, 43–45,
 61, 106, 117, 127–129, 150, 152,
 153, 158, 159, 166, 171–173
Bell, Daniel, 15, 34
Benn, Tony, 1, 20, 33, 40, 44, 46, 56,
 57, 61, 63, 88, 103, 111, 121,
 122, 130, 134, 142, 143, 147,
 149, 153, 156, 158, 161, 169,
 170, 177, 186, 193, 195, 207
Bernstein, Eduard, 13, 53
Bettelheim, Charles, 74, 85
Bevan, Aneurin, 16, 17, 76, 105, 106,
 186
Blair, Tony, 90, 175, 179, 186, 187,
 190, 191, 198, 201, 202, 207,
 214
Blue Labour, 211, 212
Brexit, 211, 215, 216

British Institute of Management
 (BIM), 132, 135, 137–139, 169,
 170
*British Road to Socialism (BRS)*, 47,
 58, 92, 150, 179
Brown, Gordon, 186–188
Bullock inquiry, 136–138, 159, 210

**C**

Callaghan, James, 22, 27, 31, 32, 88,
 109, 112, 159, 176
Cambridge Economic Policy Group
 (CEPG), 113–115
Cameron, David, 199
Campaign for Labour Party Democracy
 (CLPD), 20
Castle, Barbara, 16, 24, 36
Chamberlain, Joseph, 104
Clause 4, 17, 69, 82, 90, 158, 202,
 214
Co-operatives, 25, 59, 87, 90, 141,
 163, 209, 212
Coates, Ken, 40, 57, 63, 150, 152,
 153, 157, 166, 171–173, 193

Cole, G.D.H., 87, 98
Common Agricultural Policy (CAP), 110, 115
Commonwealth, 108, 110, 115
Communism, 58, 86, 102, 112, 117, 120, 127, 130, 155, 157, 183, 186, 198
Communist Party of Great Britain (CPGB), 2, 33, 39, 40, 42, 46, 47, 49, 58, 59, 92–94, 99, 106, 111, 112, 114, 119–122, 124, 125, 127, 128, 130, 150, 162, 165, 171, 173, 179, 180, 183, 186, 202, 203
Confederation of British Industry (CBI), 133, 136, 138, 170
Conference of Socialist Economists (CSE), 40, 50, 107, 124, 134, 150, 183
Conservative Party, 1, 16, 19, 21, 22, 26, 27, 29–31, 56, 67, 69, 82, 105, 110, 120, 123, 124, 132–134, 137, 139, 147, 161, 162, 164, 176, 179–183, 191, 195, 198, 199, 213
Cooley, Mike, 162, 163, 173
Corbyn, Jeremy, 2, 168, 187, 207–211, 213–216
Corbynism, 2, 207–216
Corporatism, 23, 78, 134, 176, 178. *See also* Tripartism
Cousins, Frank, 32
Cripps, Francis, 103, 113, 114, 128, 129
Cripps, Stafford, 76
Crosland, Anthony, 12–14, 24, 33, 53, 68–70, 74, 76, 82, 83, 95, 169, 180, 186
Crossman, Richard, 16, 19, 34

**D**
de Gaulle, Charles, 108, 111

Delors, Jacques, 110, 193, 204
Deutscher, Isaac, 119, 129
Donovan inquiry, 24, 135
Dual power, 43, 151, 153, 154, 163

**E**
Engels, Friedrich, 53, 63, 87, 98, 125, 180, 200
Entrepreneurial state, 77, 78, 80, 208
Environmentalism, 188, 192, 194, 202
Eurocommunism, 86, 93, 180, 183
European Community (EC), 109, 179, 189
European Economic Community (EEC), 2, 101, 102, 105, 108–112, 115, 117, 121, 122, 124, 126, 127, 180, 193, 194
European Union (EU), 101, 112, 188, 193, 195, 204, 215, 216

**F**
Fabianism, 33, 79, 136, 150, 180
Fine, Ben, 46, 49, 61, 200
Foot, Michael, 47, 56, 201

**G**
Gaitskell, Hugh, 17, 82, 108, 127, 180
Gesell, Silvio, 68
Giddens, Anthony, 190, 198, 203, 205
Glasman, Maurice, 211, 217
Globalisation, 83, 118, 188, 192, 211
Glyn, Andrew, 62, 115, 129, 165, 173
Godley, Wynne, 113, 114, 128, 129
Gorz, André, 35, 181, 182, 189, 197, 200, 204
Gramsci, Antonio, 59, 149, 182, 184

**H**
Hain, Peter, 45, 50, 56, 61–63, 106, 111, 116, 127–129, 139, 140,

147, 149, 170, 171, 195, 201, 204
Hall, Stuart, 35, 36, 180, 184, 186, 196, 201, 202
Hardie, Keir, 186, 202
Harrod, Roy, 113
Hattersley, Roy, 47, 185, 201, 202
Healy, Denis, 49
Heath, Edward, 22, 26, 27, 36, 108, 137, 177
Heffer, Eric, 55, 63
Hobsbawm, Eric, 35, 58, 63, 104, 126, 180–183, 200, 201, 208
Hodgson, Geoffrey, 5, 40–42, 45, 48–51, 53, 61, 62, 89–94, 99, 106, 111, 115–117, 124, 127–130, 140–142, 145, 147, 149, 170, 171, 192
Holland, Stuart, 7, 9, 10, 32, 33, 40, 41, 44, 47, 48, 51, 53, 61, 62, 65, 66, 70–76, 78–90, 92–98, 107, 109, 110, 112, 118, 121, 124, 128–130, 134, 144–147, 149, 169–172, 191–194, 203, 204, 208, 209, 217

**I**

Imperialism, 104, 119–122
Import controls, 2, 4, 102, 112–117, 121, 126, 134, 168, 192
Incomes policy, 24, 28, 31, 32, 135, 136, 147–149, 158, 159, 176, 214
Industrial democracy, 2, 4, 5, 9, 33, 43, 51, 52, 96, 131–146, 148, 150–154, 156, 157, 159, 160, 163–169, 195, 210
Industrial relations, 9, 12, 14, 15, 23, 27, 51, 69, 131, 132, 135, 138, 139, 143, 169, 212, 213
Industrial Reorganisation Corporation (IRC), 81

Inflation, 24, 28, 72, 93, 99, 103, 106, 109, 143, 148, 176
*In Place of Strife*, 24, 25, 29
Institute for Industrial Reconstruction (IRI), 78–81, 84, 96
Institute for Workers' Control (IWC), 40, 45, 133, 143, 150–153, 156, 158, 159, 161, 163
Internationalism, 33, 101, 102, 119, 120, 122, 126, 189
International Monetary Fund (IMF), 109, 121, 122, 176, 194
Italian Communist Party (PCI), 86, 98, 183

**J**

Jacques, Martin, 36, 186, 201, 202
Jenkins, Roy, 24, 70, 82, 97
Jones, Jack, 28, 29, 36, 152, 153, 158

**K**

Keynesianism, 2–7, 9, 22, 23, 48, 65–73, 75, 91, 94, 95, 99, 105, 109, 113, 114, 176, 203, 208
Keynes, John Maynard, 4, 65–68, 70, 71, 73, 75, 95, 133
Kinnock, Neil, 175, 179, 180, 183, 185, 195, 201, 202

**L**

Labour Co-ordinating Committee (LCC), 20, 40, 42, 45, 50, 61, 106, 107, 115, 129, 150, 185
Labour Party, 1–5, 7, 8, 11–13, 17, 19, 20, 23, 26, 28–30, 32–34, 36, 40, 48, 55, 56, 58–60, 82, 87, 96–98, 105, 108–110, 117, 121, 127–129, 132, 158, 164, 169, 176, 183, 185, 191, 199,

200, 203, 205, 208, 210, 211, 213–215, 217, 218
Labour Party Young Socialists, 11, 33
Laclau, Ernesto, 35, 182, 198, 200, 204
Lassalle, Ferdinand, 87
Leadbeater, Charles, 186, 189, 203
Lenin, V.I., 43, 53, 54, 58, 59, 63, 74, 96, 119, 129, 130
Leninism, 3, 53, 62
Liberal Party, 133, 169
Liberalism, 110, 123, 124, 211
Lipset, Seymour Martin, 16, 21, 35
Localism, 188
Lucas Aerospace, 162–164
Lukacs, Georg, 54, 63
Luxemburg, Rosa, 54, 63

**M**
Macmillan, Harold, 108
Mandel, Ernest, 156, 172
*Manifesto for New Times*, 175, 185–195, 202, 203
Mann, Tom, 151
Marxism, 2–5, 9, 10, 13, 40, 42, 44, 48, 50, 53–56, 58, 60, 68, 79, 86, 87, 101, 118, 119, 122, 124, 126, 146, 154, 163, 181–183, 187, 191, 197, 199
*Marxism Today*, 46, 179, 180, 182–184, 186, 200, 201
Marx, Karl, 4, 10, 44, 53, 54, 56, 63, 68, 75, 79, 87, 96, 97, 124, 125, 130, 163, 173, 180, 200
May, Theresa, 210, 217
Mazzucato, Marianna, 208, 217
McDonnell, John, 208–211, 217
Meacher, Michael, 42, 61, 115–117, 121, 129, 130, 140, 147, 149, 170, 192, 201, 204
Mesoeconomy, 71–73
Mikardo, Ian, 30

Miliband, Ed, 187, 208, 210, 217
Miliband, Ralph, 19, 35, 57, 63, 137, 169, 180, 200
Militant Tendency, 50, 56
*Miners' Next Step (MNS)*, 166, 167, 173
Mitterrand, François, 193
Monetarism, 6, 23, 67, 73, 91, 176
Monopoly, 4, 7, 71, 72, 74, 79, 80, 85, 92, 112, 121
Morrow, Felix, 155
Mosley, Oswald, 105, 122
Mouffe, Chantal, 182, 198, 200, 204
Mulgan, Geoff, 186
Multinational firms, 10, 71, 72, 83, 93, 109, 110, 112, 118, 121, 122, 188, 213

**N**
Nairn, Tom, 123, 130
Napolitano, Giorgio, 86, 202
National Enterprise Board (NEB), 77, 88, 140, 145
National Executive Committee (NEC), 82, 86, 98, 113, 177
National Front, 105, 123, 124
National Plan, 24, 88
National Union of Miners (NUM), 36, 159, 164, 165
Nationalism, 102, 105, 116, 119, 120, 122, 123, 126, 188, 216
NATO, 122, 194
New Labour, 1–3, 83, 175, 185–188, 190, 191, 195, 198, 199, 201, 202, 207, 210, 212, 214, 216
Nuclear disarmament, 2, 17, 121, 179

**O**
Oligopoly, 78, 80, 81, 88
Opening the books, 74, 146, 152, 156

**P**

Panitch, Leo, 3, 10, 17, 20, 34, 35, 37, 56, 57, 63, 148, 149, 171, 176, 199, 200

Parliament, 3, 17, 27, 44, 48, 49, 51, 57, 60, 109, 122, 156

Patriotism, 102, 104, 112, 120–122, 125, 211

*Plan for Coal*, 164, 165

Planning agreements, 2, 88, 89, 93, 140

Post-Fordism, 189

Powell, Enoch, 105

Preobrazhensky, Eugene, 54, 63

Price controls, 2, 4, 28, 147, 148, 158, 159

Prior, Mike, 106, 127, 168

Protectionism, 9, 95, 101, 102, 104–107, 117–120, 123–126, 192, 212

Przeworski, Adam, 4

Public ownership, 1–5, 13, 14, 16, 46, 66, 68, 69, 74–80, 82, 83, 85, 90–92, 94, 110, 134, 136, 147, 159, 160, 166, 179, 180, 187, 192, 207


**R**

Radice, Giles, 133, 168

Ramelson, Bert, 46, 49, 61, 91, 93, 94, 99, 119, 120, 130

Reflation, 2, 4, 72, 92, 110, 113

Regional development, 74, 124

Reid, Jimmy, 162

Revisionism, 2, 3, 5, 9, 12–19, 23–25, 34, 44, 65, 66, 68–71, 74, 76, 81, 82, 108, 169, 175, 185, 203, 213

Rowthorn, Bob, 37, 41–43, 45–49, 51, 52, 61, 62, 91–94, 99, 106, 112, 114–117, 127–129, 150, 180, 186, 193, 200, 202

**S**

Saville, John, 57, 63

Scanlon, Hugh, 28, 30–32, 36, 152, 153, 158, 172

Scargill, Arthur, 159–165, 173

Schumacher, E.F., 140

Sedgemore, Brian, 48, 62, 148, 171

Shore, Peter, 32, 47

Slater, Montagu, 120, 130

Snowden, Philip, 104, 127

Social contract, 1, 13, 23, 27, 28, 30, 31, 33, 143, 147, 148, 156, 158, 214

Social Democratic Party (SDP), 185

Social movements, 182, 185, 191, 213, 215

Soviet Union, 53, 74, 86, 90, 93, 94, 99, 156

State capitalism, 53, 71, 74, 85, 134

Strachey, John, 16, 76, 105, 106


**T**

Tariffs, 104, 105, 115

Taylorism, 140

Thatcher, Margaret, 31, 93, 137, 164, 176, 179, 180, 183–185, 193, 195, 199

Thatcherism, 36, 93, 177, 180, 184, 186, 198

Topham, Tony, 136, 150, 152, 153, 157, 166, 169, 171–173

Trade unions, 2, 8, 13–15, 17, 18, 20, 22–31, 34, 37, 42, 43, 54, 55, 59, 67, 89, 93, 132, 133, 135–148, 151–153, 156, 158–160, 164, 166, 167, 169, 176, 178, 179, 184, 185, 190, 191, 193, 195, 196, 211, 213, 214, 216

Trades Union Congress (TUC), 24, 25, 29–31, 133, 135, 137, 138, 168, 169, 193

Transitional programme, 33, 49, 50, 89, 154, 155, 193

Tribune Group, 30, 40, 48, 49

Tripartism, 23, 27, 89, 135, 144–146, 150, 176, 178, 193–195

Trotsky, Leon, 49, 50, 58, 62, 90, 154, 155, 172

Trotskyism, 3, 19, 40, 49, 50, 114, 154–156, 165

**U**

Unemployment, 15, 24, 45, 52, 67–69, 93, 99, 103–105, 108, 113, 115, 116, 125, 145, 179

Upper Clyde Shipbuilders (UCS), 161, 162, 164

**W**

Warren, Bill, 106, 127, 168

Williams, Raymond, 59, 64

Wilson, Harold, 13, 22, 24, 27–29, 81, 88, 109, 136, 159, 177, 186

Wood, Ellen Meiksins, 86, 98, 180, 181, 183, 190, 196, 200, 201, 203, 204

**Y**

Yugoslavia, 90, 156, 157, 172

Printed in Great Britain
by Amazon

80566027R00153